D1218454

THE THEOLOGY
OF ALTIZER:
CRITIQUE
AND RESPONSE

Books by John B. Cobb, Jr.
Published by The Westminster Press

The Theology of Altizer:
  Critique and Response (*Ed.*)

God and the World

The Structure of Christian Existence

A Christian Natural Theology:
  Based on the Thought of Alfred North Whitehead

Living Options in Protestant Theology:
  A Survey of Methods

Varieties of Protestantism

THE THEOLOGY
OF ALTIZER:
CRITIQUE
AND RESPONSE

Edited by

John B. Cobb, Jr.

THE WESTMINSTER PRESS
Philadelphia

ISBN 0–664–20891–6

Library of Congress Catalog Card No. 79–116529

Published by The Westminster Press ®
Philadelphia, Pennsylvania

PRINTED IN THE UNITED STATES OF AMERICA

Contents

Preface

American radical theology, or the death-of-God movement, is generally seen as a negation of traditional Christianity in the name of honesty and modernity. Often it is associated with the call for secularity, or for a political theology, or for a theology of revolution, or even for a dissolution of theology in ethical action. Alternately it is associated with support for a general religiousness characteristic of East and West alike.

This picture of radical theology is appropriate to much of what has been taking place, but it is profoundly misleading when applied to Altizer. He is a leading radical theologian, indeed *the* leading radical, but his radicalism is marked by opposition to much of what is called radical theology. His concern is not to adjust Christian theology to the predominant contemporary sense of what is credible and important. His thought is not secular, and even his call for total affirmation of the profane is for the sake of a new manifestation of the sacred. For him theology is much more fundamental than politics and ethics. It is Christianity and not religion in general to which he is committed.

Fortunately, alongside the general discussion of radical theology, there has appeared also a substantial literature of insightful criticism directed toward Altizer as an important and original thinker. As the excitement stirred up by the news media subsides and the demand for titillation by something new focuses popular attention upon other movements, the time has come for serious Christians to look more carefully at Altizer, the constructive theologian.

Altizer is a young man with much of his theological career ahead of him. Most of his serious critics, also, have been men with much of their theological work ahead of them. Many of them have already experienced a profound impact on their work through encountering Altizer's thought. Hence the discussion between Altizer and his critics is not the clash of fixed positions but the concerned interchange of growing minds. It is a living and unfinished debate.

One purpose of this book is to encourage increased attention to Altizer's systematic theology. To this end critical essays of high quality, some previously published, some new, are presented. All reflect keen interest in, and generally accurate understanding of, Altizer's position. Their several criticisms help to locate his thought in relation to the panorama of contemporary theology as well as to highlight the critical issues involved in his distinctive views.

The second purpose of the book is to stimulate and embody the living debate. To this end critical essays are followed by Altizer's responses. The tone of both the critiques and the responses is respectful, friendly, and open. But the issues raised are matters of ultimate importance toward which indifference is impossible. The book should serve to clarify issues and to involve readers in the ongoing discussion.

Some of the critiques of Altizer come from clearly defined traditions. Of those included in this book, two (Runyon and Beardslee) are Protestant, two (Meyer and Heisig) are Catholic, and one (Rubenstein) is Jewish. These are grouped accordingly. The remaining four papers view Altizer in relation to a diversity of issues. They have been grouped rather arbitrarily under two headings. Two (Noel and Gier) discuss Altizer's relation to other nontraditional options for religious thought, and two are written by historians of religions (King and Eliade), who view Altizer in perspectives provided by the discipline in which he did his doctoral study. The final essay was written by Eliade specifically for this volume and is of particular interest as it is his first public response to Altizer's book *Mircea Eliade and the Dialectic of the Sacred*.

The idea of editing this book was stimulated by the thesis of Nicholas Gier entitled "Process Theology and the Death of God" (Claremont Graduate School, 1969). In addition, Gier has played several roles in the preparation of the volume. He helped locate, evaluate, and edit materials; he contributed an essay; and sections III and IV of the Introduction are from his hand. He represents a generation who, while experiencing spiritual turmoil in college through disillusionment with traditional Christianity, found the death-of-God theologies speaking to their condition. This is a generation it is important to involve rapidly in the professional theological discussion, lest those of us "over thirty" lose touch with the shapers of the future.

The greatest contribution to the volume is that of Altizer himself. He has assisted in identifying and evaluating the critiques; he read and criticized an early version of the Introduction; and, most important, he has written substantial responses to the critical essays. It is with his encouragement that the hilarious spoof on him, and specifically on *Mircea Eliade and the Dialectic of the Sacred*, "Mercy for Miss Awdy, in a Vile Acting of the Sacred," is included as an appendix. This spoof was written by Walter D. Love, formerly a colleague of Altizer at Emory University, who has since been killed in an accident. It is used with the kind permission of his widow, Peggy V. Love.

Grateful acknowledgment is hereby also made to the previous publishers for permission to use the following essays:

William A. Beardslee, "A Comment on the Theology of Thomas Altizer," *Criterion*, Vol. VII (Spring, 1968), pp. 11–14.
Winston L. King, "Zen and the Death of God," *Japanese Religions*, Vol. V (December, 1967), pp. 1–21.
Eric C. Meyer, C. P., "Catholic Theology and the Death of God:

A Response," *Chicago Studies,* Vol. VIII (Summer, 1969), pp. 189–203.

Daniel C. Noel, "Still Reading His Will? Problems and Resources for the Death-of-God Theology," *The Journal of Religion,* Vol. XLVI (October, 1966), pp. 463–476.

Richard L. Rubenstein, "Thomas Altizer's Apocalypse," in William A. Beardslee, ed., *America and the Future of Theology* (The Westminster Press, 1967), pp. 32–40.

Theodore Runyon, Jr., "Thomas Altizer and the Future of Theology," in Jackson Lee Ice and John J. Carey, eds., *The Death of God Debate* (The Westminster Press, 1967), pp. 56–69.

Thanks are due also to my student assistant, Delbert Swanson, for help in editing and proofreading, and to Mrs. Erma Walks and Mrs. Barbara Henckel for typing. Without the cooperation and assistance of the administration of the School of Theology at Claremont, especially President Gordon Michalson and Dean F. Thomas Trotter, the project could not have been realized.

JOHN B. COBB, JR.

Claremont, California

Contributors

Thomas J. J. Altizer is Professor of English at the State University of New York at Stony Brook, Long Island, New York.

William A. Beardslee is Professor of Religion at Emory University, Atlanta, Georgia.

John B. Cobb, Jr., is Ingraham Professor of Theology at the School of Theology at Claremont, California.

Mircea Eliade is Professor of the History of Religions at the Divinity School of the University of Chicago, Illinois.

Nicholas Gier is a student in the Department of Religion of the Claremont Graduate School, Claremont, California.

James W. Heisig is Instructor in Philosophy and Theology at Divine Word College, Epworth, Iowa.

Winston L. King is Professor of the History of Religions at Vanderbilt University, Nashville, Tennessee.

The late Walter D. Love was Associate Professor of History at the University of Bridgeport, Connecticut.

Eric C. Meyer is engaged in advanced studies at the University of Münster, Germany.

Daniel C. Noel is Assistant Professor of Religion at Lafayette College, Easton, Pennsylvania.

Richard L. Rubenstein is Charles L. Merrill Lecturer in the Humanities, Director of the B'nai B'rith Hillel Foundation, and Chaplain to Jewish Students at the University of Pittsburgh, Pennsylvania.

Theodore Runyon, Jr., is Professor of Systematic Theology at the Candler School of Theology, Emory University, Atlanta, Georgia.

John B. Cobb, Jr.
Nicholas Gier

Introduction

I

The late '60s in this country will be remembered in theology chiefly for the remarkable public attention directed to radical theology and especially to the idea of the death of God. Paul van Buren, William Hamilton, Gabriel Vahanian, and others shared the spotlight of national attention, but Thomas J. J. Altizer was the most prominent figure. In these last few years he has been the most widely and most heatedly discussed American theologian.

Not only has Altizer's theology been the most widely discussed, it has also been the most influential. The furor over the "death of God" has altered the theological climate in America irreversibly. As late as the early '60s, some form of Biblical theology or neo-orthodoxy was the point of departure for most theological discussion. As the decade closed, these movements appeared to have chiefly historical interest. Even those whose present positions have developed from them—such as Langdon Gilkey, Gordon Kaufman, Dietrich Ritschl, Thomas Oden, and Peter Berger—now address themselves in a quite different way to what they recognize as a quite different situation. Much of this change was already incipiently occurring, of course, or the response to Altizer's challenge would not have been so dramatic. Nevertheless, it required public discussion to bring into dominance the mood of radicalism. For that public discussion, Altizer has major responsibility.

The claim that Altizer has been the most influential American theologian in the past few years would collapse if it meant that he was the most widely followed or even read! Although he has rejoiced to lead in the shattering of the apparent consensus of the past generation, there remains a gulf between his vast influence in negation and the limited response to his constructive solution of theological problems. Many have agreed that in our time honesty requires that we be atheists, but few have had any appreciation for the remarkable form of "atheism" Altizer actually proposes. His influence has encouraged the emergence of an ethical Christian humanism that is poles removed from his own theology.

A third claim is more subjective than the first two, but still widely acceptable: Altizer is also the most original and creative American theologian of this period. For this reason the lack of understanding of his constructive theological position is particularly unfortunate. His theological assertions differ so profoundly from the dominant theological radicalism of our time, as well as from the neo-orthodoxy and liberalism of the recent past, that some have tried to write him off as an irresponsible eccentric. But few who have studied him seriously, and even fewer who have known him well, have found it possible to dismiss his thought in this way. Whether one agrees with him or not, one discovers in his writings a coherent vision of great power. In addition, one finds that this vision has been arrived at, not by personal whim, but by an approach to Christian theology in the context of the history of religions, an approach that is widely approved but rarely attempted. Indeed, Altizer is the first major theologian since World War I to think theologically from the perspective of the study of the history of religions conceived on a world scale.

This point needs explanation. Other theologians, of course,

have approached the study of the history of religions from a theological point of view, and their theology has been influenced by what they have learned. Some have studied Christianity as one of the world's religions from the point of view of the historian of religions. Others have thought theologically from a perspective shaped by study of the Near Eastern religions of Biblical times. But these are quite different matters. Altizer is not *first* a Christian theologian who *then* is affected by studying other religions, and he is not a historian of religions who wants to place Christianity in the total context. He is a theologian whose categories and questions are shaped by profound immersion in the study of the planetary history of religions. Among past theologians, Troeltsch and Otto come closest to this theological method, but today, approximation to their approach leads to quite different results.

Whereas the first three claims for Altizer's importance may be widely admitted, the fourth may appear strange and even perverse. Of all the American theological writing of this period, it is Altizer's that embodies the most vigorous and passionate faith. The widely assumed contrary view has two major causes. First, the initial impact of Altizer has been upsetting to the faith of others. His negations have come across more effectively than his affirmations, and Altizer, convinced that what is being uprooted is in fact already dead, has done little to soften this destructive consequence of his thought. Second, many associate "faith" indissolubly with "God" and hence cannot understand the denial of God as an act of faith.

Nevertheless, a careful and open reading of Altizer will convince one that he is encountering a profound expression of faith of a sort rare in current theology. Altizer does not understand himself as a man who, because of holding certain traditional values, *still* calls himself a Christian. That point of view is easy to find in our times. It expresses a situation in which a man's fundamental self-definition is ethical, or humanistic, or scholarly, or secular, but in which he secondarily accepts the designation of himself as Christian also. In contrast, Altizer is

first and foremost a Christian. Like many passionate Christians
before him (Luther and Kierkegaard, to mention just two examples), he is intensely critical of the Christianity he finds about
him. But such criticism has no other basis than faith itself.

Furthermore, this faith is not a name arbitrarily given to
some aspect of his existence. It is faith in the Word, in Christ,
in the Incarnation of God, in the Kingdom of God. True, these
terms take on new meanings in Altizer's thought, but they are
not unrecognizable meanings. On the contrary, they are traditional meanings taken with such radical seriousness as to transform them. Even the "death of God" is affirmed, not as a concession to modern skepticism, but as the deepest Christian meaning of Incarnation and Crucifixion. Furthermore, Altizer's faith
enables him to discern in the present world what other Christians anxiously miss—the real presence of Christ. He is "persuaded that everyone who lives in what we know as history
participates at bottom in the life of Christ" and "that the task
of theology is to unveil and make manifest the universal presence and reality of Christ." (Quoted from a letter to me, July 7,
1969.)

These statements make clear that Altizer is also the boldest
evangelical theologian of our time. While most American theologians seek to provide some justification for Christians to remain
Christian, to overcome some misunderstanding of faith, or to
guide the church in the responsible direction of its energies,
Altizer addresses the "cultured despisers" with the word that
they live by participation in Christ. How successful he will be
in reaching his public cannot be foretold. It would be idle to
suppose that those whom he persuades will hurry to the local
church to share in its worship and cultural activities! But the
evangelical purpose is clear.

In the light of these judgments about Altizer, this volume is
an attempt to shift the focus of attention from his negations to
his affirmations. If Altizer's sharp critique of Christian habits of
mind has made manifest and accentuated the theological sickness of the church, perhaps the study of the theology in which

he expresses his own powerful faith will be a source of healing. But our attitude toward this theology cannot be shaped only by respect for the creativity and faith that it embodies. Once we respect it and recognize its importance, we must approach it with critical care, seeking to evaluate it with whatever norms we have available. The essays that follow embody this attitude. All take Altizer seriously. All offer specific and sharply focused criticism.

The remainder of this Introduction is intended to prepare the reader for a clearer understanding of Altizer's thought and of the issues between him and his critics. To this end, the rest of the Introduction is divided into three parts. Section II offers some comments about the general cast of Altizer's thought and its fundamental assumptions. Section III describes the development of his thought through three important stages. Section IV relates Altizer's thought to the early Barth and to contemporary secular theology.

II

Altizer is not and has never been an ontological realist. A realist conceives entities as existing in some definite and discriminable way quite apart from human experience. For example, a realistic interpretation of the sentence, "The stone is gray," is that there exists independent of human experience an entity called a "stone" qualified in a distinctive way such that the term "gray" is appropriate to it. The realist need not suppose that grayness as a humanly experienced color exactly characterizes what the stone is in and of itself, but he believes that there is a correlation between what is objectively occurring in the stone and the human experience of perceiving gray, such that the former is an independent and prior cause of the latter. The sentence, "The stone is gray," is thus taken as referring to a reality outside of human experience and responsible for the human experience of the grayness of the stone.

Altizer, in contrast, has never been interested in what things are in and for themselves apart from human experience. Indeed, he has not recognized this as a possible question. The reality with which he has concerned himself is humanly experienced reality, and that alone. This could be indicated by pointing to his enthusiasm for Hegel, but identification of reality with humanly experienced reality is much more widespread in the modern world than is Hegelianism. Idealists share this identification with empiricists, positivists, historicists, and phenomenalists.

Altizer was immersed in this perspective long before he seized on its Hegelian formulation. Probably it grew naturally out of his study of the history of religions. To understand a Buddhist or a Hindu, one does not ask how his vision of reality corresponds with what is "really" there. One takes that vision as constituting his *reality*. If that vision differs from the Christian one, then one recognizes that his *reality* differs from Christian reality. To judge the two realities by a supposed knowledge of what is "really" real, gained by some means alien to both, is to abandon the perspective of the history of religions. Furthermore, it may well be an illusion, for it presupposes some access to "reality" more basic or more reliable than that of Buddhist and Christian. That presupposition can express only a third perspective, different from both, but not for that reason truer.

Many who think that they agree with such judgments and methods still suppose that if God exists for one he exists for all whether they recognize him or not, or that if God does not now exist he never existed. Such views express the power of commonsense realism even when it is avowedly abandoned. Altizer is more consistent. God is real, actual, and existent where and when he is present in human experience as real, actual, and existent. But where God plays no vital role in human experience and vision, he is either nonexistent, as for the Buddhist, or dead, as for the modern Christian.

Similarly, many who hold to phenomenalist theories nevertheless seek to test contemporary beliefs about the past against the way the past *really* was. Altizer is again more consistent. For him, there is no meaning to the question of what the past was in and for itself. Our question is what the past is for us, in *our* reality. Viewed in this way, the past is also changing as the shape of existence in the present changes.

These paragraphs might seem to imply an extreme subjectivism. It might seem that "reality" is whatever one believes it to be. This is far from Altizer's intention. We all experience reality as much more objective than that. Whether God is now alive or dead is not a function of my private opinion on the subject. As individuals, we are caught up in a movement of history about which we do not personally decide. It is given to us. And at its deepest level it is constituted by a concretely experienced reality. That reality is obscured by our inherited beliefs and habits. It is laid bare for us by the spiritual giants of our time. In retrospect, we can often judge these visionaries with some accuracy. To judge our own time is always a risk. Altizer is convinced, however, that the judgment of the death of God is now overwhelmingly evident. On the other hand, and with far less obvious justification, he believes that Christ is very much alive; that, indeed, he constitutes the life of our history. The fact that this is not widely recognized is no evidence of its falsity.

In an attempt to understand Altizer, it is misleading to say that the death of God refers to a cultural phenomenon. Of course it does, but to state matters in that way implies that there is something else with which cultural phenomena could be contrasted, such as a metaphysical reality. For Altizer, what happens in culture, most fundamentally understood, *is* the metaphysical reality. This identity of history and metaphysics is what unites him with Hegel.

This understanding of the situation has consistent consequences in Altizer's appraisal of the work of others. He does not ask whether what they say corresponds to some nonhistorical reality, for the historical reality is all there is. Fundamentally, the question is whether the argument or thought is somehow in tune with the existent historical reality, whether it illumines this reality or participates in shaping it. This can be judged partly by the kind of reception a man's work enjoys. If those who have most deeply entered into the contemporary situation find what is said dull or vacuous, it is not saved by the amount of evidence amassed for its conclusions or the tightness of its logical arguments. The question is not so much whether an idea can be "proved" as whether it rings true.

Once again, this could easily be misunderstood in a subjectivist way. But Altizer has no patience with the lazy thinker who accepts ideas according to their emotional appeal or the force of the rhetoric with which they are presented. Value is not judged by mass acceptance. Yet any thinking is fundamentally irrelevant if it does not begin with the present situation as it is really felt and known in sensitive and informed experience.

On the basis of this account of Altizer's Hegelian idealism, we can now see why he moves as he does on specific points of special importance for theology. Of these we will consider three: first, Altizer's view of the normative relation of faith and theology to the dominant cultural movement of the time; second, Altizer's approach to Christology; and third, the *style* of Altizer's thought and argument.

1. There is little doubt that Christian morale is currently at a low ebb. Historic Christian beliefs appear either incredible or irrelevant. Those who are most sensitive and perceptive have abandoned them, sometimes because they *wished* to do so, more often because traditional faith has simply lost the power to shape vision and experience and to guide action. The great artists have developed new categories. Christians are widely perceived as a rear guard composed of those who do not trust reason, experience, and enlightened sensibility.

One response to this situation is to understand Christianity as the creation in history of a new and in some sense final mode of human existence. Elsewhere, I have characterized this Christian existence as self-transcending selfhood expressing itself in concern for the other as an *other*. This mode of being is the fundamental ground of what has been most dynamic, most creative, and most redemptive in Western history and, more recently, in the Westernized history of the entire planet. It has freed men personally and intellectually to raise radical questions and to develop whole new disciplines of thought.

Ironically, the thinking for which men have been freed by Christian existence has increasingly undercut the beliefs that are bound up with that existence. Such existence involves effort, tension, the bearing of burdens, and the postponement of rewards. These have been endurable and even enriching in the context of the historic Christian understanding of man as living from God and for God. But in the absence of some such vision, men are empty, and Christian existence cannot long endure. It will be destroyed by its own fruits.

The alternative to the disappearance of Christian existence is the emergence of a new vision capable of sustaining intentional communities whose vitality would enable them to revivify part of the remains of the institutional church. A church in which credible and relevant conviction expressed itself in consistent and appropriate disciplined action would not have to be large to be redemptively effective.

This view defines Christian faith in terms of continuity in a mode of existence, while recognizing the constantly new intellectual task of articulating doctrines required and supported by it. It can acknowledge the powerful attraction of competing ideas and visions without therefore accepting them. Thus the Christian differentiates himself and his faith from the dominant cultural currents of his time, not by ignoring them, but by discriminating appraisal, selective appropriation, and constructive reconceptualization.

This response presupposes that Christian faith has its fundamental existence in some isolation from the fundamental movement of history. For Altizer, precisely this isolation from the movement of vision and spirit is faithlessness. We have, in his view, no static essence of Christian faith or existence in terms of which to evaluate other modes of belief and existence. Where authentic creativity is to be found, there is the reality with

which faith has to do. Thus true Christianity can and must reverse itself in the most fundamental ways in order to be true to
itself. Since all that we have known as Christian existence, or
personhood, or even humanity is swept away in the new visions
of our time, faith requires that we affirm their death. The Christian is not to plan strategies for salvaging or reviving what is
dying, but rather to learn to see the new as the dialectical con-
tinuation, through transformation, of the old. In the deepest
sense, faith is the affirmation of what *will* be rather than the attempt to shape an indeterminate future.

The task of theology is to articulate the teaching of the church
only to the extent that the church's teaching grasps and expresses the reality of our historical situation. Altizer under-
standably judges that this extent is currently very slight. If
Christian theology is to escape from the ghetto in which it has
imprisoned itself, it must enter the arena in which man's reality
is being creatively discerned and shaped, and today that is far
from the church. Yet Altizer enters that arena convinced that
the reality in question, however it is now being named, is truly
Christ. Indeed, for him the very essence of faith is this conviction, and it is this faith which frees the Christian for total
openness to the reality of his time, however dark and empty it
may appear.

2. Altizer's approach to Christology is consistent with this
understanding of the nature of theology. It is to be understood
as a renewal and transformation of the Hegelian Christology
of the last century in the setting of our time.

Christian orthodoxy in its Christological dogma has held two
concerns in tension. One concern is transpersonal, sacred, or
divine reality. The other is the particular, contingent, historical
figure—Jesus of Nazareth. Much traditional theological debate
focused on the nature of the relation of the absolutely transcendent to the relative and immanent aspects of God with only
incidental reference to Jesus. This is sometimes called "Christology from above." Some of the discussion was about Jesus

and in what way he embodied or presented deity. This is sometimes called "Christology from below."

With the breakdown of creedal orthodoxy, Hegel and his followers developed a new form of Christology from above. It differed from the old in that the "above" in question was now that "Spirit" which is the subject of the total historical process undergoing transformation in and through it. But Hegelian Christology is similar to the old Christology in that the contingent particularities of the person of Jesus are of merely incidental interest. The doctrine of Incarnation is far more crucial for the Hegelian than is the historical reconstruction of the authentic sayings of Jesus.

Although Hegel has had profound influence on the course of modern thought, most of what we call liberal Christology has followed the second course. It has been concerned first and foremost with the recovery of the real Jesus and only secondarily with creedal affirmation. Hence, it has motivated the quest of the historical Jesus and the attempt to formulate Christology to conform with what is known of him.

In the years after World War I, Christians felt keenly the difference between both of these modern forms of Christology on the one hand and the historic faith of the church on the other. Karl Barth gave voice to the concern of a generation to recover lost elements of traditional belief. Against the Hegelian tendency to identify God with man and to see the doctrine of Incarnation as expressing this unity, Barth stressed with new force the transcendent otherness of God. Against the liberal tendency to dwell upon the personality and teaching of Jesus, he stressed the sheer fact of Incarnation. Thus he reaffirmed and intensified the orthodox claim that in Jesus the transcendent God became man for our redemption without thereby losing his transcendence.

The collapse of neo-orthodoxy has rapidly returned us to the alternatives against which it was proclaimed. The choice is now posed more harshly than ever. Most radicals have accentuated the liberal approach. They have simply lost interest in metaphysical claims about Jesus, viewing him as a "man for others" or a "free man" in relation to whom we can become free. Altizer, in contrast, has only incidental interest in the historical Jesus. For him, "Christ" names the central reality of the Christian imagination and hence of the Christian's history. Since "Christ" is bound up with the pictures of Jesus that have succeeded each other in our history, and since those pictures are bound up with the judgments of historians, Altizer does not ignore the work of the great New Testament scholars. But he interests himself in their vision of the past rather than in the question of the conformity of their vision to an objective past event. Thus Altizer identifies himself with the Hegelian tradition, carrying forward with greater radicality than ever its version of Christology from above.

3. An important feature of the style of Altizer's thought is suggested by the word "Totality." Altizer thinks in terms of wholes. He seeks the essence of an idea, a doctrine, a point of view; and when he finds it, he discards all the qualifications with which it is surrounded in order to elicit its pure and radical meaning.

This is the reason for much of the exasperation sometimes felt by his critics. In the course of time, many doctrines have been hammered out cautiously, replete with qualifications that adjust them to the various difficulties that have been encountered. Altizer ignores everything but what the doctrine in its purest essence communicates in our situation. Obviously the judgment here is somewhat subjective, and those who have been articulating the doctrine resent the neglect of their careful formulations.

At the same time, this is the reason for much of Altizer's power. He avoids involvement in the subtle and sophisticated arguments in which much academic theology bogs down. By going to what he sees as the heart of the matter and capturing it in pure and extreme form, he breaks open the broader question and forces total reconsideration.

His own intellectual development illustrates this violent refusal of qualification and moderate formulation. As late as the early '60s, Altizer believed Christianity to require of us a total rejection of all that the modern world understands as reality and creativity. Apocalyptic was for him the pure manifestation of Biblical faith, and apocalyptic was the rejection of this world in the name of a Kingdom of God that is wholly alien to it. The error of historic Christianity was that it compromised by coming to terms with the world and by affirming its value.

Altizer found that this position put him in an extremely painful situation existentially. He was forced to reject all that he admired most in art, literature, and scholarship. Furthermore, he recognized that although Biblical eschatology resembled Oriental mysticism in its negation of the given reality, it was a different sort of negation, which somehow also affirmed the forward movement of time and history.

Another man might have responded to this situation by cautiously modifying some of the extreme elements in his earlier position, but not Altizer. Instead, he reversed himself totally. Christian eschatology and Incarnation now are seen to mean a total affirmation of the world, a total identification of the sacred with historical reality. Christianity, instead of being at bottom identical with Oriental religion, is juxtaposed as its opposite. Historic Christianity is condemned for clinging to the symbols of a transcendent other.

The pattern of negation and reversal of which Altizer writes so much is here embodied in his own development. This can also be illustrated in his view of the traditional Christian doctrine of Creation. At one level this doctrine may be seen as a theory of the origin of the universe, but at this level it interests neither Altizer nor his critics. Fundamentally, the doctrine expresses a particular view of the reality and worth of the world and thus of human life. This view has a twofold movement of thought.

First, he who understands the world and himself as created perceives both as real and valuable. All being is affirmed as good because it is the product of God's purposeful intention and activity. In spite of all the horrors of suffering and sin, human life and its entire historical and natural context must be affirmed, and one must devote his energies to serving his fellowman in the concreteness of his bodily existence rather than seeking escape from these given conditions. Because the doctrine of Creation is thus an affirmation of the world, the early Altizer rejected it as a perversion of the apocalyptic negation of the world that was for him then the heart of faith.

Second, he who understands the world and himself as created perceives nature, history, and his own being as radically contingent, radically dependent upon God, radically subordinate to the Creator in both worth and reality. The meaning of life is not found, finally, in life itself as empirically given. Goodness, value, and meaning are found unqualifiedly, independently, or intrinsically only in God himself. The meaning of human existence is derivative. Because the doctrine of Creation thus subordinates the world to God, the later Altizer rejects it as a perversion of the incarnational affirmation of the world that is for him now the heart of faith.

In this way Altizer's thought has exemplified something of the coincidence of opposites that is so important to him. There *is* an affinity between total negation and total affirmation that separates them both from all qualified forms of affirmation and negation. Both total affirmation and total negation repudiate any discrimination between degrees or levels of truth and falsity or of good and evil. Both thus exclude the sphere of the ethical, the weighing of particular values against one another. They exclude in a profound sense positive concern for the individual in his separated individuality. They demand a solution of the human problem that is unequivocal, absolute, total. Thus the forward movement of history must be toward an end in which that movement will come to absolute rest, or at least to total moments in which all past and future are abolished.

The most thoroughgoing and disturbing result to which Altizer's program has come thus far is to be found in *The Descent Into Hell.* Here the totality toward which we are borne is identified insistently with hell and death. Not only has transcendence emptied itself into immanence, and the sacred into the profane, but heaven empties itself into hell, and life now empties itself into death. In this way, Altizer seeks to claim as an epiphany of Christ even the hell and death to which the modern spirit is drawn in fascinated horror.

III

In this section we will trace the development of Altizer's thought since the publication of his first book, *Oriental Mysticism and Biblical Eschatology,* in 1961. Three periods may be distinguished in this development. First, there is the mythico-mystical orientation of *Oriental Mysticism* and Altizer's journal articles of this time. Second, there is the historico-existentialist orientation of *Mircea Eliade and the Dialectic of the Sacred* (1963) and articles of that time. Third, there is the cosmico-metaphysical orientation of *The Gospel of Christian Atheism* (1966), *The New Apocalypse* (1967), and *The Descent Into Hell* (1970). The evolution of Altizer's thought through these three periods shows an ever-increasing awareness of the full implications of the dialectical method.

During the first period of his development, Altizer's primary emphasis is the Oriental tradition and how it relates to an understanding of Christianity. In the original formulations of both Buddhism and Christianity he sees a radical distinction between faith and philosophy. In both views there is an infinite qualitative difference between faith and being. For both, the demands of faith compel one to give up his ontological security in the world. In *Oriental Mysticism,* Altizer maintains that the teachings of Jesus and the Buddha exhort one to suspend "the quest for religious ontology and mystical knowledge."[1] The believer is called to reject everything he knows as reality—everything that has "being" for him. For in essence, being is man-made; it was created when man came into the world as a self-conscious being.

In *Oriental Mysticism,* Altizer observes that Heidegger, also, maintains that being is not an eternal reality equatable with the sacred or God; rather, it is a historical event involved in the establishment of *Dasein,* human existence.[2] Heidegger comments: "If I were to write a theology, which I am sometimes tempted to do, the word *being* would not be allowed to appear in it. Faith does not need the thought of being, and if it needs it it is no longer faith."[3] Altizer agrees by stating that "faith can never accept the ultimate reality of being. . . . The high moments of religion are those in which there is no awareness of being."[4] Affirmation of being in the form of the Promethean spirit is a rebellion against the sacred, for the sacred reality can be known only as wholly other than the man-made world of being.

In his essay "The Religious Meaning of Myth and Symbol," Altizer continues this same theme: "The sacred can be actualized only by means of a dissolution of profane existence."[5] Modern man, however, is faced with a much greater problem than archaic man with respect to apprehending the sacred reality. The primitive does not give ontological weight to his day-to-day mundane experience; this to him is unreal and illusory. For archaic man the only reality is the sacred reality of which he becomes a part through myth and ritual. As Mircea Eliade states, "For on the archaic levels of culture, the *real*—that is, the powerful, the meaningful, the living—is equivalent to the *sacred*."[6] For modern fallen man the situation is quite different: "Modern man experiences both an alienation of himself from the cosmos, and an alienation of the *sacred* from *reality*."[7] What is real for modern man is the profane, not the sacred. Altizer's thought at this stage remains in mystical and mythical categories; furthermore, he sees no real difference among the higher religions of the world.

The essay "Nirvana and Kingdom of God" is a transitional piece. It contains evidence of both his mythico-mystical orientation and the existentialist posture that is fully rehearsed in *Mircea Eliade and the Dialectic of the Sacred.* Christianity, which Altizer comes to hold as unique in his later writings, has not yet gained that status. He suggests that the Buddhist categories of faith that end in the experience of Nirvana can be used "as a mode of entry into the original form of Christianity." [8] He states that modern Christian theology is cut off from the sacred; we must now approach the sacred through non-Western religious forms. Following the theme of his earlier book, Altizer holds that all desire to be a being in the world must be annihilated; all history, nature, and being must be brought to an end. Near the end of the article, however, we sense a reversal of his former postion. Earlier, Altizer was advocating a leap of faith to the sacred from illusory being; but now he says that the Kingdom of God "will never dawn in us if we refuse our existence in the here and now." Being is not destroyed, as in the earlier view, but it is transfigured.

> It is *this* very reality in its sheer actuality and immediateness which is being transfigured by the dawning of the Kingdom; God appears here and not in a beyond. Therefore, the Christian must live *this* life, sharing all its fullness and emptiness, its joy and its horror, knowing that his destiny is to live *here* and *now*, allowing his life to be the metal which God's fire will transform into his Kingdom. And if we are to live *now*, we cannot escape the anguish of the human condition; if we are to live *here*, we cannot flee this condition by a leap of faith.[9]

We have now reached the period in Altizer's development that I have termed the historico-existentialist. While Altizer had earlier affirmed Heidegger's radical distinction between faith and being, he now denies it. Central to Altizer's new vision is Nietzsche, who said, "Being begins in every Now." Now we must say Yes to the being of the immediate moment, for it is the only reality we know. We cannot and should not return to the primordial totality of myth and mysticism. Hence, at this stage Altizer responds negatively to Heidegger: "Perhaps nowhere else does Heidegger so clearly reveal how his attachment to a traditional mystical form of the holy so deeply sets him against the historical destiny of our time, and so likewise does it set him against Nietzsche." [10] A Buddhist No-saying to the world is supplanted by a Dionysian Yes-saying to the world. Earlier, Jesus was compared to the Buddha; now, Christ and Dionysus are one. Earlier, to "cling to being" was to close oneself to the sacred; now, the dialectical affirmation of being in the immediate moment is an epiphany of the sacred. Later, in *The Descent Into Hell,* Altizer attempts to reconcile these two seemingly contradictory views.

In this second period of Altizer's development, the modern man of faith is called to meet his destiny in history, and he must meet it in the immediate moment. Altizer's position at this point is primarily existentialist; he will not affirm as yet a metaphysical approach to theology. Even though Altizer's faith has now entered history and the profane, its essence cannot be grasped in intelligible categories. A faith totally committed to the profane is still a scandal, an "ontological scandal." Eschatological faith is directed against any cosmological or metaphysical view that would attempt to resolve the paradox or scandal of faith. A radical faith, according to Altizer, "can know no *logos* of things." [11] Altizer contends that the modern man of faith must say Yes to the most illogical of all views of the world: Nietzsche's Eternal Recurrence. "Eternal Recurrence is neither a cosmology nor a metaphysical idea: it is Nietzsche's symbol of the deepest affirmation of existence, of Yes-saying. Accordingly, Eternal Recurrence is a symbolic portrait of the truly contemporary man, the man who dares to live in *our* time, in *our* history, in *our* existence." [12]

All reality, according to Nietzsche, is destroyed and re-created in every moment by an irreversible, ongoing dialectic of the sacred, which appears in our history and in our radically profane *Existenz.* The drama between old and new being, old and new man, is a continually recurrent one. In each moment, man lives in crisis and is placed in judgment. Each of his acts is an ontological crisis; in each act the ground of his being is destroyed. In the dialectic of the sacred there are no standpoints; there is only movement toward another and fuller experience of the sacred. To deny this dialectic is to lapse into the false security of a traditional ontology. Such an ontology formed the basis for the Enlightenment and now governs the completely profane mode of existence of modern scientific man. To affirm such an ontology and live such an existence is to live the horror that is the death of God. To affirm Eternal Recurrence and renounce autonomous selfhood is to live the Kingdom of God, which is in our midst.

These views are essentially an extension of the German crisis theology of the 1920's. Although Altizer's terminology is somewhat different, the dialectical method is ever present and strong; indeed, it is here more fully developed than it ever was in the German dialectic theology. Existence in faith involves a continual crisis between the sacred and the profane. One can choose to avoid the crisis that confronts one in each moment of his existence; he can choose instead an illusory but nonetheless secure form of nondialectical existence; he can choose to cling to the being of which his profane mode of existence seems to assure him. For Altizer, however, a nondialectical affirmation of the profane ends in despair and Godlessness, for the profane alone has no sacral or redemptive power. Only dialectical affirmation can break through this groundless "crust" of profane being and reveal the new sacred reality.

At this point in his development, Altizer has not yet reconciled philosophy and theology. I would suggest, however, that the roots of a dialectic ontology are already implicit in this existentialist stage. This ontology, however, is certainly not of the traditional sort. While the traditional ontology of a theologian such as Tillich tends to resolve the paradox of Christian faith, Altizer's dialectic intensifies it. In an article on Tillich's theological method, Jacob Taubes states that Tillich eschatologizes ontology and ontologizes eschatology.[13] I submit, to the contrary, that this interpretation does not apply at all to Tillich's ontology as it is fully elaborated in his *Systematic Theology*. I believe that this can be more aptly applied to Nietzsche and to Altizer.

Nietzsche's proclamation of the death of God brings to an end all concepts of unconditioned being and hence all traditional ontology. The death of God threatens our ontological security in the world. In short, it eschatologizes ontology. At the same time it gives ultimate reality to the very moment in which eschatological faith is realized. Eschatology, then, is ontologized. We are left with a dialectical inversion of all traditional thought about eschatology and ontology. In eschatological thinking, all being will be destroyed. In traditional ontology, being is grounded and sustained. In a dialectical vision, real being, i.e., the sacred, appears in the eschatological moment only after man's ontological ground in the world has been destroyed. A truly radical faith, Altizer insists again and again, must be an ontological scandal.

Altizer's book *Mircea Eliade and the Dialectic of the Sacred* is a curious work. As William Hamilton states: "In the book Altizer has not decided whether to do a book on Eliade (to whom he owes a profound debt) or an original piece of theological exposition. He comes up with a little of both, and the result is not structurally satisfactory." [14] Criticism ranged from outright rejection because the book was not Biblical or Christian enough to recognition of the genius of the work—with reservations concerning problems of coherence and intelligibility. As a consequence, Altizer, in the first book of his third period, *The Gospel of Christian Atheism,* "comes up with a little of both," and I believe the results are more satisfactory.

In this book, Altizer tries to move in two directions at once: toward a more Biblical theology on the one hand, and toward a philosophical theology on the other. His move toward a Biblical theology is brilliant but, according to some, unsuccessful. His attempt to build a radical doctrine of Incarnation on the *kenōsis* hymn in Phil. 2:7 raises criticism from many New Testament scholars. Theodore Runyon claims that Altizer's exegesis of the *kenōsis* hymn is invalid and shows an ignorance of Paul's doctrine of God.[15]

What Runyon has failed to see here is the fact that Altizer, in his own peculiar way, is much a part of the "new hermeneutic." In some respects, Altizer's disdain for the historical-critical method is equal to that of Barth. Altizer would hold that the meaning of any text changes with the evolution of human consciousness. Therefore, what this passage meant for Paul is not necessarily what it should mean for man living in the modern age. Altizer is in full agreement with Owen Barfield's discussion of the historical-critical means of New Testament interpretation. In *Saving the Appearances,* Barfield claims that historical criticism and traditional exegesis will someday be unveiled as forms of idolatry.[16] In a review article on Barfield, Altizer states: "*Saving the Appearances* may well point to a liberation of the Biblical scholar from an idolatrous understanding of the Bible as literal text." [17]

It is not surprising, then, that Altizer finds the dialectic and logic of Hegel so alluring. Altizer betrays his assumption of a metaphysics when he states, "Hegel's central idea of *kenōsis,* or the universal and dialectical process of the self-negation of being, provided me with a conceptual route to a consistently kenotic or self-emptying understanding of the Incarnation, an understanding which I believe has been given a full visionary expression in the work of William Blake." [18] In other words, Blake supplies the poetic vision and Hegel supplies the philosophical constructs to interpret that vision.

Altizer's second direction in this third phase is toward a more comprehensive overview; in other words, toward a cosmology. After attempting to find a Biblical base for a kenotic doctrine of Incarnation, he turns and finds a philosophical base for it in the metaphysics of Hegel. In the second stage of his development, Altizer achieved a dialectical resolution of faith and *Existenz;* it remains for him in the third stage to seek a grander synthesis with the world and the cosmic totality. The achievement of such a goal should be quite tenuous—especially if Altizer intends to retain the radicalism of his previous work. Such an achievement was something a Kierkegaard or a Barth had thought impossible. In essence, Altizer attempts to reconcile philosophy and theology and still retain the paradox of faith.

The third period of Altizer's development is characterized by several definitive changes. First, there has been a redefinition of the death of God. The early Altizer claimed that the death of God happened in *our* history and *our Existenz*. Only when a fully profane consciousness had appeared in history could one affirm the death of God. It was an existential, not a universal, event. Those still living under the spell of myth were unaware that God was dead, since they had not yet fallen into existential despair. With the assumption of the dialectic of Hegel, however, the death of God is now universalized; it is not only an existential event but a cosmic one. The death of God now becomes, in terms of Hegel, the self-annihilation of Spirit. Spirit, primordial and deficient of actuality, pours itself into the world and becomes flesh. This self-annihilation of Spirit, as Altizer says, is "at once historical and ontological."[19] The death of God is now seen in ontological as well as existential terms.

With these developments Altizer is now allowed: (1) to affirm the uniqueness of Christianity; and (2) to develop a doctrine of grace. The self-emptying of God into the world is a forward-moving, nonreversible process. God, or better, the Christ of radical immanence, is here to stay in our flesh and in our midst. Never again will Christianity be identified with a priestly or mythical form of religion—one that attempts to recapture a primordial beginning or totality. Because of this, Christianity, according to Altizer, is not only unique among the world's religions; it is the truest revelation of the movement and reality of the sacred. Furthermore, a doctrine of a self-sacrificing God allows Altizer to develop a legitimate doctrine of grace. This would have been impossible within strictly Nietzschean categories.

It is significant to see how Altizer now deals with the existentialist posture that characterized his second period of development. The existential phase was described in terms of Hegel's "Unhappy Consciousness," which is, as Altizer says, a "necessary phase through which Spirit passes in its development in history." It serves now as a transitional period for a future cosmic fullness of the sacred. Altizer states: "We cannot understand the 'Unhappy Consciousness' unless we realize that it too, like the 'Dark Night of the Soul,' is a transitional state between an individual and particular realization of the truth and the reality of Spirit, a realization whose very particularity demands a chasm between itself and Spirit, and a universal and total epiphany of Spirit which obliterates this chasm." [20] Spirit finally overcomes alienation and otherness and reveals itself as Absolute Spirit or God as all in all.

We have now reached a point in Altizer's third period that is crucial and distinctive, for it constitutes a radical break with his earlier positions. With his assumption of a Hegelian metaphysics to explain the self-annihilation of God, he has also adopted a finalism; in short, the dialectical process aims at an end: God as all in all. This is a cosmic end, and not just an existential crisis, as Altizer would have seen it during his second period of development. Earlier, Altizer would have said that there is no order, meaning, or direction in history or in the cosmos outside of the existential situation. Now Altizer does see direction: the self-annihilation of God has effected a dialectical process that *aims* and *ends* with God literally becoming all in all. God sacrifices himself to the world and, as a result, experiences the world fully. As a consequence of his being alienated and being faced with his "Other," God is able to realize himself in a far richer form. The God of innocence, after passing through self-annihilation, becomes the God of total experience and flesh.

To draw an analogy between Hegel's dialectic of Spirit and the evolution of Altizer's own thought is too tempting to avoid. Altizer states in *The New Apocalypse* that the unfolding of Spirit corresponds to a similar evolution within the individual religious consciousness.[21] In the *Enzyklopädie* Hegel states,

"The same development of thought which is treated in the history of philosophy is being portrayed in every philosophy, yet emancipated from that historic externality, purely in the element of thinking." [22] The early mythico-mystical view advocated a denial of the profane world and a return to a primordial Totality. This of course would correspond to the primordial Spirit, innocent and deficient of all actuality and experience.

Altizer's historico-existentialist period was characterized by a dialectical affirmation of the world of experience, which maximized a radical thrust into the profane only to transfigure its present form. The witness of modern literature and art to existential despair and alienation is central to this period. This stage would correspond to Hegel's "Unhappy Consciousness," which is Spirit particularized and alienated. John N. Findlay, one of the best among Hegelian scholars, describes the "Unhappy Consciousness" in this penetrating and significant statement: "This Unhappy Consciousness is aware only of its total *loss* of all that previously reassured and filled it: its anguish might find expression in the words of the Lutheran hymn 'God is dead.'" [23]

In the third period of his development, the cosmico-metaphysical, Altizer discovers that it is not solely the historical and the existential with which we must deal, but the cosmic as well. The existential experience of God is but a symbol of what actually will happen at the end of history on a cosmic level. Similarly, the death of God that occurred at the Crucifixion is but a particularized form of what is happening on a universal scale in our time. The vision of Hegel's Absolute Spirit or Altizer's Christ of radical immanence serves as an ideal aim for the dialectical process; it serves as an impetus for process and lures all process to its final end.

The Descent Into Hell, Altizer's most recent book, is the most systematic statement of his theology. In this work he incorporates themes from all his previous works; he also attempts some radical reinterpretation of Christian doctrine. One significant feature of the book, which sets it apart from other books in the third period, is Altizer's effort to reconcile his present thought with his early work on Buddhism. He returns to some of the early motifs and reinterprets them in the light of his second and third stages of development. To the unsuspecting reader, it might seem that Altizer has in fact returned to his first stage, but for those who view Altizer's development as an ever-increasing awareness of the full implications of the dialectical method, Buddhism is now seen as the reversible (i.e., dialectical) ground on which a new radical Christianity can be founded.

The sharp dichotomy that Altizer drew between the Buddha and Christ in his second period and in *The Gospel of Christian Atheism* of his third period is now seen in a different light. He suggests that the Buddha is a "face or form" of Christ; in fact, he states that we must come to know the Buddha as the primordial identity of Christ. To recognize this fact is to be freed from everything past and primordial. Altizer states: "Nirvana is not 'other' than Kingdom of God, just as Buddha is not 'other' than Christ: Nirvana is the primordial ground of Kingdom of God, just as the New Jerusalem is the eschatological realization of Nirvana." [24] Furthermore, Altizer now claims that Nietzsche's Eternal Recurrence is identical with the Buddhist Void.[25] Thus, his position in his second period was not dialectical enough; at that time he was not able to see the intimate connection between the primordial vision and the eschatological vision. The fully dialectical view sees that each needs the other for its own inherent fulfillment. In a similar way, the sacred needs the dialectical opposition of the profane for the fulfillment of its own intrinsic movement.

Far more pervasive, however, than this apparent reconciliation with Buddhism, are the principal themes of eternal death and Christ's descent into hell. In a series of significant and revolutionary reinterpretations of orthodox doctrine, Altizer contends that the true image of Christ is not the exalted Christ of the Ascension, returning to the right hand of the transcendent creator God; but it is the Christ of the Passion, ever more humiliated, ever more in the flesh, ever more with the suffer-

ing of mankind. The Passion of Christ is the particular form
and symbol of the passion of modern alienated man. The primary image of Christ in the time of the death of God should be
one of self-negation and self-giving, descent and humiliation.

Contrary to the orthodox view that the Resurrection inevitably
led to Christ's ascension to transcendent glory, Altizer's radical
interpretation of the Resurrection sees it as just another point
on the continuum of kenotic Incarnation: the dialectical movement from primordial, transcendent Spirit to radical immanence
and flesh. For Altizer, pure transcendence is a symbolic image
of primordial Spirit, while pure immanence is the symbolic
equivalent of the Kingdom of God.[26] Therefore, Altizer's "eternal death" is not a literal death as fallen man knows it; rather, it
is the same as pure immanence—the totality of flesh.

According to Altizer's kenotic view of Incarnation, Christ
did not become flesh only to leave it, as orthodox theology would
have it. Christ became flesh to remain flesh, to become a living
symbol for the man of radical faith living in the time of the
death of God. Therefore, the end result of Altizer's reinterpretation of Crucifixion and Resurrection is, as he puts it himself,
the "final and total loss of Heaven" and "the triumph of
Hell." [27] The judgment of hell means the transformation of
everything past and primordial, a necessary condition for the
triumph of the Kingdom of God. As Altizer phrases it, only
in the dialectical vision can we "be open to the actuality of our
dark emptiness as a sign of the light of the apocalyptic Christ." [28]
In another penetrating statement, Altizer makes the same point:
"Is the dark negativity of our emptiness so overwhelming that
no way is present to us of celebrating emptiness as a mask of
total bliss?" [29] In our time, such a question separates those who
would follow formal logic and resign themselves to a Godless
world from those who would affirm dialectical logic and rejoice
in the fact that Godlessness is a necessary precondition for a
modern revelation of the sacred.

IV

Most radical theology in our time seems to be moving toward a fully secular theology—toward a virtual identification of faith and culture. This can be said of theologians such as William Hamilton, Harvey Cox, Paul van Buren, the "Mainz radical" Herbert Braun, the late Paul Tillich, and many of those who follow and comment on the works of Friedrich Gogarten and Dietrich Bonhoeffer. Hence, Altizer's position among the radical theologians is a distinctive one—so distinctive that in many respects he is to be seen over and against the others named above. The secular theologians mentioned above hold a Promethean theology, one that celebrates the hubristic, self-assertive, autonomous man in search for the "sacred" as a fulfillment of our present secular culture. Altizer, on the other hand, has a Dionysian, fully dialectic theology that, by radical affirmation of the profane, goes beyond mere secularism and its Godlessness and discovers the sacred via a nonhubristic apotheosis.

Altizer is closer than any other contemporary theologian to the first radical of twentieth-century theology: the early Barth of *The Epistle to the Romans*. It should be clear at once that Barth certainly did not approve of any secular expression of faith and rejected violently all theo-philosophical attempts at "capturing" God. For the early Barth, God is completely hidden; he is unsayable and unnameable. There lies an abyss between man and God, the secular and the sacred; and the step over that abyss, from old aeon to new aeon, is one that God alone can take. No human expression, philosophical or existential, can bridge that gap. Our relationship to God, according to the early Barth, is a completely indirect one. It can be conceptualized only within the inner tensions of the dialectical method. The meaning of Paul's Romans "cannot be released save by a creative straining of the sinews, by a relentless, elastic application of the 'dialectical' method." [30] I would suggest that Altizer's method is

continuous with, and a fulfillment of, the dialectical method of
Barth's *Romans*.

Barth attempted to reconcile the brute fact of a Godless world
with such terms as God's hiddenness, his incomprehensibility,
and his complete otherness. In *Romans,* Barth said that the Word
of God can be uttered only when the predicate *Deus revelatus*
has as its subject *Deus absconditus.*[31] The vast ocean of so-called
reality that is the profane world of a completely autonomous
mode of human existence has left the island of the sacred completely submerged. Barth thought that the reason modern man
has no vision of the sacred is that he has inadvertently desacralized all reality in thinking that he is its center and creator.
Barth's theological efforts turned on his attempt to make faith
completely autonomous—free from human capability and ma-
nipulation, empty of all human content. The result was that
faith became a complete vacuum to be filled by revelation—by
the power of the sacred alone. Barth states: "Genuine faith is a
void, an obeisance before that which we can never be, or do,
or possess; it is devotion to him who can never become the
world or man, save in the dissolution and redemption and
resurrection of everything we here and now call world and
man." [32]

The parallels with Altizer, both in content and in style, are
striking and significant. In *Oriental Mysticism,* Altizer describes
faith as the "will to nothingness pronounced holy," [33] and in
"Theology and the Death of God," he states that "eschatological
faith is directed against the deepest reality of what we know as
history and the cosmos." [34] For both Altizer and Barth the
sacred reality is seen as completely autonomous. For both, there
is a hiatus between faith and being, faith and *Weltanschauung,*
faith and the secular. Contrary to the secular theologians, both
believe that the secular and the profane have no saving power.

For Barth, however, the sacred reality remained wholly transcendent. At this juncture Altizer goes beyond Barth by recognizing the full implications of the dialectical method. Although
the sacred must remain completely autonomous and incom-

mensurable with the profane, it is nonetheless inevitably found in the midst of the profane and not in some transcendent realm. Altizer's affirmation of the profane is a dialectical affirmation that seeks to destroy the profane in its present, all-too-pervasive form, in order that the sacred can be revealed in a new, immanent form. For both Barth and Altizer, the only true God is the revealed God; and for Altizer a new Christ of radical immanence is being revealed in this time of the death of God.

In essence, Altizer views the proposals of the secular theologians as forms of theological reductionism, a sellout of the sacred to the profane. The effort of these programs is to present theological terminology and formulations that will have "cash value" in terms of contemporary culture. This, of course, is quite alien to Altizer's theological intentions. In an article entitled "Word and History," he observes that "a dangerous rhetoric underlies many of these joyous announcements" of full secularity.[35] Altizer's view, again quite similar to Barth's, is that everything man has created for himself in terms of culture has been at the expense of the abandonment or dissolution of faith.[36] A genuine form of faith is one that keeps culture continually in crisis and under judgment.

In an essay entitled "The Sacred and the Profane," Altizer makes it quite clear that he does not want to deny the full movement and form of the profane.[37] He insists on avoiding the accusation of Gnosticism. He contends that his view is "non-Gnostic because a truly modern dialectical form of faith would meet the actual historical destiny of contemporary man while yet transforming his unique *Existenz* into the purity of eschatological faith."[38] This does not mean, however, that there will be an identification of faith and culture. Radical faith is a faith that dares to encounter and affirm the death of God in modern culture, but does not entail an affirmation of culture for its own intrinsic spiritual worth. It is a dialectical affirmation that will transform the present structures of the profane world, and thus it is a form of faith that goes beyond mere secularism. It is Altizer's conviction that a faith strong enough to affirm the death of God is strong enough to transform the radical profanity of a Godless world. He states, "Theology was born out of faith's will to enter history; now theology must die at the hands of a faith that is strong enough to shatter history." [39] According to Altizer, a dialectical affirmation will break through the Godless veil of the secular and reveal the new sacred reality: an immanent Christ in our time and in our flesh.

Altizer's theological convictions show not only passionate faith, but incomparable spiritual strength and courage as well. The theological program to which Altizer enjoins us is a task that only a few men have attempted or accomplished. First, one must unequivocally renounce one's individual selfhood as the center and ground of consciousness and experience. This proposal in itself is exceedingly difficult for modern man to comprehend, let alone instigate; for, in order to combat the onslaught of modern alienation, modern man has withdrawn to the refuge of his inner "self." The irony, however, is that once there, he discovers that he has only intensified his alienation.

Second, one must give up completely any hope of heaven or utopia, the womb or the Garden. In essence, one is called to reject all concepts of a primordial homeostasis; for, according to Altizer, all such yearnings contradict the fundamental movement of the sacred and what Blake called the great "Humanity Divine." Again such a demand threatens modern man's security and his deepest desires for a lost paradise. One must realize that this applies not only to the most fundamentalistic Christian but also to the most doctrinaire Marxist-Leninist. Perhaps we will come to realize, despite the passionate convictions of a Blake, a Nietzsche, or an Altizer, that only a few men have had the strength or the courage to will the "final and total loss of Heaven"; that most of us will inevitably cling to visions of utopia and will persistently deny the dialectical movement of the sacred and the New Jerusalem that Altizer claims is dawning in our midst and in our flesh.

Notes

1. Thomas J. J. Altizer, *Oriental Mysticism and Biblical Eschatology* (The Westminster Press, 1961), p. 166.

2. *Ibid.,* p. 193.

3. Published for private circulation, Zürich, 1952. Quoted in Jacob Taubes, "On the Nature of the Theological Method," *The Journal of Religion,* Vol. XXXIV (Jan., 1954), p. 19. Reprinted in Thomas J. J. Altizer, ed., *Toward a New Christianity* (Harcourt, Brace and World, Inc., 1967), p. 231.

4. Altizer, *Oriental Mysticism,* p. 191.

5. Thomas J. J. Altizer, "The Religious Meaning of Myth and Symbol," in Thomas J. J. Altizer, William A. Beardslee, and J. Harvey Young, eds., *Truth, Myth, and Symbol* (Prentice-Hall, Inc., 1962), p. 93.

6. Quoted in *ibid.,* p. 88.

7. *Ibid.,* p. 90.

8. Thomas J. J. Altizer, "Nirvana and Kingdom of God," *The Journal of Religion,* Vol. XLIII (April, 1963), p. 112. Reprinted in Martin E. Marty and Dean G. Peerman, eds., *New Theology No. 1* (The Macmillan Company, 1964), p. 162.

9. *Ibid.,* p. 116 (166).

10. Thomas J. J. Altizer, *Mircea Eliade and the Dialectic of the Sacred* (The Westminster Press, 1963), p. 215.

11. *Ibid.,* p. 189.

12. Thomas J. J. Altizer, "Theology and the Death of God," in Thomas J. J. Altizer and William Hamilton, eds., *Radical Theology and the Death of God* (The Bobbs-Merrill Company, Inc., 1966), p. 99.

13. Taubes, "Theological Method," p. 19 (231).

14. William Hamilton, "The Death of God Theologies Today," in Altizer and Hamilton, eds., *Radical Theology,* p. 28.

15. See the essay by Theodore Runyon, Jr., in this volume, p. 45.

16. Owen Barfield, *Saving the Appearances* (Faber & Faber, Ltd., 1957), p. 175.

17. Thomas J. J. Altizer, Review of Barfield's *Saving the Appearances,* in *The Journal of Religion,* Vol. XXXII (Oct., 1964), p. 385.

18. Thomas J. J. Altizer, Introduction to his "A Wager," in Altizer, ed., *Toward a New Christianity,* p. 301.

19. Thomas J. J. Altizer, *The New Apocalypse: The Radical Christian Vision of William Blake* (Michigan State University Press, 1967), p. 71.

20. *Ibid.,* pp. 43–44.

21. *Ibid.,* p. 47.

22. Georg Wilhelm Friedrich Hegel, *Enzyklopädie,* 6th ed. (Verlag von Felix Meiner, 1959), p. 47.

23. John N. Findlay, *The Philosophy of Hegel* (Collier Books, 1962), p. 51.

24. Thomas J. J. Altizer, *The Descent Into Hell* (J. B. Lippincott Company, 1970), p. 192.

25. *Ibid.,* p. 211.

26. *Ibid.,* p. 86.

27. *Ibid.,* p. 213.

28. *Ibid.,* p. 209.

29. *Ibid.,* p. 208.

30. Karl Barth, *The Epistle to the Romans,* tr. by Edwyn C. Hoskyns (Oxford University Press, 1933), p. 8.

31. *Ibid.,* p. 422.

32. *Ibid.,* p. 88.

33. Altizer, *Oriental Mysticism,* p. 112.

34. Altizer, "Theology and the Death of God," p. 109.

35. Thomas J. J. Altizer, "Word and History," *Theology Today,* Vol. XXII (Oct., 1965), p. 383. Reprinted in Altizer and Hamilton, eds., *Radical Theology,* pp. 121–139.

36. Thomas J. J. Altizer, "The Challenge of Modern Gnosticism," *The Journal of Bible and Religion,* Vol. XXX (Jan., 1962), p. 20.

37. Thomas J. J. Altizer, "The Sacred and the Profane: A Dialectical Understanding of Christianity," in Altizer and Hamilton, eds., *Radical Theology,* p. 146.

38. Altizer, "Theology and the Death of God," p. 100.

39. *Ibid.,* p. 110.

Part I

ALTIZER
AND PROTESTANT THEOLOGY

Theodore Runyon, Jr.
Thomas Altizer
and the Future of Theology

IN ATTEMPTING TO CLARIFY AND ASSESS CRITICALLY THE CONTRIBU-
tion of Thomas J. J. Altizer to theological discussion in our
time, I shall employ a rather broad descriptive typology. Like
all typologies, it will not do justice to all the factors, but its use
will be defensible, I trust, if it makes a few of the main issues
more clear.

Generally speaking, man has expressed his consciousness of
divine reality in two basic ways. One of these we shall call "the
way of *identity*," the other, "the way of *distinction*." According
to the way of identity, man intuits himself and the divine as
one, at least on the ultimate level; the way of distinction insists
on distinguishing the reality of God from that of man at every
level.

The "way of identity" is by far the more venerable and the
more universal. It can be observed as operative in some of religion's most subtle and highly developed forms as well as in its
most primitive manifestations. Whether primitive or sophisticated, however, the way of identity views reality as mono-

From *The Death of God Debate,* ed. by Jackson Lee Ice and John J.
Carey. The Westminster Press, 1967.

lithic. The gods do not have their reality independently from the world but rather are the personification of world forces. Man himself, at least in the primitive forms of this approach, does not differentiate himself from the cosmos of which he is a part. He understands himself, his society, and his daily life as an integral part of a world which is in its totality *sacred*. Though there may be areas of his life or his world which take on special sanctity for cultic purposes, these sacred acts and places only represent the whole of life, the whole of his world. The divine is intuited fundamentally, therefore, not as a separate object (even though the worshiper may be surrounded by idols) but as that which permeates his whole existence. Because the divine is continuous with the world, access to the divine requires no mediation. Insofar as he is able to penetrate through the superficial and actually illusory levels of his existence, man finds himself to be in immediate touch with the holy. He participates ecstatically in the ultimate principle of the universe.

Moreover, man intuits this ultimate principle to be unmoved and unmoving. This is why he joyfully embraces it as an answer to the problem of his own existence, plagued as he is by insecurity, instability, and change. By means of his participation in the ultimate, unmoving, unchanging reality, he is assured of that which is permanent in the midst of change. The enlightened man is thus able to recognize "change" as a deficient mode of being and finally illusory.

The way of identity, therefore, presents us with a monolithic approach to reality in which the gods, the world, and man all have an ultimate identity in the infinite, unchanging One which is All.

In contrast, the approach to the reality of the divine which I have termed "the way of *distinction*" draws a fundamental difference between God and the world, and exercises considerable effort to maintain this difference in the face of recurring tendencies to weaken or erase it. The typical way of asserting the distinction is by differentiating between Creator on the one hand

and creature and creation on the other. "Creature" and "creation," even when raised to their highest powers, are still qualitatively distinct from Creator, according to this view. To quote Kierkegaard, there is an "infinite qualitative difference between man and God." The divine is not available to man as an immediate principle either within himself or his world. Rather, contact between the human and the divine is characteristically understood as being initiated from the side of the divine and involves an interaction between the divine and the human which is analogous to interpersonal relations. Indeed, the way of distinction would assert that, strictly speaking, "relations" can exist only where there is difference, and thus it would be improper to speak of "relation" within an identity context. For things which, at the point of their mutual interaction, are intuited as identical are not related, they are simply one.

Having noted the fundamental contrast between these approaches in their understanding of the nature of the divine-human link, we are not surprised to find that the way of distinction has a contrasting view of change. "Relation" is understood on the model of an event in time and space; that is, it has a reality which transcends man as well as involving him, and it occurs in the flux of history. Time-space existence, therefore, as the arena of man's contact with the divine, is not a deficient mode of being, it is not illusory. It is just as "real" as is God himself. It is where salvation takes place.

This means, however, that the God who is interacting with man in this time-space dimension is just as involved in history and change as is man. He is not above the historical flux but commits himself to it; and he is known in the midst of the flux not as the static, unmoving absolute but as the Faithful One of Israel.

The Kingdom of God which Jesus proclaimed, and which he may have sensed as dawning in his own ministry, was the Kingdom of this kind of God and was to be realized in a new history. His ministry may have had ecstatic overtones, but one thing is clear, he conceived of the Kingdom fundamentally as the reconstituting of all relationships: God with man, man with his fellowmen, man with the world.

The way of distinction, therefore, puts a positive valuation on the time-space continuum and, though it sees divine redemption as the *remaking* of history into something new, it cannot conceive of divine-human interaction in other than historical terms which preserve the qualitative difference between God and man.

Now let us attempt to locate Altizer's contribution to the future of theology in terms of his typology. He is seeking to do a very daring thing, one that has exciting and far-reaching implications.

I believe it is accurate to say that Altizer's roots are in the identity approach. That approach has, in the past, spoken most directly to his religious sensibilities. The immediate awareness of the Holy, the *mysterium tremendum,* ecstatic participation in the Sacred: this is language he can understand and with which he can identify, as is evidenced by his first book, *Oriental Mysticism and Biblical Eschatology.* More recently, however, Altizer has become at least partially dissatisfied with "the way of identity." Why? Because in its traditional forms it is unable to put a positive value on the historical process. As a result, it can neither take the problem of evil in history seriously nor affirm a redeemed future in time. Christianity, however, does both. In Christianity the problem of evil, for example, is not an illusion which is to be escaped but the occasion for responsibility in this world, for struggle, and for ultimate victory. The present and future have significance according to Christian faith because they are the plane on which God is working out his will. God has a stake in history. He has a destiny.

Now we are in a position to see more clearly the uniqueness and daring of Altizer's theological venture. He stands in two theological worlds. He is unwilling to give up either, because he has a vision of combining both of them. This is not a matter of syncretism, he asserts, for the combination is demanded by the deepest religious insight of both approaches. What I have presented as two contradictory approaches he feels to be dialectically related. The way of identity, the way traditionally associated with Oriental mysticism, must be completed by a world-affirming involvement in history. Its world denial, if understood dialectically in terms of the "coincidence of opposites," is actually world-affirming, he insists. And this potential for world affirmation ought to be given theological expression, which the East has not as yet done. Precisely here lies the Western contribution, for only in the West, and—in spite of the fact that it was implicit in the Christian gospel—only in our time, has "change" become something no longer to be feared but rather to be welcomed as the bringer of hope and the unfolding of the divine (Hegel). "Modern man is the first to live so fundamentally out of the *future*," says Gerhard Krüger, "that for him the *new* as such has a magical attraction." [1] If it can be demonstrated that world affirmation is implicit within the way of identity, the Eastern approach need no longer place a negative value on change but can learn from the West that there is no necessary conflict between change and the divine, nor is there any need to view the dimension of the sacred as antagonistic to the phenomenon of change.

Equally important, however, are the implications for Christianity. The Christian proclamation will be complete only as it recognizes that the way of distinction was only a passing stage in the divine evolution. It was a projection of the alienation and repression which man experiences in his society. But now through the insight of the true inheritors of the Christian gospel, seers such as Blake, Hegel, Nietzsche, this projection can be recognized for what it is. It need no longer victimize and repress, for it is in the process of dying away. History is moving toward the ultimate dissolution of the distinction between God and man and a merging of the two in the new godmanhood of the eschatological age.

This vision of a new way of identity Altizer sees as inherent in the true meaning of the incarnation. Theology in the past, he argues, has not taken with radical seriousness the claim, in Phil. 2:7, that Christ, in entering the world, "emptied" himself

(Greek, *kenōsis*) of his divinity, pouring out his divinity into the world and assuming full and complete humanity. With this one act of self-giving, namely, the life and death of Jesus, God willed to join himself with the world, so that from henceforth he is no longer to be found in the heavens—the transcendent, domineering God is dead—but must be found where he wills to be found, that is, in his world.

It has taken Christianity nineteen hundred years to discover that the God who is distinct from man and the world no longer exists, says Altizer. The seers of the nineteenth century finally grasped the fact, and now it is breaking through to the masses. (It is in this dual sense that Altizer wants to insist that "God has died in our time, in our history, in our existence.") His point is that this death of God was implicit from the beginning in the Christian proclamation, for it was a death willed by God himself. Though we are only now beginning to realize it, as our awareness of this fact increases we move into new possibilities for becoming sensitized to the life of God in his incarnate form, that is, in the world Christologically viewed. Our eyes are opened to his epiphany, and we begin to see the dawning of that Kingdom which complete union with the divine in this world will bring, namely, the new humanity, the divine humanity, our being remade in the image of Christ, our identity with the truly Sacred.

Anyone who is serious about the task of theology in our day cannot but appreciate the breadth of Altizer's vision and the ambitiousness of his undertaking. If he succeeds, he will have accomplished what no other theologian has done: he will have joined the characteristic religious ways of the East and the West together in one consistent approach, albeit on an Eastern base but with strong Western contributions. This accomplishment would have consequences of the utmost importance for missiology and ecumenism. Thus, regardless of one's attitude toward Altizer's thought, there is no denying its seminal significance.

Let me now indicate, however, what I consider to be the chief difficulties in his approach. I shall mention just two.

My first question has to do with Altizer's interpretations of Biblical passages and of traditional Christian doctrines. Is it legitimate, on Biblical and historical grounds, to make the kind of nondialectical use of traditional language which Altizer does? He employs (*a*) the *kenōsis* passage of Philippians, (*b*) the doctrine of the incarnation, and (*c*) the eschatological message of Jesus to justify dissolving the distinction between God and the world, bringing God into identity with the world in a way which, though initially dialectical, is ultimately thoroughly monistic.

Altizer's interpretation of the self-emptying (*kenōsis*) of Christ as the merging of God with the world may be defensible if one is reading Paul via Hegel and Blake. But if one is attempting instead to get at Paul's own orientation, then it would seem that for Paul the most basic sin of man is that he confuses God with the world, the Creator with the creation:

Claiming to be wise, they became fools, and exchanged the glory of the immortal God for images resembling mortal man or birds or animals or reptiles. . . . They exchanged the truth about God for a lie and worshiped and served the creature rather than the Creator. (Rom. 1:22–25.)

How can a reading which eliminates the distinction between Creator and creation claim to do justice to Paul's theological intention?

Nor did the historical doctrine of the incarnation intend to provide a basis for a dissolution of the difference between man and God. Even in Chalcedon's tortured attempts to bend rational language to serve the cause of paradox it is evident that in the description of the new humanity, Jesus Christ, the God-man, the distinction between the divine and the human is to be maintained:

> We apprehend this one and only Christ . . . in two natures;
> . . . without confusing the two natures, without transmuting
> one nature into the other. . . . The distinctiveness of each
> nature is not nullified by the unity.[2]

Regardless of what one thinks about the adequacy of this formula, it is clear that the classic doctrine of the incarnation cannot be construed as supporting, even eschatologically, a dissolving of the distinction between God and man.

Finally, Jesus' own apocalyptic message can scarcely be credited with pointing toward the elimination of the Creator-creature distinction, for his was the proclamation of the inbreaking of the reign of the *Lord*. And "Lord" and "servant," even when transmuted by Jesus into "father" and "son," remain distinct, noninterchangeable categories. In raising the term "son" to the highest power, we still have "son" and not "father." To be sure, the inbreaking of the Kingdom meant the transvaluing of all previous religious and cultural values; but this transvaluation was one of completely reconstituted relationships, not one of mystical identity. For Jesus, the eschaton means that God will be God, and man will be man and not attempt to be God anymore. True creaturehood will be restored, which is at the same time full humanity. And thus there will be peace, joy, life!

It would seem to me, therefore, that the use Altizer makes of Jesus' eschatological message, Paul's notion of the self-emptying of Christ, and the traditional doctrine of the incarnation, is suspect in the light of their historical contexts and original intentions.

My second question has to do with the nature and extent of secularization and the response appropriate to it.

Contrary to the impression some may have received, Altizer is not uncritical of the process of secularization. True, he warmly greets the process insofar as it is releasing persons in our time from their bondage to the transcendent God (who in his dead and negated form is better identified as "Satan"). Yet, unlike those who might uncritically embrace the "secular city," Altizer recognizes that secularization is a very mixed blessing. Why?

Because it destroys not only false religion but any sensitivity to the Sacred as well. The technological world is no new savior. It is dull, flat, boring, and finally demonic, because it prevents the realization of that new humanity which is only possible where the Holy is present and participated in. Therefore, for Altizer, secularization is *good* insofar as it destroys that God who is different from man, but *bad* insofar as it also eliminates the religious instinct, the awareness of the Sacred, that divine dimension of experience which is intuited as identical with man's own ultimate being and destiny.

At this point I should like to suggest an approach which is quite the opposite. Secularization is *good,* it seems to me, insofar as it undermines excessive confidence in the religious instinct or intuition (Bonhoeffer calls it the "religious *a priori*"). The religious instinct appears to be a fairly universal phenomenon. Men have from time immemorial experienced wonder, mystery, awe, and dread in the face of the inexplicable and uncontrollable forces of nature and of their own inner nature, and have hypostatized these experiences in the gods. But critics as diverse as Calvin, Marx, Julian Huxley, and Bultmann have recognized that to give these experiences absolute status and authority is to fall into ideology. Calvin labeled the religious instinct "the idol factory of the human heart." And Marx was hopeful that as man more fully mastered his environment and destiny, residual religious feelings would wither away. The religious ideology would no longer be necessary when its source in human feelings of finitude and limitation had been overcome by man's success in organizing his world. Marx may have been overly optimistic in his prediction. Nevertheless, insofar as Marxism exposes the products of the religious instinct as ideology, as one stage in man's development which is now being made irrelevant, thus undermining confidence in the absoluteness of the religious intuition, Marxism may be Christianity's secret ally in world history. Secularization is therefore good as it undermines man's confidence in the ultimacy of the religious intuition as *the* clue to the divine.

However, from the same standpoint, secularization would be

bad insofar as it itself turns into an ideology, secular*ism,* which collapses reality into a self-contained monolith, so that there is no longer anything or anyone to call man out of identity with his world into responsibility for it.

Where the gods are identical with the world, man can have no independence from it either. The political scientist, Eric Voegelin, points out that modern technological secularism has, in effect, reversed the movement which took place in ancient Israel. That ancient movement was one in which man achieved independence from his world by being called out of his identity with the cosmos to assume a place of responsibility over it. He was called to this independence and responsibility by a God who was different from the world. Only where God remains distinct from the world is this kind of call possible. When this God dies, the cosmos is the only reality left; the process reverses, and man slips back into identity with his world, back into the pre-Judeo-Christian form of religion.[3] Yes, modern secularism remains "religious," but it is a religion of identity: one aspect, one dimension of the world is exalted, is mythologized, represents the whole. And the new, technologically monolithic world has shown an amazing propensity to spawn mythological expressions by which to give itself identity (now that it has lost its relativity to a transcendent God), myths of race, class, nation, blood, etc. Man continues to attempt to create within his windowless world some kind of absolute, some dimension of ultimacy. All he seems to be able to bring forth, however, is more fanaticism, the clash of absolute with absolute, of ideology with ideology, always attaching what is left of the religious instinct to his creations and demanding obeisance.

Altizer is, of course, just as opposed to this kind of idolatrous absolutizing of the world as is any sensitive thinker today. I do not see, however, that he has any real basis or norm within his approach of identity for calling man out of identity. The Archimedean point of reference is missing, for God has no dialectical reality apart from us as well as in our midst, no reality apart from the world as well as in it. Therefore, there is no basis from which to create what I would call genuine historical existence, nor any way to call man to what seems to me the vital need of our age, the vocation of responsible technological existence. Strictly speaking, a "vocation" cannot be self-given; one must be called to it. And where there is no one to call, the understanding of life as vocation drops away. This is precisely modern man's problem. He no longer has a context within which to understand his life as responsible to anyone but himself.

What is needed, therefore, is not a collapsing of reality into a monolith of immanence but rather the recovery of a language by which man can be called out of identity into responsibility. This I take to be the crucial task of theology in our time.

But allow me to push this questioning of Altizer a bit farther. What he understands to be the point of identity with ultimate reality, namely, the awareness of the Sacred, the sensitivity to the Word incarnating itself in our flesh, I would contend—with the Marxists—is in actuality simply our own aesthetic faculty, a sensitivity with which everyone is endowed to a greater or lesser degree. Most of us have experienced "finitude" and "ecstasy," which seem to mark off the standard range of "religious" awareness. To be sure, these experiences are also found in the "way of distinction," where they may accompany the event of relation. However, to paraphrase Martin Buber, while they may accompany the event they do not constitute it.[4] Our aesthetic sensitivities, important as they are in experiencing life to the full, are a part of the world, a part of creation. To exalt them, including the most purely "religious" intuitions, to some kind of absolute status, or, which is to do the same thing, to assume that they are *the* means of access to the ultimate, is to be involved in ideology.

My own inclination is to say that genuine historical existence, understood as relation with the Other, is possible only when all ideologies, including religious ideologies, are called into question. From where I stand, therefore, it looks as if the "radical theology" represented by Altizer is not radical enough. Its atheism is a soft atheism. It disposes of the transcendent God, to be sure, but puts in his place something that looks very much like an aesthetic ideology to which is attached the label, "Christ is alive!" In comparison with this, the hard atheism of a Sartre or a Camus, who refuses to be drawn into ideology, is still somehow more attractive.

Summarizing the crux of our difference of theological approach: From Altizer's standpoint, the God I am advocating, the God who is *distinct* from man and the world, is a repressive figure who must be killed in order that the God who in Christ is identical with the world might emerge. From my viewpoint, what needs to die, or at least to be relativized, is absolute confidence in the religious intuition of man, which in this form I take to be a deifying of the aesthetic dimension of the creature. For only when our confidence in the ultimacy of our instinctive religiousness has effectively been challenged can we begin to be sensitive to the God who is distinct from man, who calls us out of identity with our world into responsibility for it.

I have posed the issues as forcefully as possible not to deny the contribution of Thomas Altizer but to affirm it. More than any of his colleagues in the theological movement of which he is a part, he is blazing new trails beyond the provincialism of Western theology. Even if one cannot agree with the particular amalgam of East and West which he is evolving, one cannot deny the importance of the task to which he has committed himself nor its usefulness as a stimulus to the overall task of arriving at a new language—or languages—which can communicate to man once again both divine and fully human existence, the goal we are all seeking.

Notes

1. Gerhard Krüger, "Die Geschichte im Denken der Gegenwart," *Grosse Geschichtsdenker*, ed. by Rudolf Stadelmann (Tübingen: Rainer Wunderlich, 1949), p. 224.

2. John H. Leith, ed., *Creeds of the Churches* (Doubleday & Company, Inc., 1963), p. 36.

3. Cf. Eric Voegelin, *Order and History,* Vol. I: *Israel and Revelation* (Louisiana State University Press, 1956).

4. Martin Buber, *I and Thou* (Charles Scribner's Sons, 1958), p. 14.

William A. Beardslee
Dialectic or Duality?

IT IS A PRIVILEGE TO RESPOND TO THE THOUGHT OF DR. ALTIZER, from whom I have learned as much about theology during the past ten years as I have from anyone else. But I do not find my response easy to formulate. It is not difficult from the fact that in Dr. Altizer's theology I am, as a believer in the old transcendent God, unwittingly a servant of Satan—in all seriousness, that can happen to any theologian, and we need to be able to see ourselves in that light. The difficulty is simply that I do not find it easy to be sure that I have really grasped the center and thrust of his thought.

Let us first sketch very briefly some of the leading motifs of his theology. Central and basic is his dialectic. There are no fixed things. The structure of human reality is process, and this process is not additive, but dialectical, which means that time does not bring just an accumulation or enrichment as the case may be, but a reversal whereby things pass into their opposites. But the dialectic is not simply cyclical (things passing into their opposites and back again indefinitely); the dialectical is fundamentally one-directional and telic. Its central key is the dialectic of Spirit and

From *Criterion*, Spring, 1968, with a title change by the author.

flesh: Spirit, existing originally *in itself,* apart, moves into flesh where it exists *for itself,* and this consciousness of itself as "there" in flesh makes possible a richer existence in itself. The ultimate goal, which will be also an end (*finis*), will be the complete passing of Spirit into flesh. I take Dr. Altizer to hold that all important human meaning takes part in the dialectic process. For human meaning centers in faith; and we now see the dialectic of faith, that is, of Christian faith, in its radicality, namely, that the transcendence of God passes totally into the immanence of Christ, so that transcendence when perceived as such has only a shell left—the power of repression. Hence faith calls us to be completely open to the present moment, so that the energy of love may be released with no reserve or restraint imposed by past forms. The very darkness of the present moment signifies that a new epiphany of Christ may dialectically take place if we give ourselves totally to the world. Even though such a way of faith may exist principally as a *vision,* and be as yet largely beyond our grasp as a whole way of life, nonetheless it is the only framework of reference for human meaning to the man of contemporary Christian faith.

This is a very bare statement, and no doubt is inadequate. Dr. Altizer sums it up by calling on the Christian joyfully to will the death of God. I have tried to do this, and I only draw a blank; it is not possible for me. Perhaps I cannot articulate the reasons with full clarity, but let us look at some of them. What you will find is a humanistic Puritan commenting on the work of a radical theologian—in many ways no new situation, since radical theology has important roots in left-wing Puritanism, and there is a long history of bitter controversy between Puritanism and its left wing.

My first comments will deal with the structure of existence as perceived by Dr. Altizer. In Dr. Altizer's vision, repression and energy are polar opposites (it seems to me that most of the time he thinks about them dualistically rather than dialectically). Love means release of energy, openness, total presentness; and it involves, of course, complete freedom to enter into suffering as well as joy. With all of this I am in accord, but I separate myself from him when he explicates his meaning by contrasting all this with any form of withholding energy. What I see here is the fear that any structure channeling the energy of love will be antithetical to love, will be, in fact, a retreat from love or from life, and this does not correspond to reality as I see it. Life and love require structure for fullness. It is evident that the sexual symbolism so fully used by Blake (and so widely felt to be the fullest symbolism for total presentness in the imagination of our time) carries with it this sense of the dissolving of structure, of the loss of self in total union. At the same time, the inability of sex to provide a full release from selfhood could raise some questions about this model for understanding "presentness."

To me the fundamental point is that some elements of pattern or structure are precisely what enable energy to manifest itself with totality and power. At this point the "I-Thou" symbolism of Buber, Ebner, and others is more adequate than the sexual symbolism. The mutual openness of love comes to its fullest expression not in a merging in which all structure is lost, but in a patterned mutuality. It is true, as Buber pointed out long ago, that one cannot confront the "thou" in a fixed or rigid structure, but the relationship nonetheless spontaneously takes *form*, and the form includes a withholding, a shaping, even a repressing of energy. In other language, harshness and grace need each other, and they are inextricably interwoven in the very necessity of form in the relationship of love.

Related to the dislike of form in Dr. Altizer's thought is his dislike of the past, for he understands form primarily as the fixed form imposed by the past, which the present must break. This stance toward the past is extremely widespread today, and assumes varied forms. In Dr. Altizer's thought the predominant note is that time is a leaving behind of the past. Of course, he perceives our own time as one in which historical roots are not available, but he has generalized this particular situation which he finds in Western civilization into a universal dialectic, or perhaps more properly antagonism, of the past and present. Pastness is deadness, sterility, repression. To live we must live in the present, and faith is able in some sense to make the future already real in the present, so that the future is not something "out there" on a line of time, but that which reaches into the present in faith. However, for Dr. Altizer, faith does not seem to have a similar creative relationship to the past, toward which its stance must be one of breaking away and freeing itself.

It is obvious that in comparison to the openness of the present, there is a sense in which the past is dead. But it seems to me that Dr. Altizer has fallen into a naturalization of historical time, that he has been led astray by his nineteenth-century mentors, who were battling against the rigidity of a mechanistic universe, for there is no doubt that in the mechanistic and objective sense the past is dead and unchangeable. No doubt human and historical time shares this quality—a word once said can't be unsaid. But my perception of historical time is very different from Dr. Altizer's. Memory is the central focus of historical time, and in the context of memory the past is a living resource, and not just a repressive and negating factor. In my perception, time "buds" (a metaphor which I acquired from William James via Dr. Ivor Leclerc), time pushes forward as the fluid and growing tip which is supported by and draws resources from the harder but still living stem behind it. The past provides possibilities (and though memory is the central locus, these possibilities are by no means confined to what is consciously remembered). It may be that the direction of the present comes from the future, not from the past; but the past is constantly reaching into the present in countless ways, both creative and destructive. Physically, we carry the past around with us in our bodies, and meet it in our environment, so that in some sense the past is already the future—and this is so not only physically—what we have already done to our children is part of their future. But this does not have to be understood in a rigidly deterministic way. The past will bud forth into the future as part of the complex fabric of the successive presents. Each present is free within the conditions and possibilities offered to it by its past. This is the way existence is, and if you want to love it and enter into it completely, it will not do to chop off the past and regard it as simply negative and repressive.

Of course I recognize that each of us speaks from a particular and limited point of view, and we know that the experience of alienation from the past is widespread today. Lawrence Durrell had to escape what he called the "English death," and his rebellion against what seemed to him to be the rigid and lethal forms of the English past produced the volcanic eruption of *The Black Book*. Dr. Altizer's book—also black—is a kind of volcanic eruption against the "Christian death" which threatens the life of faith. But I would remind you that Durrell came to write the fantastically structured *Alexandria Quartet,* in which, even though the selves in it do not escape from the relativity of their own selfhood, nonetheless memory, and thus the past, plays a central and creative role. I venture to hope that Dr. Altizer will move beyond his negative view of past time to draw more sympathetically upon the past that lives within him as a Christian. In particular I refer to his several references to the negative function of memory and to liberation as forgetting. Thus my judgment is that the traditional view of the past as a living resource is more adequate than the contemporary one which Dr. Altizer, along with many others, so eloquently represents. This criticism is obviously closely linked to the former one, for in both cases the thesis is—in line with my Puritan tradition—that limitation and form are essential to life and that formed life is full life. Even though the quest for an adequate form for life and faith is the agonizing quest of our time, this quest is not rightly expressed as a quest for freedom from form.

Next, with regard to the very important role of the concept of "the future" in Dr. Altizer's thought, I find a very considerable ambiguity here, as to whether the future as eschatological future is grasped as vision or as analysis of actual existence in faith. Clarification of this point is important to his thinking. One vein of his thought presents the dialectical movement of the transcendent into the world as a continual one, to be consummated at the "end." On this view there would presumably still be some transcendence left, so to speak, even though the real intention of the future would be disclosed by the vision of an immanent Christ which Dr. Altizer sets forth. Thus a positive alternation between past and future would be possible. The other vein speaks of the dialectical movement as already completed, so that there is no transcendence left (except the dead shell of oppression which grips those who reach out toward transcendence in the old style). It seems that if the former vein, which is usually the secondary one in his thought, were to become primary, the whole structure would look quite different. If the total coincidence of transcendence and immanence is *vision,* and not *structure of existence,* then the traditional styles of faith and practices of faith may still have possible meaning, even though they are seen to be penultimate; and then the radical theologian can be understood as standing in a spectrum of theological positions and not in isolation.

Dr. Altizer picks out the eschatological symbols of total reversal, of forgetting, of loss of identity. But along with these the eschatological language uses symbols of fulfillment—notably the symbol of the "city," which is the profound eschatological symbol with which the Bible closes. This is a symbol of the taking up into the final reality of the hopes and strivings and work of the past—a structured symbol, in which transcendence has indeed become totally present, but in which form, pattern, dance, differentiation still have meaning. Dr. Altizer's hope moves toward a point—all his lines converge. I am suggesting that the older eschatological visions were right in projecting the lines through the point to a reemergence of moving, living pattern.

The future is problematic in another sense in Dr. Altizer's thought. He has so harshly applied the dialectic of opposites to the contrast between present and future that his eschatological future is made to contrast completely with the present. Thus the present, including what we may call the visible and human future, is forced into the category of total darkness. This absolutism has its clearest historical counterpart, not in Biblical eschatology, but in Gnosticism.

This comment leads to a related point at which I part company from Dr. Altizer, indicated by his frequent references to "Totality." To me this is a very Gnostic-sounding word raising the question whether Dr. Altizer's resolute dialectical inversion of Gnostic patterns of thought has really been successfully achieved. One way of describing Dr. Altizer's effort is to say that he recognizes that Gnosticism, as flight from reality into a private religious world (or ideological world), is the great temptation or even treason of today, and that to combat this threat he has boldly adopted a typically Gnostic pattern of thought as the vehicle for expressing total commitment in and for the world.

Characteristic of Gnosticism, as of Dr. Altizer, is the sense of a radical split within the divinity; and also characteristic of both is the faith that the radical split is overcome by acknowledging the ultimate unreality of one side of the split—in Gnosticism, the evil, worldly side will eventually become nothing; in Dr. Altizer's thought, the transcendent side has assumed the negative sign and either will become, or has become, nothing. Common to both is the quest for an ultimate beyond the god of religion, and this ultimate has in both the character of "totality." The quest is also expressed by the term "radical" in "radical theology," for it is characteristic of radical theology as Dr. Altizer uses the term that it involves a quest for totality, which denies ultimate differentiation.

There is obviously a drastic difference between Dr. Altizer's worldly totality of Christ and the Gnostic vision of a transcendent totality. But both have in common what I may call a "refusal of distance." The quest for "total redemption" on which Dr. Altizer is embarked (note the continuity with left-wing perfectionist sects in Protestant history, "antinomians") is restless with an awareness of distance between the human and the divine.

Perhaps one could say that this theology is too serious—too serious about man and hence unable to accept the distance between man and the transcendent. A little more irony about the human might allow more scope for the stance of awe which Dr. Altizer finds passé, but which is so deeply built into the various forms of the response of faith.

So far our comments have been largely a contrast of stances toward human existence: a plea for a more truly dialectical, less dualistic understanding of the relation between form and energy, a plea for a similar openness toward the past, a question about the future to the effect that the incompleteness of the present ought not to frustrate Dr. Altizer into insisting that the total *reversal* promised by the glimpsed eschatological future be the only standard or norm of faith. In a way my question about "totality" and "the refusal of distance" sums up the other questions and suggests that a stance which has a larger component of irony and understatement toward the self might be able to bear the fragmentary character of existence with less restlessness toward totality.

Can we now turn from these comments toward a more positive statement? I agree with Dr. Altizer on the crisis character of the present theological situation, in which the old expressions of faith are, all of them, called into question. I hold, with him, that a movement of deeper interaction with the contemporary world is required of theology if it is to have a future. At the same time I concur in his fundamentally confessional stance that what is particularly required of the Christian theologian is a clarification of the meaning of Christ.

At the same time I find that he has adopted a rigid dialectic that forces reality into patterns to which it does not correspond. It is clear that I hold the association of transcendence with rigid negation to be wrong. Just as in human existence the pressure of structure has always to be imposed upon energy, so too, any ultimate to which we respond will embody both the elements which are traditionally known as justice and love. Similarly I find his dialectic of past and future to be out of correspondence with reality, forcing him to reject not only the past but the non-eschatological future as positive elements in his theology.

Dr. Altizer's emphasis on process I take very seriously. The process of reality includes God himself, and he is affected, even changed, in the process. A key element in the process of reality is incarnation, the embodiment of the transcendent in the world, the actualization of spontaneous love. For the Christian, Christ is the paradigm of incarnation, or love, and Christ is to be understood as a living reality who is not unaffected by the encounter of incarnation.

Further, I concur at least in the willingness to explore an orientation toward the future which (however inadequately worked out, as noted above) is a central feature of Dr. Altizer's theology. Christ is fundamentally to be understood from the future, not the past. It is apparent that we are just seeing "the future" becoming a central theological concern. I would suggest, however, that theology needs to be more open to various modes of the future than Dr. Altizer's system allows: both to the impact of the future as presented in a corpus of Christian tradition under the theme of "hope," and to the future as it presents itself to our secular world.

Thus, to sum it up, I should think that a more adequate line of theological exploration would entail the working out of an understanding of Christ and God that views them in a framework of process, but understood in such a way that process involves cumulative enrichment and fulfillment and not simply dialectical reversal. The life that is through death is not wholly discontinuous with the life before death. It is apparent that I am sympathetic with, and open toward, the various attempts to restate Christian affirmations in Whiteheadian categories, for Whitehead's thought seems to me to offer a categorical framework which may express a grasp of process appropriate to Christian faith.

Further, faith must be understood more fully in a framework of community than is the case in Dr. Altizer's work (for him the outsider is the model of faith). A fuller grasp of the inter-active, community dimension of faith will make it possible and necessary to retain ethics in its traditional proximity to theology.

The quest for a more universal form of faith is one on which we shall be embarked for some time. It is not always possible, in the midst of the quest, to judge which are the false starts. Personally, I should find it more helpful to quarry into the old *logos* theology, and interpret it with a deeper sense of man's historicity, than to cut off the doctrine of Christ so sharply from its roots as Dr. Altizer seems to do.

Thomas J. J. Altizer
Response

I

I AM DEEPLY GRATEFUL TO THEODORE RUNYON FOR THE MANNER in which he has presented my theological quest, particularly insofar as he has seen it in terms of an attempt to join the religious ways of East and West. I am also pleased that he has chosen to do so by way of a typology posing a fundamental difference between the way of identity and the way of distinction. This is clearly a way of meeting the difference between the religious worlds of East and West at its deepest level. Not only does this means of approach allow the worlds of East and West to speak for themselves, but it is also an effective means of raising the theological question of whether or not Christianity is ultimately a universal way of faith. Few theologians would answer this question negatively, and in our day many of our most gifted theologians, including Runyon, see the universality of Christianity in terms of its necessary and inevitable expression in a historical process of secularization, a process that has perhaps already triumphed over the religious world of the East.

A fundamental problem posed by Runyon's analysis has to do with the meaning of "relation." Let us grant that in the way of distinction true relation can exist only where there is difference.

Time-space existence then not only becomes the arena of man's contact with the divine but also becomes just as "real" as is God himself. My first question is, How can the way of distinction know that historical process is just as real as God if it posits an infinite difference between man and God? If the goal and ground of the way of distinction is the restoration of true creaturehood where God will be God and man will be man and not attempt to be God anymore, than how can man know thereby that he is just as "real" as God? This problem becomes particularly acute for a theological position that repudiates both the aesthetic and the religious faculties as sources for a true or genuine knowledge of God. Are we to believe that the God of the way of distinction has revealed that the ultimate reality of the world is just as "real" as is the ultimate reality of himself?

A second question has to do with the human and historical identity of the way of distinction. Presumably the way of distinction is a religious way; or, at least, it is presented in the context of a typology distinguishing between contrary ways of man's consciousness of divine reality. Quite clearly, it is also intended to comprehend the Christian faith. But here a problem arises. If Christianity embodies a negation of religion and of the religious instinct, then how can it be a religious way of distinction? Does this mean that the way of distinction is a non-religious way and that only the way of identity is religious? If so, is Christianity the only way of distinction? No, for it would appear from Runyon's analysis that the God of the way of distinction is present and known in the worlds of Judaism and Islam. Then does anything whatsoever distinguish the God of Christianity from the God of Judaism and the God of Islam?

I am particularly intrigued that Runyon is honest enough to say that the Kingdom of God which Jesus proclaimed is an eschaton that will "restore" true creaturehood, or full humanity. Apparently it is an eschaton or an end that will reverse the Fall and return humanity to its pristine and unfallen state. Here, our end lies in our beginning, our goal is a state of primordial innocence. Moreover, the God of the end is the God of the beginning, the primordial and transcendent Creator. If so, does Jesus' proclamation and ministry embody a new revelation? Isn't the God of the way of distinction more clearly manifest in the Old Testament than in the New? If we identify God with the transcendent and primordial Creator, then isn't the fullest and most powerful witness to God present in Second Isaiah and in The Book of Job? Or in the Koran? Surely the early surahs of the Koran contain far purer images of the transcendence and sovereignty of God than does the proclamation of Jesus. Or does Jesus transcend both religion and historical revelation by abolishing all images of God? Then how can we know that God is Creator? Mustn't we then be silent about God? Isn't full humanity a state in which one ceases to talk about God and religion and all ideologies and talks instead only about man, the world, and the secular?

Are we then to assume that the pure form of the way of distinction has become manifest only through the historical process of secularization? Is the new language that will communicate both divine and fully human existence to man once again a language going beyond and transcending Biblical language? Or do we reach the true meaning of Biblical language by passing through a process of secularization that stills all human language about God, thereby allowing man to respond passively in faith to the full and final language of God? This would appear to be the real goal of the secular school of contemporary theology, and I think it does full justice to the meaning of God-language for us. Only when man can no longer speak about God can he hear and respond to the Word of God. I think that this school has truly gone beyond Barth and neo-orthodoxy by recognizing that it is only a fully and finally secular man who can speak about God. I also think that it has gone beyond neo-orthodoxy in reaching a manifestly non-Christian position. Here, God appears as being absolutely sovereign and transcendent, so transcendent that there can be no human language about God, and so sovereign that God can be known only by way of the image of the Creator, and this is an "image" that negates all human vision of God, an image totally confining man to the creaturely realm, to the secular, or to the "world." God is now real both apart and within, but he is real in our midst only insofar as he silences our religious and aesthetic faculties, thereby liberating us for a life in which only man and the world can appear or be manifest.

I delight in Runyon's excellent critique of my theological way because I believe that it makes manifest the anti-Christian consequences in our time of classical Christian language about God. Despite all its concern with the secular and the future, or perhaps because of it, secular theology is finally grounded in the God of the absolute Beginning, and it wishes to restore man's pristine and therefore prehistoric state. True faith in God is an openness to a Kingdom of God in which God will be God and man will be man and neither will speak or appear in the form or language of the other. There will be no human language about God, no human vision of God, no religious awareness of God: in short, it is only Godless man who can truly have faith in God. Jesus then becomes the one who points to the state of total creaturehood, a state of full humanity in which man is only man, and all human language about God, the ultimate, the total, the final, etc., will simply disappear. The Kingdom of God as the brave new world? Here, man can know that within his windowless world there can be no dimension of ultimacy. Or rather, the ultimacy that he has been given is an ultimacy that stills and silences every human voice about the ultimate, so that here man will listen only to God. And what will he hear? Nothing that can be expressed in a human or creaturely language; nothing, nothing whatsoever! Then man will truly be servant and God will truly be Lord.

II

William A. Beardslee speaks from a different perspective than that of Theodore Runyon, but both raise the important question of the meaning of the dialectic of faith, just as both pose the question of whether my position is dialectical or dualistic. Beardslee's astute and penetrating analysis suggests that my thinking has fallen into a naturalization of historical time by way of my inability to establish a creative relationship between the present and the past. I am sensitive to this criticism because it is obviously a just one, and I am embarrassed because Beardslee has taught me so much about the past. Am I to repay that debt by understanding the past as the ground of repression and death? As Beardslee recognizes, this understanding derives from a particular historical situation, our situation, a situation in which many Christians are unable to apprehend their historical past as a living resource for the contemporary life of faith. Have I generalized this particular situation into a universal dialectic or antagonism between the present and the past?

No doubt I have and my initial defense is that every theological position reflects a particular historical situation and whatever universality it reaches can never wholly transcend its particular and relative historical ground. If the universality of a theological position can be measured by its transcendence of this ground, then my position is all too limited and particular. There is in this context, however, the further question of the relation between our particular present and our apprehension of the meaning of form and structure. Certainly ours is a century in which the traditional Western forms have been collapsing about us, but in the arts and sciences at least, the dissolution of old forms has gone hand in hand with the birth or rebirth of new forms. May we hope that a comparable process is occurring in the arena of faith, and that it is the birth of a new form of faith that has given the old form the image of darkness and death? For a truly new form of faith can be born only out of the ashes of the old, and to the extent that the old form remains powerful and real the new form must remain unrealized and unreal (as witness, the opposition that Paul and Luther established between the law and the gospel).

It is my persuasion that the thinker who has most truly understood the revolutionary and dialectical meaning of faith is Hegel,

and that we must ever return to Hegel for a theoretical understanding of the meaning of a movement of dialectical negation.
Hegel's *Aufhebung,* or dialectical negation, is a movement of
history and consciousness wherein the old passes into the new.
It is not that the old is literally negated or forgotten, but rather
that it is transcended in such a manner as to allow its own life
and energy to evolve into a new form. The crucial point is that
it is only an act or movement of negation and transcendence
that makes possible the advent of the new. The power and the
fullness of a new form of energy and consciousness is inseparably
related to the negation that it effects of its own original ground.
We could put this position into an explicitly Christian context
by saying that the new testament will truly be new to the extent
that it embodies and effects a negation and transcendence of its
old-testament ground. This formulation would also capture the
Hegelian point that no entity is eternally given and unchanging,
just as no identity truly remains itself apart from a process of
change and transformation, a self-transformation in which each
identity becomes itself by passing through its inherent other. It is
the old testament that becomes the new testament, not in the
sense that the Old Testament gives way to the New Testament,
but rather in the sense that the old testament itself becomes the
new, but it does so only by ceasing to be old.

Thus I would maintain that it is only in the context of the
new testament that the God of the old testament can be known
as being alien and other. We can learn through Paul (as Beardslee has taught me) that it is only to the extent that we live in
faith that we are liberated from the law, only to the extent that
we live in Christ or in the new aeon that we are liberated from
the power and authority of the old aeon. The power and reality
of the old aeon are not simply or literally negated in Christ, they
remain present in what Beardslee calls the *structure of existence,*
and are negated and transcended only in what Beardslee calls
vision and Paul calls Spirit or the new creation. So, likewise, as
Beardslee points out, it is only in *vision,* or in the new creation,
that the "end" is consummated; apart from *vision* we can know

the "end" only as merely future. But a dualistic danger arises here, namely, the danger of establishing a dualistic distinction between old and new creation, as though old and new are literal and unchanging opposites. I would say that we actualize this dualistic danger whenever we impute a given and unchanging form to either old or new creation. Moreover, as I am coming to see it, it is the old creation or old aeon itself that passes into the new creation. And only to the extent that the old aeon is negated and transcended can the new aeon be actualized and real.

The danger, as I see it, of maintaining traditional styles and practices of faith in a new situation is that their very life and existence will block or reverse an eschatological and dialectical movement of faith. Doubtless, as Beardslee insists, symbols of fulfillment are essential to eschatological symbolism. But apart from a movement of dialectical or eschatological negation, fulfillment will not be eschatological; it will either fail to move from the old to the new or it will dualistically isolate the new from the old. The fundamental question here is the question of the relation between old and new in eschatological faith. In some sense the new fulfills the old, but in what sense? Surely the new does not fulfill the old in an obvious and clearly apparent sense, just as Jesus is not openly and obviously the Christ. Furthermore, the historical expressions of eschatological faith do employ the symbolic language and imagery of opposition: old and new, light and darkness, flesh and Spirit. May we say that old and new are truly opposite in eschatological faith, and that it is only on the basis or ground of this total opposition that an eschatological fulfillment can occur? Beardslee sharply opposes this position and suggests that it is in Gnosticism and not in Biblical eschatology that we find such a total opposition. Is it true that there is no dialectic of opposites in Biblical eschatology? If so, my own position is Biblically groundless.

It is true that I am fascinated by the religious symbol of "Totality." I have learned through Joachim Wach and Mircea Eliade of its immense power in the history of religions, and Hegel and Blake have convinced me that it is an essential ground of dialectical thought and vision. Must we say that eschatological faith is closed to a vision of "Totality"? Why then do we find therein such symbols as old and new creation, old and new being, and old and new aeon? Nor do such symbols play a peripheral role in eschatological faith; they are rather at its center, even if that center was lost in the established form of the Christian tradition and in its nondialectical theologies. If the idea or symbol of "Totality" is foreign to a genuinely eschatological faith, then what meaning can be present in Paul's hope and assurance that God will be all in all? Or in Jesus' proclamation that the Kingdom of God is dawning in our midst? Or in the expectation of the coming of the Paraclete in The Gospel According to John? Yes, images and symbols of "Totality" are fully present in Gnosticism, and they are not fully present in orthodox Christianity. Yes, radical theology, as I understand it, just like the radical faith that is its source, does embody a quest for total redemption, and it does deny ultimate differentiation. Does that mean that it must finally be judged to be non-Christian?

I am particularly indebted to William A. Beardslee for the way in which he has presented my own theological quest, and especially so for his point that I have attempted to invert the Gnostic vision of a transcendent totality in my quest for a totally immanent Christ. But I must resist the judgment that such a quest entails a dualistic rather than a dialectical form of faith and understanding. Let me confess that a substantial body of my work is either implicitly or explicitly dualistic. But to the extent that it is dualistic it is a failure, and I acknowledge it as such. The more I have struggled to formulate a dialectical theology the more I have recognized its overwhelming difficulty.

Is a consistent and comprehensive dialectical theology a possibility? Or is it impossible for dialectical theology to go beyond Luther and Kierkegaard? We know that a fully and totally dialectical vision is present in Buddhism. Is it impossible in Christianity? I believe that it is insofar as we remain bound to the dominant Western symbol of the eternal and unchanging distance between God and the world. I also believe that to the extent that we remain bound to that symbol we will be closed to the fullness of eschatological faith. Unless we engage in what Beardslee astutely calls a "refusal of distance," we will not be able to break away from the contingent particularity of our Christian history, a history that in any case is rapidly coming to an end. True, we must seek a community going beyond and thus negating everything that is manifest to us as a Christian and ecclesiastical community. Only such a radical negation will make possible that universal form of faith which is our goal.

Part II

ALTIZER
AND CATHOLIC THEOLOGY

Eric C. Meyer
Catholic Theology
and the Death of God:
A Response

THIS ESSAY IS AN EFFORT TO REFLECT ON SOME OF THE PROBLEMS raised by Dr. Thomas J. J. Altizer's serious attempt to show that a Catholic death-of-God theology is possible. Dr. Altizer explored this possibility in a paper that he read in the summer of 1967 at the Catholic University workshop on the problem of God in contemporary thought. The paper was printed in the 1967 summer issue of *Cross Currents* but mistakenly entitled "Catholic Philosophy and the Death of God." [1] My intention is to show why Altizer's careful arguments in favor of the possibility of a Catholic death-of-God theology are inconclusive. This essay does not purport to be a fully adequate encounter with Altizer's radical theology; but however small, I hope it will be a genuine contribution to the ongoing task of responsible theological reaction to the earnest questions and challenges put to the Catholic faith by members of the death-of-God movement.

I shall begin by underlining some of the most important things

From *Chicago Studies,* Summer, 1969, slightly modified by comparison with the typed version.

Dr. Altizer has said in addressing himself directly to Catholic theology. I will follow this by a critique of his understanding of the category of analogy in Catholic theology and of his arguments to show the evolutionary nature of God. After that, I will recall the central thesis of his paper and then summarize and respond to each of his efforts to answer the three objections he himself considers against his project of showing that a Catholic death-of-God theology is possible.

I

Altizer's probe of the possibility of a Catholic death-of-God theology is a real venture in creative ecumenical thinking. It is perhaps the most important attempt to date to bring death-of-God theology out of a purely Protestant theological world into the center of Catholic reflection as a Catholic program and not just a Protestant curio requiring at the most an occasional Catholic commentary. There is a firm and practical acceptance of the unity of Christian theology in that Altizer concedes that if death-of-God theology is not a possible option for Catholic theology, then he must reluctantly admit that *no* Christian death-of-God theology is possible and that atheistic theology is a "destructive aberration." This serious confrontation with Catholic theology, which he explicitly recognizes as a Church theology, is also an ecumenical breakthrough for Altizer's own radical theology, because it means that Altizer has relented somewhat from his very negative attitude toward the Christian Churches and Church theologies, which in *The Gospel of Christian Atheism* he pronounced thoroughly demonic because of their alleged efforts to return to or cling to past forms of God's revelation of himself.[2] He now grants that it might be possible that it is atheistic theology which is demonic. Beyond this initiation of direct discussion between Catholic theology and death-of-God theology, Altizer calls on all Catholics and Protestants to occupy a common theological frontier with regard to atheism—examining together if it be a genuine possibility that atheism might be the final stage in the development of Christian faith. Altizer doubts that real ecumenicity with the modern secular world is possible until Christianity can see how atheism might be accepted theologically.

The most important concern in Altizer's thought is the significance of the problem of atheism. He does not simply take note, as so many have, of the pervasive and seemingly irreversible rise of atheism during the nineteenth and twentieth centuries in everyday life, in literature, philosophy and, indeed, all throughout our culture. He emphasizes the Christian and theological character of the rise of atheism. Modern atheism is a Christian problem in part because it has evolved quite specifically in the Christian West and because it often bears the Christian characteristics of humanism, optimism, and a hopeful forward-orientation. The negative efforts of traditional Christian apology against atheism have only further removed Christian faith from the secular world. Even within the Christian Churches there is growing admission that it is more and more difficult to call on the name of God and that the experience of God's *absence* is overpowering. Altizer rejects many of the more recent positions toward the problem of atheism: that we need a long moratorium of God-talk, that God is somehow eclipsed for a time but will return, that what God is in himself is eternally unnameable, that what has died is some idolatrous idea of God, that there never was a God and now he is unthinkable because any need for such an idea has passed. Altizer contends that an in-depth examination of the nature and evolution of Christian faith will show that atheism can be a final stage in the development of Christian faith and theology. He argues that it is possible to reconcile Christianity and atheism because something really happens in God which explains his demise in our consciousness. In his view this happening is that the transcendent God becomes incarnate as Christ and dies once and for all to his transcendence with the death of Christ to become universally immanent in man and cosmos. As God's immanence in man continues to evolve toward

a final apocalyptic goal of the complete identification of everything, so that God eventually will be all in all, the memory of
the transcendent God becomes ever more distant and alien.

I believe it is true and important to maintain that the experience of the absence of God is today our principal problem, a
Christian problem and a theological problem that requires a positive theological answer. Nonetheless we will see that the manner
in which Altizer attempts to open up the possibility to his kind
of death-of-God theology for Catholicism must be judged inconclusive.

In his paper Dr. Altizer appeals for a systematic theological
assimilation of cosmic evolution and the developmental character of historical consciousness. He insists on a general revelation in nature (and that therefore its character must be evolutionary) and that the Church's unity with the world be thought
out. Most importantly, Dr. Altizer places the Incarnation at the
center of any theological consideration of atheism, maintaining,
orthodoxly enough, that Christian theology must be Christology.
The concreteness, fullness, and irreversibility of God's Incarnation and death in Jesus of Nazareth is one of the most striking
elements of Altizer's Christology and an important departure
from the merely moral rendition of the Incarnation's meaning
that one seems to encounter in so much of modern Protestant
systematic reflection on the Incarnation. For Altizer, God quite
actually and historically became Jesus and died in Jesus' death
to any transcendent separateness. The Incarnate Word now is
not a resurrected Jesus as in any way distinct or individual or
personal. The Incarnate Word is present as having become universally and immanently one with all cosmic and human energy
and life, and this entire dialectically evolving process of energy
and life is gradually moving forward beyond all past and present
forms to a Final Totality or coincidence of opposites that will be
in its ultimate condition a perfect identity of oneness. An important aspect of Altizer's Christological thinking is systematically to unify Incarnation and Eschatology by way of his theory
of the dialectical movement of transcendence into immanence and

on to a final apocalyptical identity. This last aspect of Altizer's eschatology is not clearly developed in his essay; however, it must not be lost sight of if we are to avoid the error of thinking that he proposes that the present immanence of the Incarnation process is the final condition of God's dying to transcendence so as to be all in all.

II

Altizer is correct when he says that Catholic theology is attempting to go beyond relating God and world in a merely negative way by its use of analogy. The analogous relation of God and world does claim to express a relation with positive content. It tries to bridge over absolute dichotomy. It does not affirm a mere dualism. The analogous relation is even "integral," at least from the side of the world in its complete dependence on God. But in Catholic theology "analogy" fully intends to preserve the polarity of that relation and even to include the negative as well as the positive aspects of the polar relationship of God and world. What is commonly attributed to God and man is said of God in a manner *essentially* different from the way in which it is said of man. Even if we might speak of both analogues as in process with relationship to one another, such a process is only similar in the analogues, not essentially the same or identical. Analogy is not the kind of a dialectical relation that terminates in complete coincidence or identification. Analogy is necessarily relational, but relation is eventually destroyed in identification, in becoming an identical one. The concept of analogy cannot be manipulated to overcome relation between God and world. It presumes and strives to cope with distinction and relation. In view of his supposed rejection of any static logic of identity and contradiction, it is not without interest that Altizer cannot acknowledge a dialectical relationship that comes to terms with a coincidence of real opposites but only with such an understanding of dialectics as will lead to its own destruction by the annihilation of the polarity in a final, posthistorical, permanent identity. In Altizer's concept of cosmic and historical process, an initial monism (the Original Totality) falls into the related parts of God and world, which slowly merge again by the entire and gradual process of Incarnation into a final monism (the Final Totality). Now, as we have said, analogy within Catholic theology is at base relational. It is not inimical to process and transformation and unification, but it is opposed to monism.

In his essay Altizer uses various arguments to contend that God's nature is dialectically evolving process, the progressive process of the transformation of transcendence into immanence. I believe that these arguments may be summarized in three syllogistic forms for purposes of a tidy discussion. Proceeding in this manner does some injustice to Dr. Altizer's fluidity of thought, but I think this injustice is neither major nor completely avoidable. Of that we will let the reader who has the industry to reread Altizer's paper as well as this critique be the final judge.

The first summary may be phrased in this way: God is "analogously or integrally" related to the cosmos. But the cosmos is in evolution and undergoes transformation. Therefore, God evolves or undergoes transformation.[3] We have already argued that the Catholic understanding and use of analogy cannot be put in service of Dr. Altizer's position because he miscalculates the Catholic stance on analogy. The Catholic theologian would conclude no more than that God may be said to evolve from the side of the cosmos' relation to God, but that evolution in God would be essentially different from what is in the cosmos. Further, since Altizer already holds that everything (God included) arises by way of the fall of creation from an Original Totality without distinctions before that fall, his argument does not proceed with the Catholic idea of the analogous relation of God and the cosmos.

The second summary may be made in the following manner: Faith bears such an essential, necessary, and integral relation to its object (God) that God cannot properly be said to exist independently of what faith apprehends him to be. But what the faith is has undergone and continues to undergo historical and evolutionary transformation. Therefore, God has undergone and continues to undergo historical and evolutionary transformation.[4] The evolutionary movement of faith is a consequence of the evolutionary movement of God.

Can we assert of anything we know (that is not purely a logical construct) that it has no existence independent from what we apprehend it to be? To say so would require that we know it with an exhaustive intuition of its total presence. This would appear to dispense with *faith* in the sense of evidence of things unseen. Besides, if we cannot validly conclude with Anselm to the real existence of God even though our idea of him as perfect being includes existence, how can we validly conclude with Altizer to the evolutionary nature of God because our current idea of him as living includes process and transformation? Still further, one must recognize that if God exists in no other way than what our faith apprehends him to be, then, because there are today simultaneously many different and conflicting faith apprehensions of God (even among Christians), God would be nothing other than many different and conflicting things at one and the same time. It was with this problem in mind that the German Cardinal Nicholas of Cusa tried to elaborate the principle of coincidence of opposites. God *in himself* exists as an identity that somehow reconciles all of the many conflicting ways in which we know him, but we do not grasp that identification itself. Altizer uses this idea, but only as the ultimate goal of a dialectical process that has already emptied the transcendent God into man and cosmos and will eventually pour every opposite into a final identity. However, if God really has no existence independent of what our faith apprehends him to be and if the evolution of faith is a consequence of the evolutionary movement of God himself, it would seem more logical to conclude that *at the present time* God is moving in many different and opposed directions. On the basis of these two *ifs*, a return to polytheism would have the edge over pantheism or atheism.

I think one must grant that God's revelation of himself, his saving presence for us, has truly evolved—at least in the Incarnation.

But one cannot argue that because God is one, therefore this presence is all there is to God (and then accuse dissenters of having to posit two natures in God—one really revealed and one still "other"). Revelation is the way in which God is present to us and for us. Catholic faith and theology see world, Scripture, Church, and Christ (*the* sacrament) as sacraments of God—as body in which, by which, and through which man (because man is body) receives God's presence and returns his love. God remains himself even in his increasing presence or immanence. The tension of this dialectic is intellectually agonizing (as is faith), but it does not stumble into the nonencounter of a deistic dualism or a pantheistic monism. It would seem to me that Altizer's position is perilously close to being the equivalent of the latter, at least in his concept of origin, of the Incarnation and the apocalypse. Pan*en*theists of the Whiteheadian and Hartshornean variety have much to offer at this junction (since a very explicit effort is made to reconcile classical theism and pantheism), but considering that position would be a digression from our purpose here.

A third summary of Altizer's argumentation is the following: The Christian must believe that the transcendent God emptied himself into Christ and became fully present in him. But Christ was fully flesh and really died on the cross. Therefore, in Christ's life and death the Christian must believe that transcendence was fully transformed into immanence and finally died to itself.[5] It is not at all clear why the Christian must accept so literal an interpretation of the *kenōsis* doctrine. Exegetical options with regard to Philippians 2 and John 1 do not demand such extreme literalness. Certainly the great Christological Councils do not present the kind of *kenōsis* Altizer says the Christian *must* believe. It would seem that by "Christian" here Altizer means the radical Christian atheist. But Altizer robs his own argument of strength when he says that the forward-moving process that is God "cannot fully and forever be identified with any one of His manifestations. . . ."[6] I would point out that he says "fully" as well as "forever." In another place he tries to say how God in some manner remains the same in that "as God moves forward his full life and energy are carried into new forms or expressions so that his energy remains itself even while undergoing transformation." [7]

Therefore, Altizer does have a kind of transcendence in his concept of God as forward-moving process, but *that* transcendence seems to have or be the very forms of cosmos and man now, even though the forms of cosmos and man are passing away as the energy moves on to a final identity of all opposites. Altizer's literal interpretation of the Incarnation in this third argument seems ultimately even more self-destructive than Origen's well-intentioned but much too literal interpretation of Christ's words to his disciples about those who have courage to make themselves eunuchs for the sake of the kingdom of heaven (Matt. 19:12). Not only does God as the transcendent Christian God die to himself in Altizer's thought, but Christ dies completely to any individual personality and continues only as the universally immanent dynamism (which Altizer names the Incarnate Word), which gradually converges everything dialectically toward apocalyptic identification. As for ourselves, every form or particle of ego or individuality or personal consciousness must be extinguished in that final absorption of every distinction. This would seem to be the castration of everything we know as self and cosmos.

III

The following quotation from Dr. Altizer's article states its thesis. I have added the numbers and capitals.

I propose to examine . . . with the purpose of ascertaining whether or not it is closed to the Catholic thinker: the possibility of an atheistic or death-of-God theology. Many critics have charged: (1) THAT A DEATH-OF-GOD THEOLOGY CAN HAVE NO POSSIBLE GROUND IN THE LIFE OF THE CHURCH, (2) THAT IT

IGNORES OR SIMPLY NEGATES THE CHRISTIAN TRADITION, AND (3)
THAT IT COLLAPSES THEOLOGY INTO A NATURALISTIC OR HUMANISTIC
ANTHROPOLOGY. Now if these charges are true I can see no possibility of a Catholic death-of-God theology, nor for that matter
could I then see the possibility of any form of Christian
atheism. But I believe them to be untrue, and I shall approach
these charges by way of taking up the question of the inherent
possibility of a Catholic atheistic theology.[8]

Here we can raise three questions: (1) Can Altizer's death-of-
God theology have a possible ground in the life of the Church?
(2) Does it ignore or simply negate Christian tradition? (3) Does
it collapse theology into a merely naturalistic or humanistic anthropology? In the rest of this article we will comment on these
questions.

1. In part, Altizer seems to be contending that God already is
dead even within the life of the Churches. He would argue *ab
esse ad posse.* He says that Catholic artists are no longer producing life-giving images of God, that Church people are themselves
admitting that even in their rare moments of prayer they cannot
evoke the image of God nor call on his name (because these are
inextricably linked with transcendence) and that many of the
Church's own radical prophets and seers have witnessed to the
death of God and to the fact that we can speak of God only when
we speak of Christ.

Could one argue that God neither existed nor was known to
Jews or Muslims because he was never pictured in their noniconic
art? Besides, the state of Catholic art would not seem to be theologically very different from the past with regard to God-images.
The old man and dove symbols were never very life-giving. Christian art has *always* found its real life-giving images in Christ. As
to the second point, *"Lex orandi est lex credendi"* for the Catholic, and the Church has consistently prayed "through Jesus Christ,
Your Son, Our Lord." Even the words of the "Our Father" were
remembered as the words of Christ addressed to the Father Jesus
reveals. Further, the liturgical revival, the growing interest in

Scripture, in retreats, and in new forms of group prayer and apostolate would seem to indicate the opposite of what Altizer argues. It may be true that *contemplative* prayer is waning today. However, even if it were clear that contemplative prayer and God as transcendent must stand or fall together (and that is not clear), one would have to point out that it is strange that, if the transcendent God died fully and finally to his transcendence in Jesus of Nazareth, contemplative prayer should have flourished so vigorously in the sixteenth and seventeenth centuries, not to mention the classical theistic theologies of the fourth and fifth centuries and the thirteenth and fourteenth centuries. Finally, is it a departure from the uncompromising Christocentrism of Pauline and Johannine theology for the Church's latter-day prophets and seers to say that we truly speak the name of God only when we speak of Christ?

In his more important argument Altizer says that God's dying to himself so as to become fully one with all men can have a ground in the very life of the Catholic Church in that the Church is not only *not* bound to any past images of herself, but her very goal and mission is to open up to and be incorporated into the entire world. The Church is to be the body of Christ. But the *total* body of Christ involves all the cosmos and all human life and energy and consciousness. Therefore, the Church is not restricted to its merely institutional forms but becomes one with all men and the entire cosmos. Underlying his argument is Altizer's basic belief that the Christ that is now present (that has negated and moved beyond the forms of the historical Jesus and the Christ of the Gospels) is an Incarnate Word that is fully immanent in the world and in all human energy and life and progress. The Church is the whole body of the present Incarnate Word. Therefore, the Church must become the whole world and must die to any form separate from the world.

Catholic theologians have often spoken of "the natural Christian" and "the anonymous Christian." Christ is confessed as both creator and redeemer, and it is claimed that he has already won the victory over death and begun the renewal of all things. I think, therefore, it must be said from the Catholic viewpoint that the saving presence of Christ is everywhere immanent (without annihilation of his personal unity), but this presence is not automatically unitive in such an *opere operato* manner that it requires no human involvement nor choice. In this sense, it seems to me that we may say that all men are potentially and even virtually members of Christ already, but the presence of Christ is not a demonic suppression of human selfhood and its freedom. Even if one attempts by subtle arguments to show that somehow men really accept Christ in their very seeming rejection of him (because the Christian witness they encounter is either unworthy or incomplete and so on), there is still always the possibility of sin, of closing in on oneself against Christ. If there were no such possibility, there would be no possibility of any free, personal acceptance of Christ either. Therefore, although the institutional Church is not exhaustively the entirety of the body of Christ, this fact does not require that the Church have no explicit and definable expression whatever nor that the Church must be willy-nilly everything. As a matter of fact, redemption or the new creation should radically change the old creation; and the completion of the new creation is not simply independent of man's response.

Furthermore, Altizer himself has argued in effect that the institutional Churches are not in the Church because they are not members of the body of the present (and therefore the only) Christ. He judged them to be fundamentally guilty of heresy by their clinging to the transcendent God and to the Christ of the Gospels. This "religious" faith and theology of return to past forms separates them from the only true Incarnate Word of Christ of the immanent present. Therefore, if it is possible to separate oneself in this way, then the whole world cannot simply be the Church.

Altizer has not shown that the life of the Church can be fully absorbed into the cosmos as he proposes. Therefore, he has not been able to demonstrate convincingly that it is really possible in this regard for his brand of death-of-God radical theology to be grounded in the life of the Church.

2. Altizer contends that Christian tradition is not simply negated but *dialectically* negated, i.e., that precisely by negating its past and static forms it is affirmed in a transformed way so as to bring the entirety of its life and energy forward into the present and future. This continuing dialectical transformation moves toward a culmination in Christian atheism precisely because authentic Christian tradition must reflect the dialectical movement of God, who emptied himself into Christ and by the death of Christ became universally immanent in cosmos and consciousness and continues there to move on toward the final identity of opposites in which God will be all in all. Therefore, although everyone experiences the absence of the transcendent God, it is only the Christian who can really know and name this absence as the death of God. Confessing God's death is, then, a Christian profession of faith which moves Christian tradition forward to the atheistic evolution of its own intrinsic destiny in a final apocalyptic Totality.

First of all, I would like to point out what seems to me the logical conclusion of Altizer's contention that tradition must follow the movement of energy beyond every particular form, in the direction of an apocalyptic identity of opposites in which God will be all in all. If this were merely another *form* of the dialectical process of energy and life—rather than the energy and life itself—it would be static and require the fixation or death of process or movement. Therefore, if the process of life and energy is not to go on endlessly negating every new form in order to move beyond it, if a final coincidence of opposites is *actually* to be achieved, then that coincidence would have to be formless or pure energy or life. But such an abstraction or formlessness of energy and life is the equivalent of the "Pure Act" concept of God, an actuality that has realized every possible form. The method of arriving at this concept is certainly different, but the result seems largely the same. This idea of God, however, is so excessively abstract and even deterministic that it seems foremost among the perishing or deceased God-concepts. Secondly, Altizer's idea of God's finally becoming all in all is an ultimate identification of opposites that annihilates all distinctions. But from our viewpoint as persons, this differs in no practical way from a final nothingness. God again becomes a monster-God that devours us. Thirdly, traditional Christian faith has always stood on Paul's either/or proposition in 1 Corinthians 15:19: "If our hope in Christ has been for this life only, we are the most unfortunate of all people." Christian tradition stands or falls on a personal salvation beyond the brutal collapse of death. We puzzle over how that trust could be realized. We puzzle over the nature of Christ's resurrection, and the locus of the resurrected Christ is extremely problematic, but in *so* merging Christ with cosmos and consciousness that he has no personality of his own in any sense, Altizer certainly seems to have negated Christian tradition. At any rate, he has not shown us convincingly that his death-of-God theology meaningfully affirms Christian tradition.

3. Altizer argues that Catholic theology has always recognized a general revelation (besides the special revelation of Scripture), that it has never separated God the creator from God the redeemer, and that it has always grounded itself in philosophy and natural theology. But if this is true, then it cannot now separate its doctrines of God, Christ, Church, and Faith from the historical development of human consciousness and the fact of cosmic evolution. But evolution involves transformation and takes us beyond past forms much as the living stream of present-day biological life has left behind the dead fossils of its past. Therefore, Catholic theology can be open to the possibility of becoming one with death-of-God theology and leave the transcendent God himself behind as a dead fossil. However, this does not mean that theology becomes a mere naturalistic or humanistic anthropology, because even while undergoing kenotic transformation God remains one with himself in the sense that the totality of that forward-moving energy and life can be said to be God and always remains the process of energy and life, and because, if I may add this point from *The Gospel of Christian Atheism,* death-of-God theology demands a real wager of faith in the totally present and immanent, evolving

Incarnate Word as the only Christ (risking complete loss if Jesus Christ is the same yesterday, today, and forever).[9]

If Altizer has not already reduced theology to a naturalism, it still seems to be the *goal* of his dialectic, for God and man are moving toward a final coincidence which will be a dialectically attained identification of opposites—not a coincidence of juxtaposition or harmony or even of union. It is not at all clear how with this eschatology he avoids the objection that he reduces theology to a naturalism. The God of the end will not be different from anything else. Even at this present, pre-apocalyptic stage of Altizer's Incarnational dialectic it is difficult to see how Altizer has avoided the charge he seeks to offset. Perhaps he might answer by describing this dialectical movement as a mutual one, as he often does in *The Gospel of Christian Atheism,* that the spirit becomes flesh and the flesh spirit. However, if this is to be more than a mere switch in poles, then both spirit and flesh must pass into one another and become some third thing (a synthesis or coincidence of the two that is a new identity rather than a tensive relation of the two in union and distinction, since Altizer appears to reject the latter idea of coincidence). But if this is the case, then man should have already correlatively died to himself as man just as much as Altizer claims the transcendent God has died to himself as God. Since Altizer claims the transcendent God has fully and finally died to himself, this hardly seems very believable.

If God dies to transcendence or separateness and becomes fully and irreversibly immanent in man and world, in the movement of human consciousness and cosmic evolution—and so much so that Altizer often repeats the words of Blake that God exists and acts only in existing and acting men, and that he can say in his essay that God has no separate nor independent existence apart from what faith apprehends him to be—then, it appears unclear why this consciousness should still be called faith, since it is the very consciousness of God become man. It would seem that the process of energy and life which God still remains is, at least in the passing present, the evolving cosmos-man form of God, even if this form is to be dialectically negated and gone beyond in the future. It is clear that Altizer is not a positivist in the normal sense of the word, but humanism and naturalism need not be so restricted. It also seems clear that *de facto* most humanists find that Altizer's explanation of our experience of being without God demands too much faith, but my point is that this demand for faith is not clear from within Altizer's own system, because he asserts that God has through Christ quite fully emptied himself into cosmic evolution and our human consciousness. If God now does not exist nor act except in existing and acting men, then faith is only another word for human consciousness.

Altizer has not effectively clarified how his death-of-God theology avoids reducing theology to a merely naturalistic and humanistic anthropology. Therefore, on this count also it does not seem that Altizer has shown us the possibility of a Catholic death-of-God theology.

NOTES

1. Thomas J. J. Altizer, "Catholic Philosophy and the Death of God," *Cross Currents,* Vol. XVII (1967), pp. 271–282.

2. Thomas J. J. Altizer, *The Gospel of Christian Atheism* (The Westminster Press, 1966). Cf. especially pp. 9–28.

3. Altizer, "Catholic Philosophy and the Death of God," especially p. 278.

4. *Ibid.,* especially pp. 275–276.

5. *Ibid.,* pp. 275–276, 279–280, 281.

6. *Ibid.,* p. 278.

7. *Ibid.,* p. 279.

8. *Ibid.,* pp. 271–272.

9. Altizer, *The Gospel of Christian Atheism,* pp. 137–138.

James W. Heisig
Man and God Evolving:
Altizer and Teilhard

On Easter Sunday, 1955, Pierre Teilhard de Chardin, the noted Jesuit scientist and mystic, died in New York City of a sudden heart attack. After a life dedicated to the discovery of God's revealing presence in an evolving universe, and yet banished and silenced in his own church, it seemed appropriate that he should depart this life on the day of the great epiphany of the Lord as victor over sin, ignorance, and the established religion. Eleven years later, on Good Friday, 1966, a new edition of *Time* magazine rolled off the New York presses with the announcement of another untimely death—the death of God. In bold red letters set on a somber black background, the words "Is God Dead?" jolted the religious sensitivities of millions during the time of the highest feast of the Christian year. Meanwhile, the principal protagonist of the new "radical" theologians, Thomas J. J. Altizer, an Episcopalian layman and professor of religion at Emory University, was busy lecturing on this bizarre theme and coming under the censure of ecclesiastical authorities. Two un-

Previously unpublished.

orthodox theological currents confronted traditional Christianity
—one convinced of God's living reality, the other preaching his
obituary. Each has had an unforgettable impact on contemporary
man; each has threatened, inspired, and deepened man's religious
understanding. Teilhard's lasting influence, as many have already
suggested, will probably lie more in the direction of his poetic
inspiration than in the formation of a systematic world view. His
expertise in paleontology and his deeply mystical spirit combined
in the project of bringing the opposing forces of Christian theology and evolutionary science into a harmonious synthesis. Yet
the continued enthusiasm and research that his writings have oc-
casioned since his death are due not so much to his scientific and
philosophical achievements as to his imaginative and visionary insight. In retrospect, it is perhaps fortunate that the forced soli-
tude of his life spared him the overexposure to mass media that
has absorbed so many a prophetic voice prematurely.

Altizer's influence for the future, however, seems precarious.
Coming from a background in comparative religion and nineteenth-century philosophy, he has attempted to bring together human existence and divine life, to show how the changes in Christian experience run parallel to the very evolution of God himself
in history. While publicity gave him nearly two years of attention, it has also diluted his thought, letting it softly drift into the
breeze of passing fashions. Few critics seem to have read him
seriously, and nothing resembling a complete critique has been
forthcoming. As a theologian putting himself at the mercy of
journalism, he has fared worse than his work deserves.

Despite one's first impression that a death-of-God theology is
hopelessly incompatible with a deeply God-centered theology,
there is much that the writings of Dr. Altizer and Père Teilhard
share in common. It is my purpose in this paper to compare their
thinking in several salient areas, in the hopes that this will help
render our contemporary Christian myths more transparent and
spell out their consequences more fully. In order to bring the
comparison into context, it is first necessary to summarize the
thought of each man.

At the risk of oversimplification, we might characterize Altizer's theology as an attempt to bring man to a radical Christian humanism that will involve the denial of all past forms of God and Christianity. The theoretical foundation for this view lies in the centrality of the Incarnation, for it is precisely Jesus Christ who has made man aware of God's role in history and the demand to incorporate it into an understanding of human history. Taking his lead from Hegel, Altizer sees the sacred—or "divinity"—as formerly identifiable with a fully transcendent and personal God. Later in its evolution, the sacred poured itself out (by *kenōsis*) into the fully profane and immanent personality of Jesus of Nazareth. This act of Incarnation resulted in the literal death of the transcendent God of the Old Testament and issued in a new "Age of the Spirit." After the death of Jesus, the process of incarnational evolution took a new turn into the "Third Age of the Spirit," resulting in the disassociation of the sacred from one profane personality and its subsequent movement toward total identification with the world by becoming coextensive with humanity. Thus man now finds himself in the process of moving dialectically toward an eschatological point, where Spirit and flesh become united in an apocalyptic coincidence of opposites.

Man's tendency to understand this world in continuous and static terms, according to Altizer, is responsible for the fossilization of past forms of Christianity prolonged anachronistically into the present. Hence, his deep concern for burying once and for all both God and church in order to align his loyalties fully with Christ—the symbol for the sacred at work in human history—as he is becoming present "in every human hand and face."

The guiding element in Teilhard's world view was his introduction of the evolutionary principle into God's relationship with man, by means of which he wove a vision that both broke from the traditional transcendence-immanence dualism and challenged many timeworn dogmas of divine providence. Beginning from empirical scientific evidence, Teilhard gradually develops a metaphysics in which man appears as the product of a dynamic, evolving universe. His law of "complexity-consciousness" returns us to a Ptolemaic world where man once again becomes the focal point of existence. This law states that there has been a tendency through time for matter to become increasingly complex in its organization, and that with this growth of material complexity there has been a corresponding rise in the level of consciousness. The causal principle of this process is what Teilhard calls "radial energy," a force inherent in the very structure of matter, propelling it toward union and eventually manifesting itself as "Love." Hence, Teilhard finds a *without* and a *within,* matter and Spirit, universally present at every level of existence.

The steps that Teilhard distinguishes in evolution include the geosphere (matter), the biosphere (life), and the noosphere (consciousness). It is on this lattermost level that the evolutionary process itself becomes self-conscious, reflects back upon itself and its dependence on a creator who made the world as a process consistent with its own principles but not totally self-sufficient. The Incarnation is the source of man's understanding of this added transcendent dimension, for it points to a reality beyond the immediate grasp of the noosphere: the union of God with his creation. The coming of Christ served both to reconcile fallen man to God and to initiate the further process of Christogenesis wherein the whole universe tends toward final union with Christ. We are now in the early stages of the Christosphere and are moving toward "Point Omega," which is Christ coming in the *parousia.* There is thus, for Teilhard, a definite rhythm to history: Creation is set into process by God at "Point Alpha," grows in perfection by becoming conscious and directing its responsibilities toward growth into Christ, and finally culminates, at Point Omega, in the Second Coming of Christ and the creation of a new heaven and a new earth.

Of the many points of comparison and contrast that present themselves, we may restrict ourselves to five general areas: evolution, the sacred and the *within,* eschatology, Christ, and God. Since these topics are all so intimately interrelated, it will soon become apparent that these divisions are somewhat artificial and constantly overlap one another.

1. Surely the most fundamental similarity, and one which these two thinkers share with most contemporary movements in theology, is the evolutionary outlook. Teilhard came to evolution through the scientific tradition associated with Darwin, Lamarck, and Huxley. Later, the thought of Spencer, Bergson, and LeRoy were to inspire him to more philosophical speculation. Altizer, on the other hand, is more a child of his time, for whom the evolutionary hypothesis is a given presupposition and requires little explication in his writings. His closest direct influence for a dynamic view of history is undoubtedly the Hegel of *The Phenomenology of Mind,* whose thought contains the obscure seeds of much later evolutionary thought. Hegel's own words seem to ring prophetically here: "We find that what in former days occupied the energies of men of mature mental ability sinks to the level of information, exercises and even past-times, for children." [1] Thus Altizer approaches the past armed with the prejudices of a twentieth-century world view, and extracts a vision that both illumines Hegel and corresponds to contemporary experience.

What is common to the two systems of thought is the added concept of time, which provides a fourth dimension and thus expands a previously static spatial world.[2] By accepting time as a factor in any metaphysics, the power of the present moment is exalted above the glories of the past, and there is implied the obligation of forming an eschatology that is both continuous with the ongoing process and irreducible to any pristine state of original innocence. Altizer's concept of the *dialectic* and Teilhard's *law of complexity-consciousness* are the basic patterns through which the temporal factor is introduced.

There are two sides to the notion of dialectic as Altizer makes use of it. First, a radical negation and a radical affirmation of the world are involved simultaneously; that is, the realms of the sacred and the profane must pass through a mutual transfiguration. They are not joined together as if in a static synthesis, but grow together in a creative tension known as the *coincidence of opposites.*[3] Second, this process of sacred and profane moving dialectically into one another is an active and forward-moving impulse that directs and defines the course of history. Because this dialectic is directed to the future rather than based on *anamnēsis*, Altizer considers the Christian understanding of the coincidence of opposites particularly nonreligious, that is to say, non-world-negating.[4]

The Incarnation is the dialectical center of such a truly nonreligious view of history. The Word, moving out of a primordial, sacred realm, undertakes a *kenōsis* into human history whereby it aligns itself to the profane by becoming flesh while not ceasing to be Spirit. In contrast to the religious way of world-negation, "What is distinctive to Christianity is a witness to an incarnation in which Spirit becomes flesh in such a manner as to continue to exist and to act as flesh."[5] At the same time, the Word continues to move ever forward, shedding previous transcendent forms and emptying itself into the profane present. The coincidence of sacred and profane in the Word-made-flesh, therefore, "cannot be truly meaningful unless it is understood as a real movement of God himself, a movement which is final and irrevocable, but which continues to occur wherever there is history and life."[6] Thus, *for Altizer, the dialectical process is the means whereby God is introduced into the world and by which history moves forward.*

Teilhard's law of complexity-consciousness, in contrast, is a means of describing the evolutionary energy in history by positing a hidden potentiality throughout the existing universe. Evolution is not a mere speculative tool for Teilhard, but an actual verifiable fact. He raises it to the level of "a general condition to which all theories, all hypotheses, all systems must bow and which they must satisfy henceforward if they are to be thinkable and true."[7] For Teilhard, the scientist, this means that the phenomena of the world must be explained in terms of the causes inherent in the world, and that no recourse is to be had to extracosmic forces. "The fundamental unity of the Universe and the inexorable interconnection and interaction of the cosmic elements . . . preclude any new being from emerging into our experience other-

wise than in function of all the present and past states of the empirical world." [8] The law of complexity-consciousness is meant to
fulfill such a causal role by (1) expressing the direction of evolution at all levels of material existence seeking complexity, and
(2) by insisting that there is a psychical energy at work in matter
by which evolution tends toward self-consciousness. *For Teilhard, therefore, complexity-consciousness is the means whereby
man was introduced into the world and whereby history continues to progress.*

Altizer's image of the Spirit expressing itself in flesh and
Teilhard's notion of the emergence of mind from matter appear
to be operating in opposite directions. For Altizer, it is the Spirit
that is primordial and guiding growth, while Teilhard prefers to
see matter as the fundamental starting point from which Spirit
later evolves. The basic difference is that Teilhard alters the
traditional concept of Creation by viewing God as permitting
things to make themselves[9] or as the great "Animator" of the
world,[10] and Altizer has God himself entering the evolutionary
scheme of history and undergoing change with man toward a
common end. A secondary consequence of the variation in the
two theories is seen in their respective attitudes to the Christian
Church. Altizer, who prefers to emphasize how the past is negated
by the present, can view the church only as the prolongation of a
"religious" world view that says No to the present and directs its
attention backwards. Teilhard, who stresses the extent to which
the present is an outgrowth of the past, always remained faithful and apparently optimistic toward the established church, looking ahead to its development rather than its dissolution. In fair-
ness to both men, it seems clear today that progress demands both
a spirit of crusading courage and the cultivation of thoughtful
traditionalism. For while a four-dimensional world can never per-
mit faith to align itself decisively to any dogmatic formulations,
it can nevertheless be presented with a heritage of symbols, Biblical and dogmatic, whose meaning must be continually supplied
and interpreted by contemporary experience.

2. If we consider next the contrast between Teilhard's idea of

the *within* and the *without* of things, and Altizer's use of the notions of sacred and profane, we shall better understand how their solutions to the problem of God's immanence and transcendence in relation to the world are different but complementary.

Both dichotomies attempt to define a polarity existing in an evolving world, a polarity whose divisions are all inclusive and yet distinct from one another. For Teilhard, everything that exists in the world has a within and a without, an inner driving force and an outer expression of it. The without is the realm of complexity in material evolution, while the within is the realm of consciousness. Thus everything that exists has some structure and a consciousness commensurate with the complexity of that structure. The within corresponds to the spiritual aspect of things, the without to their material side. Moreover, there is an energy that Teilhard posits at each pole: "tangential energy" is the force that drives matter into complexification with all elements of the same order, and "radial energy" is the dynamism drawing a thing into convergence in the future, into ever further spiritualization. Together these two energies are responsible for moving the evolutionary history of the world from geosphere to biosphere to noosphere.

Altizer's distinction between the sacred and the profane is a less specific dichotomy that is not as empirically evident as Teilhard's within and without. It grows out of the dilemma of the immanence and transcendence of God. While Teilhard begins from the observation of material phenomena, Altizer is taken with human experiences of the holy[11] that are only indirectly applicable to nonhuman life and dead matter. The sacred points to the human encounter with the realm of the Spirit, of transcendence; the profane lies in the area of immanent experience, of the flesh. What this means is that the zone of experience is either strictly scientific and looks for immanent causes, or else is open to nonscientific, transcendent origins. The profane world is not seen as a veil for the sacred,[12] but is a contradiction to the sacred and will eventually unite with it in the coincidence of opposites. In pure religion, the profane world is denied precisely so that it can be reassumed as sacred, that is, primordial. In Christianity, however, the situation is quite different. There must be a total disassociation from the concept of a totality that preexisted the separation of reality into sacred and profane so that history can be viewed as the working out of an identity of the two. There is to be a transformation of the opposites rather than a denial of one or the other. "Only at the End will flesh and Spirit become identical, and their identity will be established only when flesh has actually ceased to be flesh and Spirit has perished as Spirit." [13]

It is evident that Teilhard and Altizer are working on different levels of experience. Teilhard is concerned with setting up a tension of energies that will account for growth at all levels of existence. Altizer, on the other hand, wants to show how the originally distinct realms of transcendence and immanence come together and grow into an identity through the course of history. Thus, just as Teilhard's within and without serve to ground his law of complexity-consciousness ontologically, so too Altizer's sacred and profane further explicate his concept of the dialectic in history.

Once again differences in their understanding of evolution come into focus. Let us look, for instance, at their conceptions of modern man. Teilhard sees man as possessed of a spirituality in virtue of which he turns in love toward his fellowman, seeking collectivization, totalization, and socialization of mankind and the personalization of the Universe.[14] Altizer, on the contrary, locates man in the "Third Age of the Spirit," meaning that the sacred has already begun to become flesh (in the Incarnation), and continues this embodiment insofar as man becomes ever more conscious of his divinity. While Teilhard seems always to consider the within as a force that grows in pace with the complexity of the without, Altizer sees the within—the sacred—as seeking externalization, *kenōsis,* and expressing its incarnational presence in a without—the flesh. Teilhard's image is that of God perfecting himself and his universe in preparation for eventual union with God; Altizer's image is that of God perfecting himself by becoming the universe. For both of them, man furthers history by perfecting his own consciousness and growing into love. Altizer stands alone, however, in adding the fact that history furthers man by rendering him ever more the coincidence of the Divine and the flesh.

Finally, there is a contrast appearing in the type of tension that the two thinkers posit between the poles of within and without, sacred and profane. For Teilhard, the within and the without appear to expand in harmony, so that a constant proportion is maintained between the levels of complexity and consciousness in a given entity, while at the same time there is a seething energy beneath the surface that constantly strives to raise the whole to a higher level of integration. In Altizer, the profane remains throughout a rather passive element that grows only by its association with the sacred, and is of itself pure meaninglessness. It is only the embodiment of the Spirit into flesh that renders the realm of the profane significant. A certain corresponding "growth" in the profane in its preparation to accept Spirit would seem to be more in line with a truly dialectical process and would suggest the possibility of associating the processes of material evolution with the process of divine evolution in the world. In this way, the two patterns of within and without, sacred and profane, could be profitably united, so that Spirit would be defined as an energy central to all entities in the universe, and flesh as the context in which that Spirit enriches and expresses itself.

3. Having seen the importance of the evolutionary viewpoint and the principles by which it is guided in the two systems of thought, we think it natural that we should ask about the goal of history, that is, its eschatological dimension. Altizer makes much of this point, emphasizing that it is the central unique characteristic of Christianity and suggesting that "a major task of contemporary theology is that of recovering an eschatological vision of God." [15] Teilhard, for his part, suggests that when evolution is

viewed as the process in which the consciousness within matter emerges and is transmuted into Spirit, natural history is seen to have a different direction—or rather, since we are on the level of the noosphere, a different purpose.

Altizer goes to great lengths to show how eschatology can serve a variety of purposes in religion, but, he insists, Christianity's dynamic standpoint demands that it preach the ongoing incarnation of Spirit. As if by anticipated result, he finds that pure religions tend to see eschatology as a return to a primordial state of innocence, while Christianity favors an end that will be the natural result of a process, a perfection rather than a return. The final apocalyptic identity of sacred and profane will thus be an improvement over the original state of total separation without becoming a mere reversal to a state of primitive sinlessness.

Teilhard develops his notion of Point Omega in a similar fashion, though for him history is merely human history, for God remains transcendent and untouched by time's changes. The goal of history is Christ, and man is prepared for this eschaton by his evolution on earth. When the world reaches its end, however, it does not open up naturally into Omega, but awaits a special *parousia,* involving a new tension and a new choice. "The end of time will then draw near," Teilhard predicts, "and a terrifying spiritual pressure will be brought to bear on the limits of the Real, born of the effort of souls desperately straining in their desire to escape from the Earth. The pressure will be unanimous. But the Scriptures teach us that at the same time it will be rent by a profound schism between those who wish to break out of themselves that they may become still more masters of the world, and those who, accepting Christ's word, passionately await the death of the world that they may be absorbed with it into God." [16] In addition, Point Omega, seen as fulfillment, changes the traditional concept of Point Alpha, which must then be seen as the initiation of a process, an invitation to freedom placed within matter itself by God, and not a state of preternatural holiness disrupted by our first parents. By identifying the cosmic Christ with

Point Omega, Teilhard implies belief that the Incarnation is part of an overall plan arranged from the beginning but permitted to work itself out through time.

The differences in the two eschatological visions again hinge on the role of God in history. Mankind, according to Teilhard, grows in history until the *parousia,* when it is subsumed into Christ who has preexisted human history. Altizer prefers to see man and God moving together toward an apocalyptic unity that will not involve any sort of *parousia* or special divine intervention. The details of each theory are clearly extrapolated from what is already implied in their fundamental positions toward evolution. Thus it is clear that Altizer would direct history to a final out-come effected by natural causes, while Teilhard's insistence on the continued transcendence of God would involve man's somehow being raised up by an act of God to a new level of being. While there is a definite significance to the symbol of *heaven* for Teilhard, Altizer can see only a *new earth.*

The basic similarity in their thought lies in that both are aiming at a linear or spiral concept of history, not a cyclical one. In order to see salvation history as an ongoing event rather than a once-and-for-all occurrence, Altizer's image of the Incarnation might help to clarify Teilhard's view of the redemption. Altizer shows how the movement toward an eschaton that began with the Incarnation of God into Jesus has been impeded by the stubbornness of the human consciousness, by man's refusal to recognize the Incarnation because of his tendency to maintain trans-temporal values and to deny profane existence its new importance. For Teilhard, this would mean that the work of salvation wrought in Jesus Christ is not an accomplished fact but a continuing process. Redemption, therefore, has not occurred to the extent that man withholds love from his fellowman, despite his sentiments of gratitude and acceptance. I remain unredeemed insofar as I refuse to cast my life into the course of saving history. Such an interpretation would seem to be more consistent with Teilhard's system than the traditional Pauline conception of a strictly objective redemption.

4. Teilhard and Altizer agree in placing the Incarnation at the center of history, although their understanding of Jesus Christ differs considerably. For Altizer, the Incarnate Word represents an irreversible movement of the Godhead to incorporate himself into the world of the profane. He is God freely become man in order to redeem humanity from utter profanity and lead it on the road to its final end. Of course, Altizer's conception of the *kenōsis* necessarily excludes a transcendent being who continues in existence after the coming of the Lord. For Teilhard, on the other hand, Jesus Christ is a high point in the noosphere, wherein God intervenes to give a new direction to struggling man. As perfect God and perfect man, Jesus Christ represents an anticipation of the eschaton in which God will raise man up to union with himself in love.

The differences in approach become more apparent if we distinguish Jesus from Christ. Jesus, the historical person who walked the earth twenty centuries ago and died on a cross, has ceased to exist for Altizer. Absolute Spirit—Hegel's term, which Altizer adopts to serve his conception of the sacred or God—had to sacrifice itself in order to gain itself. It had to become flesh in order to enrich itself. "This self-sacrifice enters consciousness when Spirit first appears in its kenotic form as the man, Jesus of Nazareth. . . . God *is* Jesus, proclaims the radical Christian, and by this he means that the Incarnation is a total and all-consuming act: as Spirit becomes the Word that empties the Speaker of himself, the whole reality of Spirit becomes incarnate in its opposite." [17] With the death of Jesus, therefore, God has also died. Altizer is quite clear about this. The Christ who lives on is not the bodily exalted Jesus of traditional Christianity who was raised from the dead on Easter morning. Rather it is the presence of the sacred, of the Absolute Spirit, in the humanity of history, working itself out in total profanity, enriching itself in the world of men. The Resurrection is the exaltation of Jesus into the Christ. Jesus becomes Christ after God and Jesus have died.

Teilhard, however, sees the distinction between Jesus and Christ as one that occurs only in the minds of men. Jesus was the Christ from the moment of his conception, but it took the events of salvation and his bodily resurrection from the dead for him to be recognized as such by men. Jesus the man died and Jesus the man was raised from the dead. According to Teilhard, Christ-Omega was operative in the cosmos before the Incarnation and will continue to be at work until the *parousia*. The actual Incarnation was a spatiotemporal intervention of God into the world, although the Word had been organically related to the world from the moment of Creation. The importance of the historical person, Jesus of Nazareth, is that he becomes the focal point of human history and gives meaning to evolution. "The mystical Christ, the universal Christ of St. Paul, has neither meaning nor value in our eyes except as an expansion of the Christ who was born of Mary and died on the cross."[18] Jesus Christ, therefore, is both immanent in the world and transcendent from it.

In addition to their differences concerning the historical Jesus, Teilhard and Altizer also differ in their understanding of the presence of Christ in the world. Teilhard characterized the presence of Christ-Omega as "a supreme, physical influence over all of cosmic reality without exception."[19] He states elsewhere that since there is only one overall plan to the movement of the universe, "no element or movement could exist in the world at all, apart from the *informing* action of the main center of all things. Coextensive with space, coextensive with time, Christ . . . is likewise coextensive with the values ranged between the heights of the spirit and the depths of matter."[20] His influence is immanent, while his personality is transcendent.

Altizer's Christ, however, is immanent both in its influences and its total reality. In place of the person of Jesus who once housed the kenotic sacred, the universal humanity now assumes the reality and dynamism of Christ and activates that power by ever becoming more conscious of its divine nature. "Radical faith calls us to give ourselves totally to the world, to affirm the fullness and the immediacy of the present moment as the life and the energy of Christ. Thus, ultimately the wager of the radical Christian is simply a wager upon the full and actual presence of the Christ who is a totally incarnate love." [21] *For Teilhard the world is diaphanous of a transcendent God,* who reveals his presence by means of signs whereby the evolutionary process points to something beyond itself. *For Altizer the world is coextensive with God.* God and world are growing jointly through the intermediary of human consciousness. While Teilhard recognizes the work of Christ-Omega throughout the universe, Altizer prefers, with Blake, to see Christ "in every human hand and face." [22]

Both views clearly opt for seeing Christ as an intervention of God into history—an intervention that is a unique factual occurrence and that gives new direction to the evolutionary process on the conscious level. Altizer, who views Jesus' death as final and irrevocable by any sort of resurrection, is attempting to thrust Christ fully into the current of history, while Teilhard's treatment of Christ as immanent through his Incarnation and transcendent through his Resurrection, leads to a perturbing paradox. For if Jesus was fully man, then men after him should necessarily evolve beyond him. But since he is a perfect man, the linear view of history is broken and replaced by a cyclical view which begins and ends with Christ, the Alpha and Omega. The evolutionary process then becomes a concession to the world, interesting and unpredictable, but ultimately to be superseded by the divine plan.

Although the radical Christian vision as Altizer has outlined it to us seems alien to Christian tradition, its undeniable strength lies in its ability to reconcile the radical humanity of Christ with the centrality of the Incarnation for human history. Even a program as contemporary as Teilhard's limps at the thoroughgoing immanence of God in Jesus and somehow seems to shrink from the possibility that the evolutionary process underlying human development should include God as well. If God's perfection could be disassociated from any *aseitas,* then perhaps we could better understand the meaning of the Incarnate Word who died in Jesus and yet arose in Christ to live on in the lives and history of men. This brings us to our final points of comparison.

5. We come to the God-concepts of Teilhard and Altizer with a number of loose ends to tie together. Much has already been said to describe their differences and similarities, but it must somehow all be synthesized.

Teilhard's God is Biblical to the core, a God who is covenanted to his people through love and whose providence guides mankind out of sin and ignorance and into life. He departs from much pietistic tradition by making Creation and divine providence subservient to the evolutionary world process, rather than viewing God's activity as a sporadic set of interventions designed to inform man of some eternal truth or to keep him traveling the straight and narrow. Defending his view against the established doctrine brought him only allegations of pantheism and endless misunderstanding during his lifetime.

Altizer goes farther by seeing God as involved totally with mankind in the world process, undergoing irreversible transformations, and being enriched by progressive incarnational movements. In exchange for growth, God abandons his past forms of existence, among them the transcendent personality that Christian tradition has come to revere as the God of the Old Testament. In some sense God—or more accurately, Spirit— is now intimately united with man and accompanies him on the path to a common eschatological end.

Once again we come to the realization that Altizer's God is evolving, while Teilhard prefers to leave evolution to the realm of man under the watchful eye of an immutable God. Even Christ-Omega existed from all eternity and entered the center of history merely according to divine plan. Nonetheless, there is a sense in which Teilhard's work justifies Altizer's image of God, and Altizer's thought clarifies the implications of Teilhard's scheme.

Were we to extend Altizer's concept of the sacred to include a basic love-energy at the heart of all matter in the universe, then we would be freed from the confusion of speaking of Christ "in every human hand and face." We could see divinity at work in the world by total association with the world's evolutionary energy. As that energy achieves self-consciousness (as it did in Jesus' awareness of his own divinity), then the divine can seek the apocalyptic coincidence of sacred and profane in the realm of human history. We could then affirm the "Third Age of the Spirit" without insisting that there was a time when God was totally transcendent of the world, as Altizer is forced to do when speaking of the Old Testament.

On the other hand, by assuming with Altizer that the sacred is somehow growing in the universe, we might profitably extend Teilhard's concepts of the within and the without to include God himself. In this way, the Divine Within would be the radial energy of love that God shares with the whole universe, and the Divine Without would be his material creation, groaning for self-consciousness and development, achieving its first self-reflective glimpses of divinity in the man Jesus, and growing into that awareness through the course of history.

What seems to happen when we combine Teilhard's vision of the evolution of man toward the Christ-Omega with Altizer's vision of the evolution of the sacred toward the apocalyptic coincidence of flesh and Spirit is that we end up with a total pantheism, not qualified by a transcendent God, either in past or present form. It is a dynamic pantheism that leaves the burden of growth and responsibility for the eschaton squarely in the hands of man and out of the control of a supernatural divine plan. Whether or not such a view is to be considered Christian will demand some further thought. What it does do, it seems to me, is to present the inevitable consequences of combining the visions of Teilhard and Altizer at the point where each becomes weakest: the artificiality of the three "Ages of the Spirit" and the continued transcendence of a triune God.

NOTES

1. Georg Wilhelm Friedrich Hegel, *The Phenomenology of Mind,* tr. by J. B. Baillie (Harper & Row, Publishers, Inc., 1967), pp. 89–90.

2. For an excellent summary of the "added dimension" of time, cf. Eulalio R. Baltazar, *Teilhard and the Supernatural* (Helicon Press, Inc., 1969), pp. 91–139.

3. Cf. Thomas J. J. Altizer, *Mircea Eliade and the Dialectic of the Sacred* (The Westminster Press, 1963), pp. 81–104.

4. Thomas J. J. Altizer, *The Gospel of Christian Atheism* (The Westminster Press, 1966), pp. 32–48.

5. *Ibid.,* p. 41.

6. *Ibid.,* p. 43.

7. Pierre Teilhard de Chardin, *The Phenomenon of Man* (Harper & Row, Publishers, Inc., 1965), p. 217.

8. Pierre Teilhard de Chardin, *The Vision of the Past* (Harper & Row, Publishers, Inc., 1966), p. 104.

9. *Ibid.,* p. 25.

10. Cf., for example, Pierre Teilhard de Chardin, *Letters from a Traveller* (London: William Collins Sons & Co., Ltd., 1962), p. 143.

11. Altizer, *Mircea Eliade and the Dialectic of the Sacred,* p. 24. Altizer depends on Eliade for the position that all hierophanies are to be viewed as *human* events, created by man's existential choice.

12. Thomas J. J. Altizer, "The Sacred and the Profane: A Dialectical Understanding of Christianity," in Thomas J. J. Altizer and William Hamilton, *Radical Theology and the Death of God* (The Bobbs-Merrill Co., Inc., 1966), p. 143.

13. *Ibid.,* p. 154.

14. Pierre Teilhard de Chardin, "Comment je vois" (unpublished, 1948), p. 7. Cf. also his *The Future of Man* (Harper & Row, Publishers, Inc., 1964), pp. 214–215.

15. Thomas J. J. Altizer, "Nirvana and Kingdom of God," *The Journal of Religion,* Vol. XLIII (April, 1963), p. 113.

16. Teilhard, *The Future of Man,* p. 307.

17. Altizer, *The Gospel of Christian Atheism,* pp. 66, 68.

18. Pierre Teilhard de Chardin, *The Divine Milieu* (Harper & Row, Publishers, Inc., 1960), p. 117.

19. Pierre Teilhard de Chardin, "Mon Univers," *Science et Christ* (Paris: Editions du Seuil, 1965), p. 85.

20. Pierre Teilhard de Chardin, "Christologie et Evolution" (unpublished, 1933), p. 9.

21. Altizer, *The Gospel of Christian Atheism,* p. 157.

22. For Altizer's concept of "Universal Humanity" as taken from William Blake, cf. his *The New Apocalypse: The Radical Christian Vision of William Blake* (Michigan State Unversity Press, 1967), pp. 57–75, 140–147, and his *The Gospel of Christian Atheism,* pp. 69–75.

Thomas J. J. Altizer
Response

IF OURS IS AN AGE OF ECUMENICAL THEOLOGY, IT IS SO ABOVE ALL in the Catholic-Protestant theological dialogue, a dialogue that so far has only just begun. Already it is possible to say that Catholic and Protestant theologians commonly meet on the basis of a mutual disenchantment with their own traditions, and a corresponding enchantment with the tradition of the other. Today Catholic theologians are for the most part excited by Biblical theology, and Protestant theologians are rapidly discovering a new form of metaphysical theology, each thereby appropriating the tradition of the other. At the same time few contemporary Catholic theologians display a firm sense of the meaning and authority of their own tradition, and Protestant theologians seem to be abandoning all sense of a specifically or uniquely Protestant tradition and authority. Is it possible that each is now recovering the ground of the other?

I

It is a distinct pleasure to respond to the critique of Father Eric C. Meyer, who was the first Catholic theologian to respond seriously to my work, and who in many ways knows my own position, or, at least my route to it, better than I do myself. However, I am embarrassed that he has focused his attention upon my essay, "Catholic Theology and the Death of God." This essay was written as a lecture to be presented to a Catholic theological audience, and its major purpose was to elicit a response from radical American Catholics, and to see if it might be possible to establish a dialogue between radical Protestant and radical Catholic theology. The argument claims far more than I can substantiate, and perhaps it might best be interpreted as the attempt of a radical Protestant theologian to think from the perspective of a radical Catholic position.

Accordingly, I seized upon the Catholic theological category of analogy or *analogia entis,* assuming, first, that it is the primary foundation of the Catholic understanding of God, and, second, that only a radical reconception of this category can make possible a genuinely Catholic form of radical theology. I am aware that what I present as the meaning of *analogia entis* is at odds with the Catholic theological tradition, and most particularly so with its Thomist expressions—but I am persuaded that no radical Catholic theology is possible apart from a radical break from or radical reconstruction of that tradition. Indeed, it is the latter course that seems to me to be the distinctively Catholic way. For this reason alone, I regard John Henry Newman's *The Development of Christian Doctrine* as the most important of all modern Catholic theological works, or at least, the most significant until Teilhard de Chardin's *The Phenomenon of Man.* Newman's work is so revolutionary that it is still not fully understood, and perhaps someday he will stand forth as the Darwin of theology. Until we learn to rethink the whole meaning of the movement and development of tradition, and to identify tradition with its movement and development, there will be no role for tradition or the past in any truly contemporary form of theology.

My own approach to a radical Catholic understanding of analogy or *analogia entis* was by way of giving it a dialectical meaning, and a meaning that hopefully would be dialectical and historical at once. This would mean that God and the world are apprehended as dialectical opposites, as opposites that bear both a positive and a negative relationship with each other, and whose relation or opposition varies in accordance with a historical movement or evolution. Now no fully dialectical way is possible which assumes that what we experience and understand of God is *essentially* different from what we experience and understand of man and the world. It is just this scholastic ground of the Catholic doctrine of analogy which I attempted to oppose, and my opposition was intended to be based upon a theological ground far more fundamental than any that is present in either medieval or modern scholasticism. This ground is, quite simply, Christian faith in Christ, for I am persuaded that no full or genuine understanding of Christ is possible so long as the scholastic principle that there is an essential and eternal difference between God and the world is accepted.

Father Meyer is quite correct in indicating that my understanding of analogy is grounded in my understanding of the Incarnation. This means that I regard the Incarnation as a coming together of God and world, as a *coincidentia oppositorum,* as a coincidence or coinherence of the opposites, God and the world or creature and Creator. Moreover, I regard the Incarnation as a historical movement and process; it does not reveal the illusory opposition between God and the world, but rather effects an actual reconciliation between estranged and alienated opposites, between an alien and transcendent form of God that is estranged from the world and a fallen and broken form of the world that is estranged from God. Thus I would insist that the Incarnation *is* a coincidence of real opposites. But as a consequence of the Incarnation, the real opposition between God and the world is negated and transcended. From this point of view, the scholastic principle that there is an essential *and* eternal difference between God and the world must necessarily result in a denial of the event or the reality of the Incarnation. And this is the fundamental charge of radical Christianity against orthodox Christianity: that the latter is quite simply non-Christian.

Insofar as the Catholic doctrine of analogy has always, so far as I know, appeared in a scholastic form, the particular challenge that I faced was one of formulating at least the outlines of a nonscholastic but nevertheless Catholic doctrine of analogy. I continue to believe that this is possible, even if I have wholly failed in my premature and all too sketchy attempt. I also believe that the idea of evolution or development is an essential key to a nonscholastic doctrine of analogy, if only because it is the modern understanding of organic and historical evolution that brought to an end the scholastic idea of Being (as is so brilliantly demonstrated by Arthur O. Lovejoy in *The Great Chain of Being*).

How is it possible even to speak of the evolution of God from a Catholic point of view? Father Meyer says that evolution in God would be essentially different from what it is in the cosmos. If this is so, how can we assign any meaning to the evolution or even the movement of God? Father Meyer compounds the difficulty when he says that God *in himself* exists as an identity that "somehow" reconciles all of the many conflicting ways in which we know him, but we do not grasp that identification itself. If we cannot grasp God's identity, how can we know that it exists? If we cannot know what God is in himself, how can we know that God in himself actually moves or evolves? Will we not then be forced to say that the evolution of God is no more and no less than the evolution or development of man's understanding or consciousness of God? God then becomes the one exception to the universal principle or process of evolution. In other words, God is all the more fully banished from the reality of everything that we know as man and world.

The great claim of the doctrine of analogy has always been that it makes possible a genuine knowledge of God. It seems clear to me that no such knowledge is possible so long as the reality of the world is essentially different from the reality of

God. And it must be *essentially* different once the world is known as an evolving process and God is known as an immutable and impassive Being. How can there possibly be a true analogical relationship between an evolving process and an unchanging Being? This is a problem which has driven scholastic theology to the wall, and it is not insignificant that Catholic theologians have been hostile toward the idea of evolution, just as it is not accidental that when a Catholic vision of evolution did appear in the work of Teilhard de Chardin, it contained no idea or vision of *analogia entis*. I would suggest that there can be no new or modern Catholic doctrine of analogy apart from a new and radical Catholic understanding of God as a developing or evolving process, a process that is a primary exemplification of rather than the one exception to the principle of evolution. I would suggest also that one way into such a new doctrine of analogy is a new understanding of man or history as the image of God, wherein historical development and evolution could be seen as a reflection or embodiment of the development and evolution of God.

There is no possibility of understanding history as the image of God unless we reach a new theological understanding of both imagery and the imagination. Father Meyer does not stand alone when he says that with regard to God-images there is no significant theological difference between Christian and Jewish or Muslim art. But he goes on to suggest that God-images have never been very important in Christian art, since Christian art has always found its life-giving images in Christ. One appreciates that "always," particularly when remembering a Dante, a Michelangelo, and a Milton. Perhaps Father Meyer is here speaking from a Protestant point of view, and from an all-too-modern Protestant perspective at that. Can we imagine how much of the Catholic tradition has been forgotten when it is said by a Catholic theologian that God-images have never been very important in Christian art? For purposes of brevity, let us simply take up the problem of medieval painting and sculpture, and ask if God-images here play a significant role, and, more particularly, ask if we can here discover a significant relation between God-images and Christ-images, a relation reflecting a uniquely Christian apprehension of the evolutionary movement and transformation of the divine process. For evidence, I shall limit myself to André Malraux's *Metamorphosis of the Gods,* not only because Malraux cannot be suspected of either a Catholic or a Protestant bias, but far rather because this is the most illuminating study that I have discovered of the theological significance of the plastic arts.

Malraux points out that in the early Byzantine period, in both the East and West, a vision of transcendence was the foundation of Christian art. Christian mosaic art represented Jesus, but it did not attempt to *portray* him, as Gothic art was to do. For the function of art in the ancient Church (as it continued to be in the Eastern Church) was to depict the sign, not the event, and solely in a transcendent world symbolizing the world of God. While noting that God remained the dominant presence in Christian art throughout the fifth century, Malraux makes this extremely important theological point: "It seems that in art —and probably in religion too—Christ tended to become the more Jesus, the more God the Father receded into the background." [1] Byzantium was obsessed by God's inscrutable aloofness, but medieval Western Catholicism found God's presence immanent in all things. Nevertheless, we do not find Jesus in any great Romanesque work, for only stage by stage did the image of Christ break free from the image of the Father in the history of Western art. As Malraux sees it, the history of medieval sculpture is one of a progressive incarnation:

But whence could the artist get convincing forms in which to clothe these symbols, except from such of their aspects as linked them to Christian faith? He did not invent them, he discovered them. The populace did not know them, yet it recognized them—and the Church called them into being, the artist created them, so that they should be recognized by the people. But it recognized Christ solely in terms of communion and this is why no other art in any other civilization ever caused the sacred to embody so much of the human and so fully expressed the sacred through the human.[2]

A comparable humanization of the sacred was taking place throughout the Christian West during the Middle Ages, but Malraux insists that it was not the human but the sacred that "disappeared" in Gothic art.

Gothic lay piety replaced the earlier article of faith, "God is love," by "God is Jesus." More and more the image of the Savior replaced the Carolingian "Hand of God," as though the Incarnation were now known to go back to the Creation. The former distance between God and his attendant elders, between the Pantocrator and his angels and elect, simply ceased to exist in Gothic art. The Romanesque Christ *is;* the Gothic Christ *acts:* "What belonged to God, as *God,* has passed away." [3] With the "passing" of the sacred, the living God ceased to be shrouded in awesome mystery, and now could be loved through the mediation of Jesus. Transcendence now became the transcendence of the love of Christ, a love of which human and earthly love is but a pale reflection. Thus the world of God the Father was eclipsed by the world of the Incarnation that succeeded it:

> Everywhere mystery was giving place to love, the aloofness of God to the nearness of Jesus, adoration to communion, repining for the Fall to that sense of Christ's victory which pervaded Gothic Christendom no less than the sense of his divinity. One would almost think that the West had only just had news of that victory, as it had just learned of the conquest of Jerusalem, and that the purpose of the company of statues that now was mustering in the glimmering recesses of cathedral porches was to reveal to men as living presences the figures of their collective dreams.[4]

With the advent of Giotto and the triumph of "Giottism," Byzantine art was swept away in the West, and within thirty years all traces of the East had vanished. Hand in hand with this Western victory over its Eastern Christian roots went a new discovery of nature, not the nature that has been present in modern art, but rather a nature charged with Christ's presence. Thus Giotto brought to painting a power that was new in Christian art: the power of locating without sacrilege a sacred scene in a world resembling that of everyday life.[5] Thereby Giotto discovered the gospel as being latently present throughout the created world. For the first time sacred scenes related no less to the world of man than to the world of God. By bringing the divine onto a plane nearer to that of man, this new "pictorial fiction" raised painting to the status of a major art and gave Christian painting a special accent distinguishing it from all other religious painting. For Malraux, Giotto brought an end to the Byzantine tradition in the West; but he fulfilled the Gothic tradition. Fifteenth-century painting then celebrated the redemption of all creation, even if the divine could no longer be expressed otherwise than by "appearance."

Now I would not insist that it is necessary for any theologian to accept Malraux's conception of the metamorphosis of the divine in Western Christian art. But I would insist that it is necessary for any contemporary Christian theologian to open himself to the possibility of conceiving faith as a metamorphosis or evolution of consciousness reflecting and embodying a comparable or analogous evolution of God. If God has become man or Word has become flesh in consciousness and experience, then it is precisely the truest or fullest expressions of consciousness and experience that the theologian can identify as "faith." Then faith could be understood not only as a witness to or participation in the reality of God but also as an actualization and realization of the life and movement of God. Only when the Incarnation has fully and finally been realized in consciousness and experience will a final *coincidentia oppositorum* actually be achieved. Father Meyer most astutely suggests that such a *coincidentia* would have to be a formless or pure energy or life, and a theology embracing it would be equivalent to the abstract and scholastic conception of God as "Pure Act." I would suggest, rather, that scholasticism apprehends the abstract potency of the

Godhead, while a radical and dialectical theology is in quest of the meaning of the final actualization and realization of that potency, and therefore in quest of the meaning of the ultimate victory of Christ. From this point of view, scholasticism is an apprehension of the primordial reality of God, of God apart from Christ, and radical theology is an apprehension of the eschatological reality of God, of the God who is all in all in Christ.

II

The greatest joy of ecumenical dialogue comes when encounter between two conflicting traditions produces a mutual enrichment of each. While I am in no position to say whether or not Teilhard de Chardin's evolutionary theology might be enriched by relating it to my own, I know all too well that mine can be enlarged and illuminated by relating it to his, and not even my own love of Teilhard has taught me this so forcefully as has the essay of Father James W. Heisig. I am particularly grateful for the manner in which Father Heisig relates Teilhard's conception of the within and the without to my understanding of the sacred and the profane. Moreover, I suspect that I am not simply projecting my own problems into Teilhard's position when I think that he was never able to resolve the ultimate or eschatological relationship between the within and the without. In one sense, Teilhard was a Hegelian, if only because he understood evolution, at least in part, as the evolution of consciousness. As he himself said in the Postscript to *The Phenomenon of Man:*

> Reduced to its ultimate essence, the substance of these long pages can be summed up in this simple affirmation: that if the universe, regarded sidereally, is in process of spatial expansion (from the infinitesimal to the immense), in the same way and still more clearly it presents itself to us, physico-chemically, as in process of organic *involution* upon itself (from the extremely simple to the extremely complex)—and moreover this particular involution "of complexity" is experimentally bound

up with a correlative increase in interiorisation, that is to say in the psyche or consciousness.[6]

Are we to understand that the involution of complexity is identical with the evolution of interiorization? Is the Omega point the manifestation of God as the ultimate identity of both the within and the without?

At one point I believe that I am closer to Teilhard—or, at least, to the Teilhard whom I understand—than Father Heisig admits. It appears to me that the Teilhardian within and without can have meaning *and* reality only in relation to each other, and therefore neither can be real apart from the other. This, at any rate, is the way in which I approach the meaning and reality of the sacred and profane, and thus I would resist Father Heisig's point that I understand the profane as a passive element that evolves only through its association with the sacred. True, I believe that of itself and in itself the profane is pure meaninglessness. But I would say exactly the same of the sacred. Each is meaningless and unreal apart from the other, and it is only the conjunction or *coincidentia* of both together that creates or is the ground of what appears to us as meaning and reality. While what we know and experience as the growth and enlargement of the profane is manifest to us as the diminution of the sacred, I would insist that faith apprehends this loss of the sacred as a metamorphosis or transformation of the sacred into the profane. Or, in more explicit theological language, the death of God is the actualization of the movement of Spirit into flesh. May one then hope that the apparent dominance of the without in our world is at bottom a reflection and consequence of a transformation of the within into the without? Was Teilhard both prophetic and apocalyptic in his vision of the essential correlation between spatial expansion and cosmic interiorization? Is the Omega point the manifestation of a totally profane without as a totally Christic within?

If the possibility actually exists that we can understand "love energy" as the heart of matter, then we would be freed to reach a cosmic understanding of Christ. Blake and others (perhaps Rilke and Joyce) reached a vision of the cosmic Christ; but an imaginative vision remains distinct as such from a cognitive understanding. Even Father Heisig concedes that the enthusiasm that Teilhard's work has aroused is due to its imaginative and visionary insight rather than to its scientific and philosophical achievement. Here lies one of the great dangers of Teilhard's vision, particularly since he chose to clothe it in the language and the imagery of modern science. So desperate are many of us for vision that we will embrace it at almost any price, including the price of the abnegation of critical thinking and understanding. It should be clear by now that Teilhard's vision can offer an authentic way to a Christian future only if it is buttressed by a philosophical understanding, which Teilhard himself only partially and precariously achieved. As every visionary has cried, we will perish without vision, but we will also perish if we attempt to exist by vision alone.

Not only does authentic vision demand a philosophical or a purely theoretical ground, it also demands a theological expression, and most certainly so if it is to bring illumination to a communal and social body. Once the theologian could speak of the church as a truly human communal and social body, and perhaps the Catholic theologian can still do so, but I see no way by which the Protestant theologian at this time can speak both honestly and positively about the church. The point that most excites me about Father Heisig's essay is the new and revolutionary meaning that he appears to bring to the ancient image of the church as the body of Christ. I suspect that the Catholic has always most deeply identified the church as the true and universal body of all humanity, and has furthermore understood the church as being a fully natural as well as a spiritual body. But Father Heisig indirectly and implicitly suggests that the church might best be understood as the "Divine Without": "groaning for self-consciousness and development, achieving its first self-reflective glimpses of divinity in the man Jesus and growing into that awareness through the course of history."

True, Father Heisig identifies the "Divine Without" as God's material creation. But I for one, and I presume Father Heisig as well, can associate no empirical or scientific meaning with any idea of such a "Divine Without." Could we not far more easily believe that the "Divine Without" is an image of the church, and of the church as the cosmic body of Christ? Moreover, if it is still not possible to assign an empirical or scientific meaning to Teilhard's vision of cosmic movement and evolution as culminating in "interiorisation" and "hominisation," may we not nevertheless regard it as an authentically Catholic and yet revolutionary vision of the church? It is surely no accident that R. C. Zaehner, one of the most gifted of contemporary Catholic religious scholars, and one who has devoted himself to the study of a non-Christian religious world, should have called in his most recent work for a revolutionary synthesis between a Teilhardian vision and Marxism. What Teilhard has given us in his vision of the "within" is a revolutionary idea and image of the church: here the church becomes understood and affirmed as a new and cosmic body of humanity. This is at least one way of understanding Teilhard, albeit a peculiarly Protestant way, and it might open a way for a Protestant appropriation of the dynamic pantheism for which Teilhard and his contemporary Catholic followers call. If Protestant understanding, at least in its living expressions, has lost all sense of the life and reality of the church, perhaps Catholic understanding can lead the Protestant to the reality and life that we have lost. For we have lost both the communal and the cosmic presence of Christ, and now perhaps Catholicism can teach us what it has always known: that all fully natural life is human life, and that life is the body of Christ.

Notes

1. André Malraux, *Metamorphosis of the Gods,* tr. by Stuart Gilbert (Doubleday & Company, Inc., 1960), pp. 132 f.

2. *Ibid.*, p. 213.
3. *Ibid.*, p. 219.
4. *Ibid.*, p. 244.
5. *Ibid.*, p. 337.
6. Pierre Teilhard de Chardin, *The Phenomenon of Man* (Harper & Brothers, 1959), p. 300.

Part III

ALTIZER
AND JEWISH THEOLOGY

Richard L. Rubenstein
Thomas Altizer's Apocalypse

I

I AM DELIGHTED FOR THIS OPPORTUNITY TO RESPOND TO DR. ALTIZER'S
work, which I have admired, and to speak on the issue of the
"death of God" theology. I believe that what these theologians
are saying about the death of God *as a cultural event* is irrefutable. I start with this premise. I do not like to use the phrase
"God is dead" for the reason already suggested by Dr. Altizer:
in some sense this symbolism is specifically Christian. In Christianity, the Christ who is both God and man dies. In some
versions of Christianity he is also resurrected. I hesitate to use
the term "death of God" because I am reluctant to associate myself with an exclusively Christian symbol arising out of the
crucifixion tradition. Jesus as a man or Jesus as the Christ has
little significance for me. It is difficult even to assert that he was
a great teacher, because we really don't regard him as such.
Nevertheless, what Hegel, Nietzsche, and Dostoevsky understood by the death of God—the absence of any sense of meaning,
direction, or value derived from a *transcendent theistic source*—

From *America and the Future of Theology,* ed. by William A. Beardslee.
The Westminster Press, 1967. Section I has been modified by the author;
Section II has been added by the author.

is certainly an accurate description of the way we experience the world.

I also welcome the "death of God" theologians because I believe they start with the real spiritual problems of the twentieth century. They begin where twentieth-century man finds himself. They attempt to offer theological insight concerning human existence in the twentieth century as it really is.

Nevertheless, while I believe that the death of God is a cultural fact, I cannot share the apocalyptic enthusiasm that Professor Altizer seems to attach to this event. As I read Dr. Altizer's paper,[1] I was reminded of Paul Tillich's comment in *The Courage to Be* (Yale University Press, 1952) that the God of theism is dead and deserved to die because he was an enemy of human freedom. I also thought of something that Jean-Paul Sartre has said repeatedly. For Sartre, there is no doubt that God *is* dead. According to Sartre, we live in a universe that is utterly devoid of meaning and hope. We are condemned to be free. While Dr. Altizer sees the death of God as liberation and apocalyptic promise, Sartre, I think more correctly and with deeper insight, understands this event in terms of condemnation and anguish.

This problem was already understood by Søren Kierkegaard, who turned away in radical fright from that which Professor Altizer takes as a portent of apocalyptic liberation. Kierkegaard understood that the death of God meant absolute despair and hopelessness. He could not accept this. After he had pushed the negation of Christian belief to the dialectic extreme of absolute despair and absolute hopelessness, he turned and made the leap to the Christ. What is important in Kierkegaard is not necessarily his leap, but his understanding that funerals are sad events— even the funeral of God. Albert Camus has commented in his *The Myth of Sisyphus* on Kierkegaard's dialectic turning away from despair toward faith. Camus accepts Kierkegaard's either/or of faith or ultimate hopelessness, but sees no way of avoiding a life without hope. I do not believe it is necessary to live entirely in the dimension of despair. Nevertheless, although I can accept the proclamation of the death of God, I cannot accept the apocalyptic enthusiasm that comes out of it.

There is one twentieth-century prophet of the death of God who is strikingly absent from Professor Altizer's thought, and from the list that he has given us. He is the one who has suggested that religion actually begins with the death of God, the first object of human criminality. I refer to Sigmund Freud, author of *Totem and Taboo* and *Moses and Monotheism*. The fundamental insight expressed in *Totem and Taboo* and *Moses and Monotheism* is not that religion actually began with the brothers of the primal horde cannibalistically consuming their father, but that human civilization rests in part on the fact that men are driven to *both* express and repress their parricidal inclinations.

Freud's myth is instructive, because it suggests the futility of seeking an end to repression and limitation in the death of God as Professor Altizer would do. The sons murdered the father because he had access to the women of the primal horde. In order to possess them, they had to displace the father. But once the deed was done, they realized that they were bound to destroy each other unless they arranged some instrumentality whereby social cohesiveness would not be threatened by sexual competitiveness. According to Freud, this was accomplished when the sons instituted the law of exogamy. Those who had participated in the crime were compelled to go outside of the tribe to find their mates. Having murdered the father for withholding the females of the horde, they then prevented themselves from possessing the very same wives and daughters, just as the father had done. They discovered that the father was not the author of repression and limitation. Reality itself demands limitation and discipline whether there is a God or not.

We must be distrustful of all Promethean proclamations of freedom that come with the death of God. Albert Camus undoubtedly understood this when he suggested that Christianity is guilty of the sin of *hubris*. As Martin P. Nilsson has suggested, *hubris* is not the sin of overweening pride but of taking upon oneself more in the order of being than one has a right to. Inevitably, *hubris* is followed by *nemesis*. The scales are righted. The harmony of things is restored. Anaxagoras saw all existence as a kind of *hubris,* and death as the payment by which we render final account. Insofar as the primary parsimony of nature is violated by life itself, we are in a sense taking upon ourselves more in the order of being than we have a right to. Death is a restoration of the disturbed harmony. Camus insists that men must take seriously the old Greek insights about *hubris* and *nemesis*. The idea of an apocalyptic humanity, overreaching itself in a new liberation, is an illusion. It is an attempt to seek for the impossible: a new aeon, a new being, a new heaven, and a new earth.

I feel strangely as if Dr. Altizer and I are Christian and Pharisee in the first century all over again. Incidentally, when I say Pharisee, I simply mean rabbi because all rabbis are of the Pharisaic school. Basically, what was the issue between them? Jesus represented the promise of a new beginning, a new fulfillment, a radical change in man's tragic and broken condition. The sad answer of the rabbis was that nothing new has happened. The world in its sadness goes on. The rabbis did not recognize any "good news." In another context, Dostoevsky's Grand Inquisitor was to have more faith in the ongoing institutions to which he had become accustomed than in the radical insecurity of the Christ returned to earth with the promise of a new start for mankind. There is tragic resignation in the refusal to accept novelty and hopefulness. Unfortunately, it is inevitable. The Pharisees and the early Christians saw the problem in terms of whether God had sent his Anointed, thus beginning a new era of hope for mankind. One group said, "Yes, he has come. The new aeon has begun." The other said, "No, he has not. Things are no different today than they were yesterday." Today, both Dr. Altizer and I stand in the time of the "death of God," and we find that Christian and Jew are still arguing about the new being and the new aeon. The Christian hopefully proclaims the new aeon, and the Jew sadly says: "Would that it were so. Would that there were less evil. Would that there were less human vice. Would that the complexities of the passions we are now free to express were less tragic than they are. Unfortunately, the complex, tragic nature of man continues unchanged."

It is my opinion that Albert Camus was correct when he suggested that, of all the evils in Pandora's box, none was so great as hope. I reject *ultimate* hope completely. I don't mean that I cannot hope that tomorrow I will have a good day or that in the years ahead I may enjoy a measure of fulfillment in life. I reject hope in the sense that I believe that out of Nothingness we have come and to Nothingness we will return. This is our ultimate situation.

I find myself drawn to the "death of God" theologians. If I have to choose sides, I'll choose my sides with them, because the radical recognition of God's absence as a cultural fact offers the only basis for theological speculation in our time. Nevertheless, I don't like to use the words "death of God"—I've joked about this with my students, though with serious intent. They have said, "Well, are you a 'death of God' theologian or not?" My answer is, "I am a 'holy Nothingness' theologian."

Let me attempt to suggest an alternative myth to the one implicit in what Dr. Altizer is saying. It's a myth that Dr. Altizer will undoubtedly recognize, with his understanding of mysticism and eschatology. It is the myth of Lurianic Kabbalism. Isaac Luria (d. 1572) was a Jewish mystic of the sixteenth century. After the catastrophes of Spanish Jewish life and the expulsion of the Jews in 1492, he developed a radical theory of creation. According to Luria, the world came into being when God created it *ex nihilo,* out of nothingness. This nothingness was not exterior to God. God created the world out of *his own nothingness* through an act of self-diminution not unrelated to the idea of God's kenotic emptying of himself to which Dr. Altizer alludes. Whatever has been created out of God's nothingness is caught in a dialectic dilemma from which it can never escape. Insofar as it is aware of its true origin in the divine nothingness—no-thing-ness would be better than nothingness—it yearns to return to its source. Insofar as it desires to maintain its separate identity, it is in alienation, separated from God's nothingness. According to Luria, all existence is in an unavoidable dialectic conflict between the tendency toward self-maintenance and the yearning to return to the nothingness that is our true origin and our real essence. Eventually, of course, God's nothingness will be victorious. With the self-division of God, in Luria as in Hegel, negation comes into existence. The price paid for creation is negation. And, negation brings evil in its train. That does not mean creation is evil; it does mean that a *part* of creation is inevitably evil and that there is, as Melville understood, a demonic side to God himself.

God cannot create without creating evil. This evil is overcome neither in an earthly Jerusalem nor in a new aeon. It is overcome only when we return to the no-thing-ness that is both our source and our end. Life has its very real joys. Nevertheless, the price we pay for existence is pain, suffering, anxiety, hopelessness, and evil. It is for this reason that I cannot accept Dr. Altizer's apocalyptic image. It seems too hopeful. It seems too quick a dance of joy at the great funeral.

Dr. Altizer has also spoken hopefully of America's vocation as being cut off from the past and oriented toward the future. I believe that few aspects of American life are as problematic as our lack of a sense of history. This has frightened Europeans as divergent in loyalties as Albert Camus and Charles de Gaulle. They regard America as an adolescent nation precisely because of our lack of a sense of the past and the continuing inheritance of the dilemmas of the past in the present. In the long run, it is America's destiny to become Europeanized. What we are experiencing in Vietnam is a sense of limit, defeat, and the ironies of history. For several centuries we were able to separate ourselves geographically from the problems of European man. When we did not find things to our liking, we went farther west. That time is past. Eventually we will find that our situation is as tragic, as replete with evil as well as good, as the European situation has been throughout its entire history.

One of the things I like about the academic life is that it has given me an opportunity to spend my summers in the Mediterranean world. There is swimming; there is beauty; there are joys of the flesh. All the joys Dr. Altizer believes are available to Americans after the death of God are freely given in the Mediterranean landscape. But, as Albert Camus pointed out in "Summer in Algiers," what you buy with the flesh you pay for with death. The beauty of the Mediterranean is the beauty of Earth, the great mother goddess who gives birth to her children, allows them their moment in which to be fruitful and beautiful, in order that she may in her own time consume them. Earth, the great mother goddess, is a cannibal goddess. She alone is our true progenetrix. She is our final destiny. We have no reason to rejoice before her.

Dr. Altizer has a highly original interpretation of the meaning of Captain Ahab's quest for the great white whale in *Moby Dick*. According to Dr. Altizer, "Ahab's mad quest for the white whale can be seen as faith's response to the death of God, wherein the man of faith becomes the murderer of God so as to make possible a historical actualization of God's death in Jesus, and thus an apocalyptic consummation of God's original self-sacrifice or self-negation." Dr. Altizer sees Ahab as a paradigmatic figure. He seeks the death of God in order to bring about the apocalyptic liberation from the restraints of the dead God, which is America's true mission. I agree with Dr. Altizer's high regard for *Moby Dick*. There is, however, one crucial speech of Captain Ahab's which Dr. Altizer seems to ignore. It is the speech at the very end in which the mad captain tells Starbuck of his forty years upon the sea. He declares that he did not marry until past fifty. His wife was not truly his wife, but a widow. He had hardly put a dent in the marital pillow before returning to sea. Having pursued his mad quest for forty years, he would not now desist from seeking the whale, in spite of Starbuck's pleas.

Melville was not unfamiliar with Biblical imagery and symbol-

ism. I do not believe that his use of Ahab's forty-year sojourn
on the seas was accidental. The forty years on the sea represent
Ahab's years in the wilderness. The great white whale is the
Captain's Promised Land. As much as he hates the whale, as
much as he wants to destroy the creature, he yearns unknow-
ingly to be consumed by it. Erich Fromm has made a very
interesting point about the story of Jonah and the whale: When
Jonah is swallowed by the whale, he returns to the womb. God
has charged Jonah to preach to the people of Nineveh. Jonah
avoids his task. His ultimate withdrawal from adult responsibility is symbolized by his being consumed. The whale is the
only creature large enough to enclose an adult man. The yearning to return to the source is a yearning to end the agonies and
the problematics of the human condition. What troubles Captain
Ahab is precisely the fact that we live in a malignant universe,
in which human existence is filled with anxiety. As he says in
one place, it is a cannibal universe underneath the calm, placid
sea. There is only one escape. It is not the New Jerusalem. *Moby
Dick* does not end with the New Jerusalem. It ends with Ahab
consumed by the whale, destined to be dissolved in the cannibal
sea. Ahab returns to the nothingness out of which he has come.
What Ahab fears and hates is that for which he also yearns.
I hope that Captain Ahab is not the paradigm of the new American, as Dr. Altizer suggests. There are many Europeans who
fear that it is. If Ahab is the paradigm of the new American,
we will not have the tolerance for the ambiguity, the irony, the
hopelessness, and the meaninglessness of the historic eras that
dawn ahead of us. Lacking this tolerance, we will choose self-
destruction rather than the pain of an incomplete and not entirely desirable existence.

Incidentally, not only does the imagery of arising out of
nothing and returning to nothing make its appearance in the
Kabbalism of Isaac Luria, and I suspect in Melville, but also in
the psychoanalytic insights of Sigmund Freud, especially in *Beyond the Pleasure Principle,* in which Freud sees life as a struggle

between the desire to maintain individual identity and the desire to return to the source from whence we have come.

I wonder whether America can accept the death of God. I hope that it can, although I doubt it. I understand that Dr. Altizer has been getting a lot of angry letters lately. Every American accepts the death of God in one sense. Dr. Altizer is right in characterizing our refusal to accept this event as "bad faith," *mauvaise foi,* as Sartre uses the phrase. The fact that Dr. Altizer and the other "death of God" theologians show the naked mirror of the self to America does not mean that America will thank them. Who knows what forms of secular tyranny and secular security America may choose rather than endure the awesome anxiety of a hopeless and meaningless cosmos? Dostoevsky saw this in the legend of the Grand Inquisitor. Men will choose bread, miracles, and security rather than truth and freedom. The sad few who acknowledge the truth will not rejoice in it.

Let me add a warning: Two years ago (1963) I was invited to lecture at a German theological conference in Recklinghausen. One of the questions I was asked was, "What do you think about eschatology?" My answer was, then as now, "Eschatology is a sickness." I want to say to all of you as Christians—and this is a difficult thing to say—it was our Jewish sickness originally. We gave it to you. You took us seriously. Would that you hadn't! Would that you hadn't for your sakes and ours! But as a Jew who has known this sickness, let me warn you. Do not be tempted by it if you become post-Christian. If you are Christian, you cannot avoid it. If you become post-Christian, choose pagan hopelessness rather than the false illusion of apocalyptic hope.

One of the insights I find psychologically most completely on target in Christian theology is the old Augustinian-Calvinist notion of original sin. It is an anthropological insight that cannot be negated even in the time of the death of God. Perhaps especially *in* the time of the death of God, we must not lose sight of the fact that man does not cease to be a guilty or sinful

creature. Original sin suggests an important impediment to apocalyptic enthusiasm at the death of God.

In conclusion I want to tell you of the way Isaac Bashevis
Singer ends his novel *The Family Moskat.* The Germans are
before the gates of Warsaw in September, 1939. One of the
brothers, realizing that Hitler is at the gates of Warsaw, affirms,
as Jews have for thousands of years: "I believe in perfect faith
that the Messiah will come speedily in our days." The other
brother is astonished and says: "How can you say this?" The
first replies: "Surely he will come. Death is the messiah." There
is only one way out of the ironies and the ambiguities of the
human condition: return to God's nothingness, the radical nonbeing of God and death.

II

Four years have passed since I offered my reflections on
Thomas Altizer's theology at Emory University. The respect I
expressed for Professor Altizer's work at the time has continued
to grow. Some of the elements in Altizer's theological vision
seemed very strange, but I was convinced that they were a
healthy corrective to a shared understanding of the religious
situation, which had outlived its usefulness.

Since that time Altizer's thought has been immensely deepened.
It is my conviction that his latest work, *The Descent Into Hell,*
is one of the most important and exciting theological statements
since the work of Paul Tillich. Altizer is a dialectic theologian.
His vision unites mystical, apocalyptic, and eschatological themes.
Few of the modern greats in philosophy, theology, or literature
are absent from his synthesis. What Hegel did for his time,
Altizer is in the process of doing for his. This is an achievement
of enormous scope.

When I reacted to Altizer in 1965, I was puzzled by his eschatology. I shared with Altizer his basic image that the cosmos
was the expression of the self-emptying of the primordial Godhead. I was convinced that Altizer's doctrine of *kenōsis* was

both accurate and inevitable. It seemed ironical to me that a Christian theologian who took seriously the ultimate unity of all things in God was regarded in the popular imagination as a Godless iconoclast. Nevertheless, I failed to understand the meaning of the New Jerusalem that Altizer proclaimed as the ultimate fulfillment of "the death of God." When Altizer asserted that Christianity involved a forward-moving negation of all past epiphanies of the sacred, in which the future was the only meaningful temporal category, he seemed to be a restless Faustian. His theology appeared to be the religious counterpart of America's involvement in the exploration of outer space. There is an element in American culture that is forever compelled to negate the limitations of any given existential situation. The quest for Eldorado has been so deeply engrained in the American psyche that many Americans could never tolerate a final closing of the frontier. American ingenuity and technology had to press on to outer space when no new locale remained on earth where the nomadic American could perpetuate the illusion of beginning anew once more. After California proved to be a smoggy, angry, problematic New Jerusalem, the planets promised an infinity of opportunities to negate the limitations of the past. Altizer's call for a liberation from the restraints of the past appeared to be a quintessential expression of the American as Faustian man. I wondered whether there would ever be a moment for Altizer when he could say, "Linger a while, thou art so fair."

There was another element in Altizer's thought, brilliant as it was, that gave me pause. Altizer called upon the Christian to participate in the death of God so that total liberation could be realized as America's destiny. It was my conviction that, in so doing, Altizer was bringing to the light of consciousness one of the most potent though hidden strains in the Judeo-Christian tradition, the quest for the achievement of infantile omnipotence. The myth that the death of the father is a prelude to liberation is one of the oldest of all human dreams. Nevertheless, it is a pathetic falsification of reality. Limitation is inherent in the structure of things. Total liberation can be achieved only by bringing reality to an end. That is why I saw Captain Ahab's "Promised Land" as return to the nothingness out of which he had come. Total liberation means the dissolution of all craving and sensation. The content of Altizer's New Jerusalem could not be a perpetual negation of the past; it could only be nothingness.

In his latest work, Altizer faces the question of the content of the New Jerusalem. His solution is startling yet inevitable for a thinker of Altizer's competence. Instead of shying away from the conclusion that nothingness is the only possible content of the New Jerusalem, Altizer embraces it. He does so by offering a unique synthesis of Buddhism and Christianity. It is now apparent that Altizer is not a Faustian. He asserts that the Christian must recognize the Buddha as "the original name and identity of the New Jerusalem or the apocalyptic Christ." Altizer maintains that

> Nirvana is not "other" than Kingdom of God, just as Buddha is not "other" than Christ; Nirvana is the primordial ground of Kingdom of God, just as the New Jerusalem is the eschatological realization of Nirvana.[2]

Altizer has thus faced both the nothingness of liberation and the Nothingness of God. He envisages the eschatological nothingness as a "total and primordial bliss" rather than a contentless void. Christ and Buddha, the New Jerusalem and Nirvana, are revealed as ultimately one.

Nevertheless, Altizer insists that the New Jerusalem can be realized only by "the final or ultimate death in consciousness and experience of every fragment or memory of the original Totality." Like Hegel and Teilhard de Chardin, Altizer sees *Endzeit* as radically different from *Urzeit*. I believe this is one of the most problematic aspects of all three related visions. It is possible that Altizer's denial of the ultimate sameness of *Endzeit* and *Urzeit* may simply be an expression of Christian sensibility I cannot penetrate. Nevertheless, my inability to distinguish final Nothingness from its initial counterpart compels me to maintain, as I did in 1965, that if there is a Redeeming Messiah, he can only be the Angel of Death. Furthermore, I prefer the limited gratifications of an unredeemed existence to the consuming bliss of Nirvana. When God truly becomes "all in all," the diverse structures that constitute reality will finally collapse. This will not be bliss but extinction.

Although I would no longer want to characterize the difference between Altizer and me as that between Christian and Pharisee, I cannot share his apocalyptic quest for "Totality," even though our visions of God and the world share many elements in common. Totality will envelop and consume all of us soon enough. In the meantime, I am convinced that gratification can be as real as craving and that love does not require the total obliteration of otherness as Altizer maintains. On the contrary, it is precisely the wholehearted celebration of the otherness of male and female that makes sensuous love realizable. The chasm separating male and female expresses both the fact that every individual can experience only a very partial segment of reality and the fact that each person is an epiphenomenal expression of the unitary, underlying nature of all things. There is a dialectic interweaving of individual separateness and ecstatic union in genuine love. One must be able alternatively to lose and to recover oneself. Altizer seems too impatient to terminate the tension between the individual and the encompassing "Totality." There are joys to finitude. They are problematic and imperiled. They are ultimately doomed to extinction. They are nevertheless very real. I would not exchange the small moments of bliss I have known for the consuming Bliss of the New Jerusalem.

Notes

1. This paper was originally a response to Thomas J. J. Altizer, "Theology and the Contemporary Sensibility," in William A. Beardslee, ed., *America and the Future of Theology* (The Westminster Press, 1967), pp. 15–31.

2. Thomas J. J. Altizer, *The Descent Into Hell* (J. B. Lippincott Company, 1970), p. 192.

Thomas J. J. Altizer
Response

RICHARD L. RUBENSTEIN HAS HAD A GREATER AND MORE IMMEdiate impact upon the world of Christian theology than has been effected by any recent radical Christian theologian, and doubtless this is true because, in the words of Langdon Gilkey, he presents the sharpest and most devastating challenge to the traditional or Biblical conception of God. More than any Christian thinker in our time, Rubenstein speaks both as a man of faith and as a man of the world. Just as his faith is real, or so it must appear to the Christian if not to the Jew, so likewise the world of which he speaks is real, and real precisely in its imperviousness to everything that the Christian has been given as the gracious or providential love of God. What seems paradoxical to the Christian if not to the Jewish mind, and paradoxical in a nontheological and nondialectical sense, is that Rubenstein has found a religious way that can be lived at the center of a Godless world. Of all the contemporary radical theologians, the one I feel closest to theologically is Rubenstein, and this is because both of us have chosen the project of attempting to effect a synthesis between a radical form of mysticism and a radical form of modern Western atheism. We would not seem to be far apart in terms of our fundamental allegiance to either Freud or Nietzsche, and perhaps we are not far apart in terms of our dependence upon either Kabbalism or Madhyamika Buddhism. What most decisively distinguishes us is our respective identities as Jew and Christian. Indeed, I have learned more of my Christian identity through encounter with Rubenstein than I have by way of encounter with any Christian theologian.

If only through Rabbi Rubenstein, the contemporary Christian can learn that his hope is both absurd and impossible. Or, at least, hope is impossible and absurd if it is an eschatological or apocalyptic hope, and it is precisely Christianity's eschatological ground that most fundamentally distinguishes it from Judaism. There is a Protestant theological principle that is commonly identified as extending from Paul and Augustine to Luther and Kierkegaard that identifies the absurd as being integrally and necessarily related to faith. Only through the gift of faith can we know the full reality of guilt and meaninglessness, for only the perspective of the new Adam or the new man of faith has sufficient distance from the old Adam to realize the full weight of brokenness. Perhaps Paul Tillich will prove to be the last theologian who could speak in this manner, and he did so only by employing the language of Hegel, Nietzsche, and Freud. For in our time it has become all too clear that it is the non-Christian thinker and visionary who has most profoundly realized the absurdity of the human condition. Can the Protestant theologian continue to maintain the integral relationship between faith and the absurd? Or between faith and depth? I believe that he both can and must, but he can do so only by evolving both a fully dialectical and a fully apocalyptic form of theology. Indeed, I believe the greatest challenge before us is one of understanding the integral and mutual relationship between apocalyptic faith and a dialectical mode of thinking and vision. It is at this point that Rubenstein can point the way for the Protestant theologian, and he can do so by his identification of the New Jerusalem as nothingness.

Notice that for Rubenstein the death of God can truly be greeted only with despair, but this is a despair that drives us to nothingness as our ultimate situation. Our only hope can be one of returning to our true sources in the divine nothingness or no-thing-ness. For evil can be overcome only by returning to the nothingness that is both our source and our end. Our end is our beginning, *Endzeit* is *Urzeit,* our origin is our goal. Every hope that is a hope in an end other than in the beginning is a hope in a literal as opposed to a primordial nothingness, a hope in "nothingness" as opposed to "no-thing-ness." Finally, the Christian hope in the Kingdom of God or the New Jerusalem is a hope in such a "nothingness," for it is a hope that contradicts the inherent nature of reality. The goal of total liberation is a pathetic falsification of reality and it can be achieved only by bringing reality to an end. Hence eschatology is a sickness, a sickness in both a Freudian and a Nietzschean sense, for it arises from what clearly appears to be an infantile or resentful attempt to abolish reality.

Now I believe that these judgments are both humanly and theologically true, and it is only by accepting their truth that Christian theology can establish its reality in our world. I also believe that it is an inescapable historical truth for us that the proclamation of Jesus and hence the original ground of the Christian faith announced the immediate dawning of total liberation, a liberation that is inseparable from the abolition of reality. An inevitable temptation of Christian theology, and particularly so in our own time, has been to think that the idea or symbol of an actual end of the world was no part of the original proclamation of Jesus, and rather derived either from the apocalyptic religious world that so dominated Jesus' disciples or from the all-too-human or fleshy component of their minds and hearts, which was impervious to the higher call of the Spirit. To this day, the greatest achievement of theological mediation in this direction is Bultmann's method of demythologizing, which assumes that any objective meaning of the gospel, any meaning that speaks of the world or reality as such, including the idea that the end of the world is at hand, belongs to the world of myth and not of gospel, and therein is consigned either to the premodern age of humanity or to the realm of the old Adam or "flesh" (*sarx*).

For Bultmann, Jesus, unlike the prophets, directed his preaching to individuals and not to a community. Therefore, Jesus "dehistorized" God and man; that is, he released the relation between God and man from its previous ties to history (*Historie*). Again, in contrast to both the Old Testament and Judaism, Jesus "historicized" God—in the sense of *Geschichte* as opposed to *Historie*—by "desecularizing" man.

For Jesus, however, man is de-secularized by God's direct pronouncements to him, which tears him out of all security of any kind and places him at the brink of the End. And God is "desecularized" by understanding His dealing eschatologically: He lifts man out of his worldly ties and places him directly before His own eyes. Hence, the "de-historization" or "desecularization" both of God and of man is to be understood as a paradox (*dialektisch*): precisely that God, who stands aloof from the history of nations, meets each man in his own little history.[1]

Here, it is apparent that Bultmann is engaged in the process of demythologizing through his translation of Biblical eschatological categories into the categories of Kierkegaardian subjectivity, wherein the inner now of *Geschichte* not only replaces but also negates the outer now of *Historie*.

Rubenstein can teach the Christian that the God who stands aloof from the history of nations is the God who stands aloof from Auschwitz, and that the price of accepting a dehistorized or subjective God (the God who is absolute Subject and only Subject) is the abandonment of the objective world or reality as such to the realm of "flesh." Precisely this, of course, has been the path of modern Protestantism, and beyond Protestantism, of Christianity at large; and therein, in the words of Kierkegaard, Christianity has become historically exactly the opposite of what it is in the New Testament. Already beginning with Franz Kafka, it has been the Jew who has most poignantly unveiled the bad faith of the modern Christian world's belief in God, and no doubt the Jew has most clearly and truly seen this bad faith, because he exists as an exile in the Christian world, an exile whose humanity is negated by the Christian faith and hope. As never before in the history of the Christian consciousness, the modern Jew has appeared and has been real as the suffering servant, the broken one in whose agony the world can behold and know the pain of humanity. If the Christian continues to believe in the gracious and providential love of God after Auschwitz, then not only is he once more denying the humanity of the Jew, but he is also inevitably denying the pain of all humanity, refusing the authentic or ultimate reality of a pain that cannot be relieved or assuaged by a dehistorized or dehumanized God. The Jew presents the Christian with the image of his brother, the brother from whom he is estranged by his very faith in God, and a brother who will never be real to the Christian until the Christian repudiates and negates every idea or symbol of salvation confining liberation to an interior, a subjective, or an esoteric realm.

But there is no way to an idea or symbol of a total liberation as opposed to an interior or subjective liberation apart from accepting the full scandal of the gospel: the scandal of a faith proclaiming that the world and reality as such are in process of coming to an end. The New Jerusalem is quite literally nothing if its advent has no actual effect upon or no integral relation to reality as such. So long as reality remains untouched by the New Jerusalem, then the New Jerusalem is untouched by reality, and the inner realm or "little history" that is celebrated by its proclaimers is not only an innocent illusion but, more fundamentally, a perverse veiling of reality. Finally, the Christian must say Yes or No to the question of the actual advent of the New Jerusalem: for if the Messiah or the New Jerusalem lies wholly in the future or primordially in the past, then Christ is neither actually nor historically real. Moreover, the Christian today can make such a decision only with the realization that to affirm the presence of the New Jerusalem is inevitably to engage in a pathetic falsification of reality, and a falsification that can truly be known to derive from an infantile or resentful attempt to abolish reality. For we know, and know as man has never known before, that faith can only know as Spirit what flesh has repressed and reversed as flesh, and that the flesh that is negated by Spirit is the flesh from which flesh itself is alienated and estranged. Spirit is born only at the cost of self-alienation, and to speak of the total triumph of Spirit is to speak of a final self-dissolution or self-annihilation. In short, to speak of the presence of the New Jerusalem is to speak of the end of reality as such.

Certainly an eschatological symbol of the end is an integral ground of the original Christian faith, and in our own time we have increasingly come to realize that such a symbol of the end is an integral and immediate ground of modern Western dialectical thinking and vision. If the modern imagination is eschatological or apocalyptic to the extent that it evolves out of a negation and reversal of our given world of consciousness and experience, then so likewise is it dialectical in the sense that it is grounded in a movement of negation and transcendence. Wherever we turn to the fullest and most total expressions of modern imaginative vision, as, for example, in Blake, Proust, and Joyce, we find that a new and total world of vision is established and maintained only by way of a dissolution or reversal of our given selfhood. Everything that an autonomous and uniquely individual form of selfhood knows and experiences as reality is here negated, reversed, and transcended; and this fully parallels primitive Christianity's eschatological negation of the world in faith. If anything, the fullest expressions of the modern imagination are even more apocalyptic in form, movement, imagery, and symbolism than is the New Testament; or so, at least, it would appear to the Christian today who inherits almost two millennia of demythologizing an originally apocalyptic faith.

Only the dualistic form of the modern Western consciousness, which is grounded in an absolute distinction between the subject and the object of consciousness, instills us with the seemingly irrevocable sense that the world or reality stands wholly outside of consciousness itself. Once this dualistic form of consciousness is negated and transcended by a dialectical movement of thinking or vision, then the world or reality no longer stands forth as autonomous and apart, and is known or experienced as being integrally and necessarily related to the center and ground of consciousness. Then a reversal of consciousness inevitably makes manifest and real a reversal of the world or of reality as such, and the world or reality as it was previously manifest to consciousness comes wholly to an end. We need not conceive such a reversal of consciousness as purely imaginative or visionary, as witness Marx's dialectical understanding of the integral and necessary relationship between consciousness and society, and Marx's revolutionary understanding of society was a consistent enlargement—if reversal—of Hegel's dialectical method. So likewise Kierkegaard's dialectical understanding of faith establishes the subjective truth of faith as a consequence of the negation of objectivity, and the passion and inwardness of faith is established only by virtue of the absurdity of its objective meaning or ground. We might also note that Nietzsche's higher or Dionysian vision of Eternal Recurrence—which he judged to be the ultimate expression of Yes-saying or total affirmation—can be reached only by passing through a full and total realization of the meaninglessness and chaos of the world or reality as such. Surely all of these expressions of modern dialectical thinking have an eschatological ground: a ground in an absolute negation and reversal of what apocalyptically can be named only as old aeon or old creation.

Yet Christians have learned again and again in our world, and perhaps most so at the hands of the Jew, that a world lies about us that is wholly impervious to faith or vision. In one sense, the Jew knows a world that the Christian has never known, or never known by way of his Christian consciousness and sensibility, and that is the world which the Christian judges in faith to be old aeon or old creation. What the Jew as Jew apparently has, and what the Christian has lost if he ever had it, is a sense of the world as creation and only creation, and thereby untouched by the announcement or gospel of total vision or total liberation. In our time, if only because of Auschwitz, the Christian is being forced to respect the judgment of the Jew as Jew, and to acknowledge that it is possible in good faith to judge that neither a messiah nor full liberation has yet entered or affected the world. Thereby a theological chasm is once again arising between the Christian and the Jew that is perhaps as great or even greater than it has been in the past, a chasm leading the Christian to question his knowledge of Yahweh, and to recognize that the Scripture which he knows as Old Testament is not the Scripture which is known to the Jew. At the very least, the Christian is coming to see that the Christian God is not to be theologically identified with the Lord of Israel, and that the God whom the Christian knows in Christ is absent from Israel, and absent because Israel has preserved its covenant with the Lord.

Even when the Jew speaks of the absence or the silence of God, he can still presumably speak as a Jew, and exist in a world that in some sense he can know as creation. Perhaps because he was forced to exist for so many centuries as an exile in alien religious worlds, the Jew has been prepared to live in faith in a Godless world, and therein to preserve the name of the Lord, even if that name must now be named as no-thing-ness. Nevertheless, if the Christian recognizes the good faith of the Jew in preserving the divine name in a Godless world, he must acknowledge his own bad faith in attempting to exercise the same vocation. For not only does the Christian not know the God of the Jew, but as a Christian he is inescapably a son of that Christ who proclaimed and made manifest the full advent of the Kingdom of God. Once faith is grounded in the dawning of the Kingdom of God, there can be no true openness to a God or Lord standing outside of the world and time, and hence no openness to the reality of God in a Godless world. To know that Christ and the Kingdom have actually come is to actualize in faith the name of God in such a manner as wholly and finally to dissociate the name of God from any realm or mode that is beyond and apart. Therefore, when the Christian acknowledges his own existence in a truly Godless world he must repudiate both the name and image of God. Indeed, when the good faith of the Jew unveils the bad faith of Christian belief in God, the Christian can become more truly open to the Christ who points to the end of the old creation, the end of reality as such, and ushers in that new creation of total liberation, which no longer can even be named as reality.

Notes

1. Rudolf Bultmann, *Theology of the New Testament,* Vol. I, §3:3, tr. by Kendrick Grobel (Charles Scribner's Sons, 1951), p. 25.

Part IV

ALTIZER AND SOME MODERN ALTERNATIVES

Daniel C. Noel

Thomas Altizer and the Dialectic of Regression

IN AN ESSAY WHICH SERVED AS A SORT OF MANIFESTO FOR THE THE-
ological radicalism of a few years ago, William Hamilton selected
himself, Paul van Buren, and Thomas Altizer as being most
representative of the "death of God" movement.[1] Hamilton's
placement of Altizer centered around an appraisal of the latter's
Mircea Eliade and the Dialectic of the Sacred.[2] His characteriza-
tion is, in most respects, an accurate one. He notes (pp. 31–33)
Altizer's "mysticism" and dependence on Eliade, Kierkegaard,
N. O. Brown, and Nietzsche. Hamilton is perhaps too quick
to label as incipient Gnosticism some of the ideas Altizer has developed out of Brown, for any position which seeks to move
through and beyond modernity is aiming at a synthesis which
would combine a nonregressive reappropriation of what has been
lost to modernity, in addition to a retention of what has been
gained by it.

From *The Journal of Religion,* October, 1966, with title change, revision,
and abridgment by the author.

On the other hand, a man who has gone to some lengths to criticize "modern gnosticisms" [3] should be brought up short when he falls into the same heresy. With this in mind, let us take a careful look at Altizer's work.

I

The general movement of Altizer's thought in *Mircea Eliade and the Dialectic of the Sacred* begins with Eliade's distinction between the sacred and the profane, moves beyond Eliade via a vertiginous dialectic, and after scattering, tornado-fashion, seven or eight prospects in its zigzagging path, settles upon Norman O. Brown and the Nietzsche of "Eternal Recurrence" as indices to a properly dialectical *coincidentia oppositorum* of the sacred and profane. Centering on the associations between Eliade, Brown, Nietzsche, and Altizer, we will seek to appraise the validity of Altizer's proposed *coincidentia* in the mode of temporality, probably the most crucial one, and certainly representative of his project as a whole.

Norman O. Brown describes Eliade's antithesis between archaic and modern time as follows: "Archaic time is cyclical, periodic, unhistoric: modern time is progressive (historical), continuous, irreversible." [4] Eliade has idealized archaic man, says Brown, "by attributing to him the power to abolish time and [Brown quotes *Cosmos and History*] 'live in a continual present' " (p. 277).

Brown, let it be clear, *shares* Eliade's intention to abolish time with archaic man and "live in a continual present," except that he feels that Eliade's primitivism cannot achieve this because it fails to take into account a necessary precondition: the abolition of guilt, which Brown has Freudianly undertaken.

Brown distinguishes between his "eternal Now," which is achieved by accepting the "actuality of living-and-dying, which is always in the present," and Eliade's "continual present," which, as a flight from death, becomes a regressive attachment to "the womb from which life came" (pp. 284–285). But Brown's distinction here invites closer scrutiny.

Regardless of how it is most successfully to be realized, is Brown's "eternal Now" any less static, finally, than a regressively entered womb-sea of primordial timelessness? Is not Brown's "eternal Now," no less than Eliade's "continual present," merely the circle of static timelessness set spinning like a wheel? As William Earle has written of Nietzsche: "[The free spirit] may be fettered by fear and concern for the future, for its own death. But let it finally accept death, for the wheel of existence turns and all things recur." [5] The acceptance of death as living in "the Now" is tied, either as cause or effect, to the wheel of recurrence.

Henri-Charles Puech, in his significantly titled essay, *"La Gnose et le temps,"* makes the following statement about "wheels of recurrence": "The circular movement that ensures the maintenance of the same things by repeating them, by continually bringing back their return, is the most immediate, the most perfect (and hence the most nearly divine) expression of that which, at the pinnacle of the hierarchy, is absolute immobility." [6] In Brown's dialectic of life and death, something has been left out of the affirmation of death. William Earle touches upon this missing element in his paraphrase of Nietzsche, quoted above: "fear and concern for *the future,* for *its own death."* (My italics.) While it may be in some sense true to say, with Brown, that the "actuality of living-and-dying" is always in the present, fear and concern for one's own death is always fear and concern for the *future,* and acceptance *of* death is always acceptance *of* the future, however immediate.

With this element excluded from Brown's dialectical affirmation of death, the "eternal Now" becomes what it is more honestly in Eliade: an Eternal Return *in illo tempore,* a return to eternity, a regression. What does Altizer do with these concepts?

The prospects are favorable, at points in *Mircea Eliade and the Dialectic of the Sacred,* for an avoidance of Brown's regressive direction. Altizer is aware that for Brown "unrepressed life would be timeless or in eternity," and he notes that "Brown seeks a libido that is unaffected by the Oedipus complex; and this means a libido that has not murdered God, a libido that is unfallen and still in union with the sacred" (p. 174). However, Altizer excuses this regressiveness by referring to the inadequacy of Brown's Freudian terminology. This is too charitable, for one can use the Freudian language as strictly as Brown does and still express the program for a nonrepressive, nonregressive coincidence of opposites.

If I may be permitted some italicized revisions, Altizer's comment on Brown would look like this: *Post*repressed life would be a *coalescence of time and eternity*, involving a libido that has been *cured* of the Oedipus complex, which is to say a libido that has *no guilt over having murdered* God, a libido that is *fallen* and still in union with the sacred, i.e., *a libido that is in the (realized?) eschaton.*

In whatever terminology it is couched, Altizer does not recognize Brown's regression. It is, then, no surprise to see him run into the same problem. He exults over Nietzsche's words on Eternal Recurrence in the third part of *Zarathustra:* "The imagery itself is cyclical, moving to and from the idea of the circle [from *Rad* to *Ring*]" (p. 185). The merry-go-round of timeless childhood beckons. Altizer senses the peril, for before he climbs aboard he says of Nietzsche that "unlike his dialectical predecessors he has isolated this immediate moment from any metaphysical relation with an order or *logos* that transcends it" (p. 186). But Nietzsche has also, we might add, made it eternal by isolating it from the movement of his history.

Still troubled, Altizer attempts to dissociate Nietzsche's Eternal Recurrence from Eliade's Eternal Return: "Briefly stated, Eternal Return transforms time into eternity" (p. 193). But we can see that that which Eliade transforms into eternity, and that which Nietzsche transforms eternity into, is not time, the future time of history, the time of entropy and the arrow, but the *point,* "the Now." Whether one moves from hub to spinning periphery or vice versa, one is still on the stationary carousel, and so, by now, is Altizer.

The ruthless illogic of his unintentional negation of time really catches up with Altizer in the culminating statement he offers in support of his claim that the Nietzsche he follows does not fall prey to Eliade's regression. Note that the two movements referred to are presented as antithetical:

> What the sacred myth [Eliade's] knows as a repetition continually regenerating the "irreversibility" of profane time into the presence of a transcendent eternity, the profane myth [Nietzsche's] knows as a repetition continually transforming the transcendence of eternity [into the "irreversibility" of a profane time? No:] into the absolute immanence of the radical profane. (P. 194.)

The forward-moving linearity of profane time has been lost here, but it is conversely evident that the logic of Altizer's intentions, if correctly followed, would have included it (although at the expense perhaps, of Nietzsche). Altizer is on the right track when he critically remarks of Eliade that "he is unable to say Yes to the future, to envision a truly New Creation, to look *forward* to the Kingdom of God" (p. 195).

This is reminiscent of Brown's statement in *Life Against Death* that "competition between . . . [current psychoanalysis and current neo-orthodox Protestantism] to produce an eschatology for the twentieth century is the way to serve the life instinct and bring hope to distracted humanity" (p. 233). Somehow, however, both Brown and Altizer have been fed a poison which has paralyzed their proposed utopias and turned them into neutral Nirvanas. We must move on to examine some possible antidotes.

II

First, let us wonder about this "dialectical" method which Brown and Altizer so enthusiastically employ. Brown says: "By 'dialectical' I mean an activity of consciousness struggling to circumvent the limitations imposed by the formal-logical law of contradiction" (pp. 318–319). He then goes on to say that "there is an important connection between being 'dialectical' and dreaming, just as there is between dreaming and poetry or mysticism" (pp. 320–321).

But *these* activities, if dialectical, are not so in the sense of "struggling to circumvent the formal-logical law of contradiction." Brown himself notes that "the dream does not seem to recognize the word 'no'" (p. 320). Surely this is a recognition called for in a dialectic which is "struggling." Further, Brown cites Freud's essay, "The Antithetical Sense of Primal Words" (p. 321), to imply contradictorily that the "reasonableness" of language, which he elsewhere equates with what the dialectical imagination of poetry is striving to *circumvent* (p. 319), is actually a subordinate quality of language. The basic character of language is dialectical only in a "natural" way, shown in the rhythmical reverberations, the loving strife, between a word's "concrete" and "ethereal" meanings, between "vehicle" and "tenor."

In spite of these acknowledgments, Brown's dialectic in practice is the spastic, "circumventing" one of his original definition. Fighting his own buoyancy, Brown employs a method which proceeds without the help of its strongest allies: the irrational basis of consciousness and the metaphorical basis of language.

Altizer finds the origin of dialectical thinking in the West in Heraclitus (pp. 81–82). Granting this, it also must be stressed that with Heraclitus dialectical thinking would not be struggling to overcome the law of contradiction, because reality itself was *polemos, eris, enantios.*[7] Altizer sees with Cassirer and Heidegger that *Seinsvergessenheit* and the logic-ization of *logos* came in after Heraclitus, but he insists on using a tainted dialectic which in effect assigns metaphysical primacy to post-Parmenidean concepts of contradiction. Like Brown, Altizer overlooks a resource which he has just looked over.

Language as metaphor, consciousness as resting on the unconscious, reality as Heraclitean fire: Can these three concepts provide an antidote to the regressive tendencies with which Brown's and Altizer's intentions have been drugged? This question may be answered if we discard the soiled term "dialectical thinking" and do some "metaphorical thinking" with three men whose words about the above-noted concepts may also offer counsel to Altizer's Christology.

III

Owen Barfield is a British literary theorist and philologist who has extrapolated from Goethe, Coleridge, Wilhelm von Humboldt, and Friedrich Max Müller in order to argue that language is basically and naturally metaphorical.[8] Reasoning from this thesis, Barfield has also had some provocative things to say about the evolution of consciousness.[9]

Both Brown and Altizer have, since the publication of their books discussed above, recognized the importance of this latter side of Barfield's thought. When the editors of *The American Scholar* asked him what book published in the past ten years did he find himself going or thinking back to, Brown replied: "I want to name Owen Barfield's *Saving the Appearances*." [10] Altizer writes of the same work: "I believe that this book is potentially one of the truly seminal works of our time." [11]

And yet, while Brown's most recent work, *Love's Body* (Random House, Inc., 1966), indicates he is familiar with Barfield's discussions on language as metaphor, Altizer does not seem to see the necessary connection between this concept and *Saving the Appearances*. It is hard to understand Altizer's oversight here, since even without reading Barfield's primary studies of language he could make this connection by a careful reading of the last nine chapters of *Saving the Appearances*.[12] Altizer should also be aware that Robert Funk's development of the idea of the New Testament parables as metaphors and in turn as linguistic counterparts of the incarnation is as much a result of Barfield's influence as Gerhard Ebeling's.[13] At any rate, it is interesting to speculate on what a thorough acquaintance with Barfield's theory of "poetic diction" would do to Altizer's "dialectical" method (and *will* do, I assume, to Brown's).

The most insistent supposition is that such an acquaintance

would provide Altizer with a methodology consistent with his own Christological and eschatological *desiderata*. Altizer already must have glimpsed a correlation between these and Barfield's "evolution of consciousness," for he paraphrases and quotes Barfield as follows:

> The mission of Israel is identified as a withdrawal from participation [in Lévy-Bruhl's sense] so as to prepare humanity for that day when it would be totally isolated from the world and yet called to the task of realizing a new unity with the world (our time). Only the Incarnation can explain [it is the only hypothesis capable of *Saving the Appearances*] the new and final participation lying upon our horizon: "In one man the inwardness of the Divine Name had been fully realized; the final participation, whereby man's Creator speaks from within man himself, had been accomplished." The Word became flesh so as to make possible in the course of time the transition of all men from original to final participation.[14]

Barfield's conception of the incarnation as a freeing of man, in the course of time, to say the Divine Name ("*I* am . . .") here coalesces with Altizer's idea that the death of God frees us to see the contemporary reality of a continuing incarnational *kenōsis* leading to a nonhubristic apotheosis of man.[15] Barfield has achieved with his metaphorical sensitivity a pre-view of a "final participation" which is the *coincidentia oppositorum* Altizer was insufficiently able to apprehend with his dialectical method. At both of these points of coalescence between Barfield and Altizer, however, there lies the thought of another man: Carl Jung.

IV

In writing recently of Jung's reputation, Floyd Matson has observed that "it is often overlooked that he has consistently turned for guidance to the future no less than to the past. . . . His emphasis, in both theory and therapy, is upon the creative potential of personality—the distinctively human capacity which he has been content to identify by the archaic titles of 'spirit' or 'soul'—as against the quest for scientific causality which in his view can only reinforce the 'primitive tendencies' of the psyche." [16]

If Jung's choice of words is not always the most felicitous, he nonetheless demonstrates that future-oriented approach which Altizer incompletely discerns as necessary for the realization of the new creation. And it is Jung, with his awareness that the logical ego-consciousness rests on an irrational and unconscious fundament, who has taken over from Heraclitus the knowledge that reality itself is of the nature of a strife of opposites. Jung has seen that psychologically this means that an overemphasis on either side of a polarity such as conscious-unconscious, or sacred-profane, will lead not to a dialectical *coincidentia oppositorum* but to a reinforcement or *enantiodromia* of the (untransfigured) other pole, that is, to an inundation or regression. [17] It will be helpful to keep these Jungian motifs in mind as we explore the somewhat surprising parallels between Jung's notion of "individuation" and Altizer's idea of an ongoing kenotic incarnation.

Jung's conclusions about an imperfect incarnation requiring a second birth of the divine child are probably no more heterodox than Altizer's talk about *kenōsis*, [18] and no less valuable as contributing to a Christology for the death-of-God theology. Jung's and Altizer's thoughts here are, in fact, but one melody played in different keys. This is readily apparent from a reading of Jung's *Answer to Job* and Philp's *Jung and the Problem of Evil,* with its illuminating correspondence from Jung.

If we may be permitted to quote at some length, Jung's position will largely explain itself. Jung writes: "From Job it is quite obvious that Jahwe behaves like a man with inferior consciousness and an absolute lack of moral self-reflection. In this the God-image is more limited than Man. Therefore He must incarnate" (Philp, p. 224). Philp addresses Jung and quotes *Answer to Job:*

The crowning point of your line of argument in *Answer to Job* is the place of individuation which you represent as the satisfying answer to Job. As the first Incarnation was, you say, imperfect, we have to wait for the Holy Ghost to produce a second birth and this in fact is described in the Book of Revelation: "Ever since John, the apocalyptist, experienced for the first time (perhaps unconsciously) that conflict into which Christianity inevitably leads, mankind has groaned under this burden: *God wanted to become man, and still wants to*. That is probably why John experienced in his vision a second birth of a son from the mother Sophia, a divine birth which was characterized by a *coniunctio oppositorum* and which anticipated the *filius sapientiae,* the essence of the individuation process." Allowing for the symbolism involved, this is how the second birth takes place: "The dogmatization of the *Assumptio Mariae* points to the *hieros gamos* in the pleroma, and this in turn implies, as we have said, the future birth of the divine child, who, in accordance with the divine trend towards incarnation, will choose as his birthplace the empirical man. The metaphysical process is known to the psychology of the unconscious as the individuation process. (P. 172.)

Finally, Altizer should want to applaud what Philp criticizes here in Jung:

I think, too, that the dogmatic interpretation which you give of the Incarnation is very narrow. You insist that it was not a real Incarnation because of the Virgin Birth of Christ and the Immaculate Conception of Mary, but I have the conviction that —without realizing it—you are working this out to fit in with another part of the structure you wish to erect, and that this particular way of looking at the Incarnation of Christ is necessary so that there will be room in your reconstruction for the continuing Incarnation which finally, you believe, is to culminate in the Christification of many through the process of individuation. (P. 163.)

Jung's melody is, in a more Catholic transposition, the same unorthodox one that Altizer plays in a Protestant key. Similarly, like Barfield's reading of the incarnation as a prefiguration of "final participation," Jung's way of looking at the incarnation is a hypothesis for "saving the appearances," which to Jung are the psychologically empirical "facts" of religious evolution. And while we are drawing parallels, there are several others which it will be fruitful for us to expose at this juncture.

Jung is related to Barfield not only by virtue of what he has to say about the incarnation but also in respect of his call for a "withdrawal of projections." This latter is essentially consonant with Barfield's call for a "withdrawal from [original] participation" in representations which have become detached from us, and have thereby, with our tendency to hypostatize them, become "idols." The possibility is negligible that Jung's term "projection" indicates a lack of agreement with Barfield that there *was* a time when man did not merely project *onto* but participated *in* his *umwelt*. Of the "euhemeristic" view of mental evolution which culminates in an understanding of "the whole metaphysical world [as even *originally*] a psychical structure projected into the sphere of the unknown," Jung writes:

> The danger of this viewpoint is an exaggerated scepticism and rationalism, inasmuch as the original "supreme powers" are seemingly reduced to mere representations. This leads to a complete negation of the "supreme powers (Scientific Materialism)." (Philip, pp. 242–243.)

Here again the melody is the same; but the keys are, this time, Jung's German Romantic background, with its emphasis on the chthonic, and Barfield's English Romantic background with its stress on the perceptual.[19]

Barfield may be linked to the later Heidegger (to bring a third "antidote" into the interstices of these observations) by the place of importance they accord to language. Barfield's insistence on the more-than-utilitarian implications of regarding language as metaphoric is matched by the later Heidegger's statement that language is the "house of Being." Barfield's "poetic diction" parallels the later Heidegger's call for a true "naming of the Gods" which would be a poetic, rather than metaphysical, "dwelling on the earth." The similarity of their uses of etymology as an anti-positivistic language-clarifier is likewise revealing.[20]

The later Heidegger, in his turn, can be related back to Jung as a sort of nondirective Jungian therapist of Being, who, entering into "proximity to the source," lets *Being* be. Likewise, it is Jung, who so often has been accused of "reifying" the unconscious, who says of it:

> It is the source of all sorts of evils and also on the other hand the motherground of all divine experience and—paradoxical as it may sound—it has brought forth and brings forth consciousness. Such a statement does not mean that the source originates, i.e., that the water materializes just in the spot where you see the source of a river; it comes from deep down in the mountain and runs along its secret ways, before it reaches daylight. *When I say: "Here is the source," I only mean the spot where the water becomes visible.* The water-simile expresses rather aptly the nature and importance of the unconscious. (Philp, pp. 12–13, my italics.)

In this unphilosophical phrasing of the matter we see a vivid demonstration that in his conception of the unconscious Jung no more intends a "simple locating" than does the later Heidegger in his search for being.

V

It is ironic that in his unpublished doctoral dissertation,[21] in two subsequent articles,[22] and in *Mircea Eliade and the Dialectic of the Sacred* (none of which displays an acquaintance either with *Answer to Job* or the Philp volume), Altizer has persisted in calling Jung a modern Gnostic whose work amounts to an undialectical world-negation and a flight into a discarnate eternity.

Jung is aware of such charges, and he meets them head-on:

The people calling me a gnostic cannot understand that I am a psychologist, describing modes of psychical behaviour precisely like a biologist studying the instinctual activities of insects. He does not *believe* in the tenets of the bee's philosophy. When I show the parallels between dreams and gnostic fantasies I *believe* in neither. (Philp, p. 239.)

The irony is that far from amounting to a kind of neo-Gnosticism, Jung's thought—together with that of Barfield and the later Heidegger—could help prevent Altizer from producing, *malgré lui,* a dialectic of regression.[23]

The valuable aspect of a primitivism such as Eliade describes is that *with* rituals, guides, witch doctors—*with,* in short, "outside help" (help from outside the self)—one can achieve a *periodic* or *sequential* or *momentary coincidentia* by regressing into the womb-sea of the archaic with someone nearby to pull one out. Rescue, then, is a momentary rebirth, and regression which is not final becomes regenerative.[24]

Always in this momentary rebirth there must be a rescuer or a rescuing agent: Ariadne's thread, Dante's Virgil, the pattern traced on the floor of the palace at Knossos for ritual dancing, the emblem on the doorway of the temple, the design in the ground outside the sacred cave, the ritual solution of a puzzle, etc. The examples can be quite diffuse, but, personified or otherwise, the pre-enactment of or guide to the successful (rescued) regression seems a universal aspect of a long pre-death-of-God stage of religious evolution.

But with the death of God (the biggest of the problem solvers) there can no longer be any outside help of a directive kind. Christianly, "conversion experiences" (one or many) give way to "becoming Jesus." Outside help must now be introjected as self-help, and the self must *become* the rescue, the ritual, the thread, etc. Preeminently, this means that redemption is within.

In Philp's work on Jung, the author quotes these words from Amy Allenby's *Jung's Contribution to the Religious Problem of Our Time:*

Consequently, modern man is no longer able to leave it to the medicine man or to the Christ-figure to achieve the transcending of the opposites on his own behalf. He has, in a sense, to become his own healer, he has to win the crystal or the alchemical lapis for himself. . . . This profound experience has been called by Jung "the process of individuation." (Philp, p. 181.)

Two points must be quickly made about Jungian individuation as self-help. In the first place, it is a *gain* over the periodic regression and rebirth (with help) process of pre-death-of-God religions. In the sporadic syntheses of the latter, there always lurked the danger that rescue would be ineffectual or too late. (Pip is rescued too late by the *Pequod* and is thereafter unintelligible; rebirth can be miscarriage.) Furthermore, and this relates to the second point, individuation, seen as becoming one's own redemption, is not *periodic or sporadic* but *ongoing and continual*.

Second, the suspicion that the concept of individuation is considered by its proponents a "state" or *finished* process is countered precisely by the realization that individuation as self-help, in conjunction with the future-orientation of Jung's thought, means that the goal is *in the going*. This applies whether the goal is a *coincidentia oppositorum,* a "final participation," or a new creation.

This "on-going" quality of the individuation process has been brought out most suggestively by the American Jungian Ira Progoff, who writes:

> In the act of doing the work that leads to the development of persons, the intimation of reality that is the driving image behind it makes reality present, just as Mecca becomes present in the midst of a pilgrim's journey. In this sense, too, wholeness of personality is not a goal that is off in the future; it is a condition of being that becomes present in the course of the work that seeks it.[25]

"Mecca as the road" also means that here we have no imperialistic or messianic *hubris* that proclaims itself as having "arrived." If the Mecca of Altizer's thought is a Garden reentered without vomiting the apple—that is, if he intends no regressive dialectic—then in the perspective of the "on-goingness" made possible by the continuing incarnation we can see his goal as a go-ing. Remembering this, and with the aid of the resources proposed above, is it possible that, more than anyone emerging on the American scene, it is Thomas Altizer who can lead us theologically "down the Garden path"?

NOTES

1. William Hamilton, "The Death of God Theology," *The Christian Scholar*, Vol. XLVIII (Spring, 1965), p. 28, n. 3. Subsequent references to this article will appear in the text.

2. Thomas J. J. Altizer, *Mircea Eliade and the Dialectic of the Sacred* (The Westminster Press, 1963). Subsequent references in the text.

3. Thomas J. J. Altizer, "The Challenge of Modern Gnosticism," *The Journal of Bible and Religion*, Vol. XXX (Jan., 1962), pp. 18–25.

4. Norman O. Brown, *Life Against Death* (Vintage Books, Inc., 1959), p. 274. Subsequent references in the text.

5. William Earle, "The Paradox and Death of God," in William Earle, James M. Edie, and John Wild, eds., *Christianity and Existentialism* (Northwestern University Press, 1963), p. 82.

6. Henri-Charles Puech, *"La Gnose et le temps,"* quoted in Mircea Eliade, *Cosmos and History: The Myth of the Eternal Return,* tr. by Willard R. Trask (Harper & Brothers, 1959), p. 89, n. 59.

7. See Philip Wheelwright, *Heraclitus* (Atheneum Publishers, 1964), p. 140.

8. See especially Owen Barfield, *Poetic Diction: A Study in Meaning* (McGraw-Hill Book Company, Inc., 1964), and his "The Meaning of the Word 'Literal,'" in L. C. Knights and Basil Cottle, eds., *Metaphor and Symbol* (Butterworth & Co., Ltd., 1961).

9. See Owen Barfield, *Saving the Appearances: A Study in Idolatry* (Faber & Faber, Ltd., 1957).

10. Norman O. Brown, Letter in "The Revolving Bookstand," *American Scholar,* Vol. XXXIV (Summer, 1965), p. 478.

11. Thomas J. J. Altizer, Review of Owen Barfield, *Worlds Apart: A Dialogue of the 1960's* (Wesleyan University Press, 1963), in *The Journal of Bible and Religion,* Vol. XXXII (Oct., 1964), p. 385.

12. Even more recently, Altizer has acknowledged indebtedness to Barfield in one place and has striven to "meet Barfield's challenge" in another. However, his continuing to seek a "dialectical vision" and especially his reaffirmation of the selfsame Nietzschean doctrines we have criticized above show that Barfield's linguistic insights have yet to make any impact upon him. See Thomas J. J. Altizer and William Hamilton, *Radical Theology and the Death of God* (The Bobbs-Merrill Company, Inc., 1966), pp. 120, 148; and Thomas J. J. Altizer, *The Gospel of Christian Atheism* (The Westminster Press, 1966), pp. 12, 147–157.

13. See Robert W. Funk, "The Old Testament in Parable," *Encounter,* Vol. XXVI (Spring, 1965), pp. 261–262, n. 72; and his "Saying and Seeing: Phenomenology of Language in the New Testament," *The Journal of Bible and Religion,* Vol. XXXIV (July, 1966), pp. 197–213. These points are expanded upon in Robert W. Funk, *Language, Hermeneutic, and Word of God* (Harper & Row, Publishers, Inc., 1966).

14. Altizer, Review of Barfield, p. 385.

15. See Thomas J. J. Altizer, "Creative Negation in Theology," *The Christian Century,* Vol. LXXXII (July 7, 1965), pp. 864–867.

16. Floyd W. Matson, *The Broken Image: Man, Science and Society* (George Braziller, Inc., 1964), pp. 208–209.

17. H. L. Philp, *Jung and the Problem of Evil* (Rockliff Publishing Corporation, 1958), pp. 114–115. Subsequent references in the text. Quotations are used by permission of Barrie & Jenkins, Ltd.

18. To find out just how far Altizer is from orthodoxy on this point of *kenōsis,* see F. W. Beare, *A Commentary on the Epistle to the Philippians* (Harper & Brothers, 1959), pp. 73–88, and the appended note, "The 'Kenotic' Christology," by Eugene R. Fairweather, pp. 159–175.

19. See René Wellek, "German and English Romanticism: A Confrontation," in his *Confrontations* (Princeton University Press, 1965), pp. 3–33.

20. A relevant presentation of the relations between Barfield and the later Heidegger is the essay by John J. Mood, "Poetic Languaging and Primal Thinking," *Encounter,* Vol. XXVI (Fall, 1965), pp. 417–433.

21. Thomas J. J. Altizer, "A Critical Analysis of C. G. Jung's Understanding of Religion," unpublished doctoral dissertation (University of Chicago, 1955).

22. Thomas J. J. Altizer, "Science and Gnosis in Jung's Psychology," *Centennial Review* (Summer, 1959), and his "The Challenge of Modern Gnosticism."

23. What I have said about the relation of Altizer to his three-fold "antidote" may also be applied, *mutatis mutandis,* to Brown. Even with regard to Jung, whom Brown joins Altizer in anathematizing, I would be prepared to defend the proposition that should the traveler follow Brown's redrawing of Freud's pioneering map, he would proceed from Vienna to Bollingen.

24. See Geoffrey Peterson, "Regression in Healing and Salvation," *Chicago Theological Seminary Register,* Vol. LV (Feb., 1965), pp. 16–21.

25. Ira Progoff, *The Symbolic and the Real* (The Julian Press, 1963), p. 215.

Nicholas Gier
Process Theology
and the Death of God

As ironic as it may seem to many, I will begin with the assumption that Thomas Altizer's death-of-God theology offers a solution to modern man's experience of Godlessness. Altizer's theology is founded on the conviction that the dialectic theology of the 1920's was not dialectical enough. It is Altizer's claim that Barth, Bultmann, Tillich, and the other dialectic theologians were never able to transcend an inherited Lutheran dualism. Their use of dialectic, says Altizer, was limited to an attack on secular expressions of faith, and thus it could not offer any new vision of the sacred.[1] For Altizer, any dialectical method that is not fully dialectical is not dialectical at all. Either it remains a strict supranatural dualism, which is most characteristic of Barth, or it lapses into a monism, as it does most evidently in Tillich.[2] Altizer opts for a full, radical dialectic that holds within its dynamics this "categorical imperative" of faith: If we affirm the death of God fervently enough, a new revelation of the sacred will appear. This is a solution to a Godless world, but is it a viable one? That is the question posed in this essay. It is a critical inter-

Previously unpublished.

pretation of death-of-God theology from the point of view of process theology.

There are other interpreters of the contemporary theological scene who maintain that it is process theology which offers the most viable solution to the problems of a Godless world. Mack B. Stokes, in an article entitled "The Non-theistic Temper of the Modern Mind," argues that the most effective counter-measure for a world of unbelief "can best succeed with the aid of personalistic modes of thought which are informed and enriched by some of the insights of Whitehead and Hartshorne."[3] Bernard E. Meland, in a critical response to Paul van Buren's positivistic stance in an article entitled "The Dissolution of the Absolute,"[4] maintains that the rejection of all traditional absolutes is part and parcel of process philosophy. However, he hastens to add that process philosophy substitutes a "vision of a More in experience" that is quite compatible with theological formulations in which we can still speak meaningfully in terms of God.[5]

In an essay entitled "Post-Christian Aspects of the Radical Theology," Maynard Kaufman suggests that all the valid insights of death-of-God theology can be retained without the loss of a doctrine of transcendence. Kaufman affirms that the radicals' emphasis on a suffering God can best be expressed in terms of the dipolar view of God that comes out of process philosophy.[6] Finally, Altizer himself recognizes that it is process theology "that is expected most profoundly to challenge a death of God theology." Altizer states that he sees himself in a quite different light than his radical compatriots, who "have avoided the problem of God and have given themselves to other and seemingly more pragmatic theological tasks." He sees himself on common ground with the process theologians because they too speak directly to the problem of God. Altizer anticipates that the challenge from process theology will come in the form of its "new and potentially radical understanding of God."[7] It is the purpose of this essay to indicate the form that such a challenge could take.

I

When I first proposed a comparison between process theology and death-of-God theology, one response was: "The radicals will refuse to meet you at the ontological or metaphysical level. Talk about philosophical theology is inadmissible for them. It was interred along with the body of God!" In the Introduction we have shown that Altizer must be seen apart from the radical secular theologians and their rejection of philosophical theology. Altizer accepts a Hegelian metaphysics and aims at developing a fully dialectic ontology, a task that he has done with some success in his most recent book, *The Descent Into Hell*. The fact that Altizer eschews the "pragmatic theological tasks" of the secular theologians and finds common cause with the process theologians in their search for a new doctrine of God betrays a sensitivity to ontological and metaphysical problems that is virtually absent in modern secular theology.

Before our proposed dialogue can be said to be on firm grounds, we must ask another even more relevant question: How do the process theologians respond to the affirmation that God is dead? The phrase "death of God" is, in many respects, an unfortunate use of words. Used as a slogan by those who must popularize and sensationalize, it has led to the detriment of radical theology rather than to an enhancement of its real contribution to an understanding of modern culture. The phrase misleads, confuses, and offends. Altizer means that God died in Jesus and that death is now being realized and universalized in modern culture. In short, it means the death of the traditional, impassive God of transcendence and the birth of a new Christ of radical immanence.

Although his apocalyptic and poetic style does joggle the strictly rational mind, Altizer does not intentionally mislead or confuse. However, I believe he does intend to offend. Altizer insists on retaining the phrase "death of God" in lieu of less shocking terms such as God's "hiddenness," "eclipse," "absence," etc. In an article entitled "Creative Negation in Theology," [8] Altizer criticizes those who say that God is merely in eclipse or in hiding. He also rejects the views of those who say that God is beyond the capacity of human expression or that modern man is incapable of believing in God. All these formulations about God's disappearance from modern culture, says Altizer, do not get at the heart of the matter. They simply are not radical enough. Underlying them is a sort of "fudging" liberalism, which sees clearly the plight of modern despair and Godlessness but hopes vainly for the reappearance of the traditional God of the past. This attitude among a great many secular theologians reveals an archaic mode of faith whose object is, as Altizer puts it, the "primordial God of the beginning."

A good example of such formulations is Heidegger's statements concerning the eclipse or absence of God. In *Vorträge und Aufsätze* he states: "But absence is not nothing; it is actually the appropriating presence of the hidden plentitude of what is past, and hence it is the collected presence of the divine things of ancient Greece, of prophetic Israel, of the sermon of Jesus. This no-more is in itself a not-yet of the veiled coming of his inexhaustible presence." [9] This statement about God's absence is completely antithetical to Altizer's intentions when he uses the phrase "death of God." Such descriptions as these are undoubtedly the reason he avoids the terms "absence" or "eclipse." We will see later in this essay that Altizer opts for a complete rejection of past forms of the sacred. The death of these past forms of God must be final and irrevocable. As Altizer states in "Creative Negation in Theology": "He is truly absent, he is not hidden from view, and therefore he is truly dead. Once we accept the death of God as a final and irrevocable event, then we can open ourselves to the full actuality of our history, as an epiphany of the Word of faith." [10] For Altizer, faith in Heidegger's God of "hidden plentitude" is not faith at all. It is simply a nostalgic yearning for a past primordial totality that can never be experienced by modern Christian man. For Altizer there is no way back to the Garden. The only way is the way forward—through a historical movement in which all transcendent reality is being completely destroyed.

How do the process theologians respond to this? First, it must be said that, strictly speaking, a process theologian cannot admit that God is dead. The organismic view of God sees him as inextricably linked with the processes of cosmic experience. In Whiteheadian terms, God is required as initial aim for each and every occasion of experience. Simply put, then, if God were dead, the universe and everything in it would be dead. Therefore, the process theologian cannot accept the death of God as a metaphysical or cosmological assertion. Altizer insists that his affirmation of the death of God be interpreted in this manner. For Altizer, a realm of transcendence that once was and once defined God is ceasing to exist. How process theology responds to this "death" of all transcendent reality is the first major problem discussed in this essay.

Despite his refusal to speak of the death of God in metaphysical terms, a process theologian, such as Cobb, will not at all reject the irrefutable evidence of the absence of God in modern culture. Indeed, as one can gather from Cobb's article "From Crisis Theology to the Post-Modern World," to live in modern culture is to live the death of God in a very real, i.e., existential, sense. Both solutions to Godlessness—process theology and Altizer's death-of-God theology—involve going beyond mere secularism. Both solutions go beyond an affirmation of modern culture in and for itself to a new post-modern world. Both views hold that modern man has committed himself to an inadequate mode of understanding the world. Both views inveigh against empiricism, Newtonian science, and sensationalism, which seem to have such a hypnotic grip on the mind of modern man.

Interestingly enough, the Whiteheadian view of Godlessness is quite similar in many respects to the view given by Heidegger above. The absence of God does not mean that God is completely dead; it means that he is unavailable, and what is more, unattainable by man's present mode of understanding the world.

Accordingly, the process view holds that if man can see his world intelligibly again, he will again find purpose, meaning, and faith in the God that was present to "prophetic Israel" and present in the "sermon of Jesus." Both the Heideggerian and Whiteheadian views attempt to witness to God's inexhaustible presence, which is apprehended only by an adequate understanding of the world. As Cobb affirms, "If Whitehead's vision should triumph in the years ahead, the death of God would indeed turn out after all to have been only the 'eclipse of God.' " [11]

The "eclipse of God," then, is perhaps the most appropriate term to use in relation to process theology. If God were completely dead, modern man would experience total relativism or chaos. The fact is that we have not reached total relativism, because we are still able to communicate. There still appear to be nonrelative points of reference, points of transcendence if you will, which keep our world from lapsing into the chaos of total relativism. In reference to this point, Cobb makes this penetrating remark: "We do still live in a world formed by a past that remains alive even in its decay." [12] With this statement the second major problem discussed in this essay is introduced. One of the crucial differences between the radical view and the process view is that Altizer would have us reject completely any "world formed by a past." The process view must insist on the retention of the past as a basic philosophic tenet.

The third major problem posed is the problem of the self. Presumably, the complete destruction of all transcendent reality would mean total alienation among all individual centers of consciousness. To be sure, modern man experiences alienation to a degree far greater than his predecessors did. Altizer observes quite correctly that Western man seems to have lost his former assurances of self-groundedness and self-sufficiency. To borrow the language of the existentialists, he seems to be suspended over an abyss of nonbeing. Indeed, it is Altizer's prediction that the total collapse of the autonomous self is on the immediate horizon of modern man.

It is Cobb's argument, however, that man does not, in fact,

experience total alienation. He is still able to come in contact
with and relate to other individuals with some success. Furthermore, he is still able, however feebly, to orient himself to a
"More" in his broken experience, which seems to assure him of
a transcendent reality of some sort. To rephrase Cobb, modern
man's individual self is still intact and "remains alive even in its
decay." While the process view remains confident that a Whiteheadian concept of the individual can lead to a new, post-modern
selfhood, Altizer would have us renounce all individual claims
to autonomy for the ushering in of the new, purely immanent
totality that is the Kingdom of God.

II

Without question, the most pervasive theme in all of Altizer's
thought is the call for the death of transcendence, the death of
God. The destruction of all transcendent reality is absolutely
necessary in order that the sacred can come alive in the flesh
in a fully immanent form. The notion that God is ultimately
mysterious, distant, and transcendent is the product of a fallen
consciousness. In *The Descent Into Hell,* Altizer claims that the
more divided and fallen is consciousness, the more divided and
alien to each other are the centers of consciousness, and the more
God will appear in a purely transcendent form. In short, a fallen
consciousness can conceptualize only a fallen deity, and all notions that God is distant and alien must be dialectically reversed
if we are to see a new revelation of the sacred in our time. That
which engages this dialectical reversal is the affirmation of the
death of God. Such an affirmation releases a formerly oppressed
and fallen humanity to participate in an ever-ongoing, nonreversible dialectic, in which all reality will be pure and immanent experience and in which Jesus will be in "every hand
and face," not in some past, and therefore lifeless, form. In *The
Descent Into Hell,* Altizer claims that those who believe in the

transcendent Creator God "will be totally unprepared for a Kingdom dawning at the center of life and the world." [13]

Maynard Kaufman agrees wholeheartedly that God must now be seen in an immanent and experiential form, but he does not see why this necessarily entails the end of God's transcendent reality:

> In terms of Whitehead's or Hartshorne's dipolar concept of God, it is not necessary to negate the primordial or transcendent nature of God in order to perceive and affirm the consequent or immanent nature of God. But this can be done only if this doctrine of God is understood cosmologically rather than historically. The agonizing either-or quality of the wager which Altizer proposes is therefore slightly misplaced and its pathos is unnecessary. We do not simply face a choice between "the primordial and transcendent reality of God and the kenotic and immediate reality of Christ." [14]

Before discussing the full implications of Kaufman's challenge, we must present an explanation of process theology's theory of dipolarity.

In the theology of Charles Hartshorne, the primordial nature (PN) of God is that determinable potentiality which underlies the actuality of the world that has already been realized in a determinate form. It comprises a unity that transcends the manifold of the cosmic process; it is the one from which the many is derived; yet, it remains independent and unaffected by the derived plurality. The PN transcends our present reality in the sense that it contains the possibilities of an infinite number of worlds, of which our present world is only one possibility. The PN is the abstract constituent of all possible reality, and therefore it must transcend any form of particular, historical reality. In other words, the PN is a universal object for all possible subjects of experience, actual or not yet actual. It is the divine object in and for the divine subject, which is God's consequent nature (CN).[15]

By positing an abstract nature of God, Hartshorne has introduced an aspect of God that is independent, complete, transcendent, and absolute; yet, he calls his view of theism "surrelativism." An absolute in a relativistic metaphysics seems to be contradictory. However, Hartshorne is a shrewd logician, and he resolves the apparent contradiction ingeniously. Together the PN and CN of God comprise all reality whatsoever. Together they are all-inclusive. But, as Hartshorne affirms, "the all-inclusive in its inclusiveness cannot be absolute," because the CN of God contains things that are finite, contingent, and changing. But since the PN and CN together include "all things, they can perfectly well *include* something absolute." [16] This "something absolute" is the PN of God. Since the PN contains all possible experience, it lacks no possibility; it contains an infinity of possibilities. In this sense it is complete and absolute. Hartshorne writes: "The absolute can exist in the supremely relative, in serene independence, serene exemption from relativity." [17] "Surrelativism," then, does not hold that everything whatsoever is relative. "The Divine is to be conceived as relative beyond all other relative things, but this relativity itself must have an abstract character which is fixed and absolute." [18] If everything in the world were relative, the word "relative" would be empty of meaning. Unless something were necessary and absolute, nothing could be significantly contingent. This is the logical basis for Hartshorne's forceful insistence on the irreducibly dipolar nature of reality; each and every form of reality is defined and limited by its polar opposite. This is also the reason why process theology must retain a doctrine of transcendence.

The PN of God, though an absolute, is not seen as a "beyond" —something utterly transcendent and alien from our experience. This "above and beyond," "distant and cold" type of transcendence, against which Altizer so bitterly inveighs, is not present in process theology. There is no completely sovereign Creator God who is removed from the processes of life—no oppressive authority of the wholly Other. "The PN," says Hartshorne, "is not before or apart from but *with* all process." [19] Thomas W.

Ogletree, in an excellent essay entitled "A Christological Assessment of Dipolar Theism," develops this point further: "When Hartshorne speaks of the absolute pole of the divine being, his intent is not to isolate God from process, but to identify one of his aspects with those factors which are the precondition for there being anything whatever. . . . In this function, *he is independent of the contingencies of process, even while he is embodied in them.*" [20]

The Whiteheadian conception of the primordial nature of God also combines these notions of independence and intimacy. For Whitehead, God is intimately related to our experience in every moment, for he is responsible for the eternal ordering of all possible actual experience. In short, it is precisely because of God's eternal ordering of possible experience that a tomorrow appears, or, for that matter, that the next actual occasions in my personal experience are continuous with the present ones and not a part of the asphalt street outside my window. It would be difficult in my mind to conceive of a concept of God in which he would be more near, more related, or more intimate. Cobb writes: "I suggest that the otherness of God expresses itself, paradoxically if you will, in his absolute nearness. Every other entity can be somehow distanced, either as temporally past or spatially separate, but God's presence is absolutely present. He is numerically other, and qualitatively, incomprehensibly other. But this other is spatiotemporally not distant at all." [21]

Edward Farley, in his book *The Transcendence of God,* describes Hartshorne's view of transcendence as "unrivaled superiority." It is a form of transcendence that cannot possibly be viewed as a physical separateness or alien otherness. Indeed, it involves just the opposite. The PN and CN of God include together all reality; nothing could be separate or beyond ordinary reality, as was thought in the traditional formulations. Farley states: "Transcendence for Hartshorne thus does not mean mystery, otherness, independence, or beyondness, but rather, *superiority.*" [22] God in his PN is unrivaled because he is free from the contingency of actual experience without being beyond it.

God in his PN is superior too because he contains all possibilities whatsoever within his nature. Contrary to the traditional views, God is transcendent not because he is the *absolutely* perfect being, but because he is the *most* perfect being. In other words, his perfection does not lie in pure attributes derived from the *via negativa,* but in those attributes derived through the *via eminentia.* For God in his CN is the most "perfect" sufferer and the most perfect participant in all experience whatsoever. In direct contrast to traditional notions of God, God is unrivaled not because he is free from all desire, but because he experiences all desires and finds divine satisfaction in each of them.

In Hartshorne's formulations, the PN of God is the divine object of all experience, while his CN is the divine subject of all experience. The PN is everything in potency and possibility, but nothing in actuality; the CN is everything in actuality, but nothing in potency. The PN contains an infinite range of possibility; the CN is comprised of a finite actuality. The CN of God is the cumulative actual being of the cosmos at any given moment, as apprehended by God in his PN. In an obvious sense, the finitude of actuality that comprises the CN is far less than the range of possibility available in the PN. In a subtler sense, on the other hand, even the most trivial item of actuality, let us say a rock, is "more" than all the PN put together, simply by virtue of its existence and actuality. However, that one item of actuality owes its present status and will derive its future status from the eternal ordering character of the PN of God.

Again we see the irreducibly dipolar nature of process theism. The polar aspects must work together in a dialectic—a dialectic that never closes and never reaches a synthesis; for, if it did, dipolarity would collapse into the nonpolarity of sheer actuality or sheer possibility, either of which would mean the end of ordered reality as we experience it.[23] The dialectic does close in Altizer's vision; transcendence empties itself and pours itself into immanence. The PN empties itself completely into the CN. A world of sheer actuality, pure experience, is the result. The dipolar view of reality must insist, however, that one needs both the abstract, highest common factor of potential reality and the concrete, *de facto* actuality of the present moment. Central to the logic of dipolarity is the conviction that nothing can have meaning in pure form. Pure actuality is just as meaningless as pure potentiality. Each must be seen in contrast with the other. The essence of all actuality, according to Hartshorne, is to be non-exhaustive of potency, and this potency is the result of the infinite range of possibility that the PN of God offers.

III

Now let us turn more directly to Altizer's death-of-God theology. In his pivotal remarks above, Kaufman contends that the dipolar view of God makes the metaphysical "death of God" unnecessary. In Altizer's view there will be a total cosmic reversal. There will be an actual ontological change in the universe, a change that occurred in a particularized form in Jesus and is now becoming universalized in the modern world. That which was originally transcendent is now becoming immanent; two formerly separate realms of reality are now becoming one: the sacred is now in the midst of the profane. If the logic of dipolar theism is sound, it shows us that there need not be this death of God or the coming eschatological reversal for which Altizer so fervently calls. According to the dipolar view, the PN and CN of God work together simultaneously; and, moreover, there was never a time when they did not so act. Furthermore, transcendence in the process view, either Whiteheadian or Hartshornian, does not at all have the distant and unrelated characteristics of the type of transcendence that Altizer rejects. As we have observed earlier, it is difficult to conceive of a form of transcendent reality that could be more in our midst or nearer to the actuality we now experience.

Not only does the theory of dipolarity make Altizer's cosmic reversal unnecessary, it also makes any ontological or fundamental cosmic change impossible. Indeed, there is always ontic

change: the possibilities of the PN are always becoming actualized in God's CN. But there could never be a time when the
PN could empty itself of all possibility. First, the mutual in-
compatibility of the manifold orders of possibility would prevent
such a once-and-for-all actualization; but second, and more important, is the fact that the PN of God is inexhaustible. The
PN could forever empty itself of possible orders of existence and
still retain an infinitude of potentiality. Therefore, in no sense
whatsoever could the primordial transcendent nature of God
become fully immanent. The PN could never be "left behind
in an empty and lifeless form," as Altizer would see it. The
Incarnation then, in the process view, is not a "total and all-
consuming act"; the "whole reality of Spirit" never becomes
"incarnate in its opposite." A transcendent reality could never
become pure actuality or a reality only "as it is immediately
experienced and perceived." [24] Process theology would indeed
give complete measure to the fullness of the divine reality that
appeared in the Incarnation, but this in no way exhausts the
PN of God, who is, as Hartshorne puts it, "the self-surpassing
surpasser." The fullness of the divine that appeared in the Incarnation would be surpassed by an even fuller epiphany of the
sacred at a future moment in time.

With regard to the related doctrines of Incarnation and Christology, there is a crucial difference between the two views. While
a Whiteheadian would hold that God has always had an incarnate form (the CN), Altizer proposes that God, previously not
incarnate, became incarnate in Jesus. Incarnation is an actual
event in the history of Spirit: God "empties" himself completely
of his transcendent form and is now becoming totally incarnate
in the world. In a sense, a process Christology could be termed
kenotic. The Whiteheadian God "empties" himself of a manifold
of possibilities for the actual experience of the world. Altizer,
however, interprets this term in a far more radical sense. For
him, *kenōsis* is a total process in which a pure transcendent
reality is becoming pure actuality. Runyon has aptly termed it
"Incarnation without a stopper."

This is a point at which I believe Altizer has misinterpreted Meister Eckhart. In *The New Apocalypse,* Altizer claims that Eckhart anticipated the death-of-God theology with the first thoroughgoing kenotic Christology.[25] Eckhart saw the Godhead as eternally begetting the Word in the soul of each individual. Altizer rightly interprets this as a kenotic view—the pouring out of transcendence into immanence. We cannot, however, interpret this as a complete emptying of the primordial Godhead. In fact, a further reading of Eckhart would show that the Godhead is inexhaustible and remains intact despite the eternal generation of the Son. It would be inconceivable for Eckhart to say that the Godhead would eventually be "empty and alien." Accordingly, this interpretation of Eckhart would then be more compatible with the process dipolar view. The primordial Godhead is never lost in an empty and lifeless form. The Godhead could never be exhausted by any particular actuality; it could never be exhausted by eternal generation into immanence; it could never be limited by any particular world because it would hold within itself all possible worlds.

Runyon has also called Altizer's view a "monolith of immanence." By systematically eliminating every form of transcendent reality in a nonreversible dialectic of pure experience, Altizer has brought many problems to the fore. It is not too surprising that they are the same problems inherent in Hegelian metaphysics. First, we must recognize that the Hegelian view holds a doctrine of strict internal relations. Such a view maintains that everything, including universals and God, are subjects of experience and hence are concrete and actual. There are no externally relatable objects, no terms of experience that do not serve as subjects also. An entity's true nature and identity are seen only in the complex of relations (all internal) that it experiences.

It is also true with the process view that an entity's nature is determined primarily by its relation to other entities; indeed, the whole of Hartshorne's philosophy turns on the concept of reality as a social process. Reality is a living organism whose parts have no reality outside of the organic environment. Yet there must be something more. As Runyon says of Altizer, there must be an "Archimedean point of reference," or otherwise "God has no dialectical reality apart from us as well as in our midst, no reality apart from the world as well as in it. Therefore, there is no basis from which to create what I would call genuine historical existence." [26] There must be some objects of experience to which entities can relate themselves *externally*. Otherwise, a world of pure experience degenerates into a Heraclitean flux of meaninglessness or a Hegelian determinism, where possibility is seen as necessity.

Hartshorne contends that the absolute idealists mistakenly identified the all-inclusive with the absolute, and "through this identification, they lost their insight into the inclusiveness of the supreme." [27] The supreme to which Hartshorne refers here is his own concept of the primordial nature of God, which we have discussed above. The PN is absolute because it always retains its self-identity; as Hartshorne says, it never "acts out of character." [28] The self-identity of Hegel's Spirit was lost when Spirit, originally primordial and deficient of actuality, decided to unfold itself for a world, and, according to the laws of the dialectic, could never return to its original state of self-identity. According to Hartshorne, an all-inclusive, pure actuality such as Hegel's is the least absolute reality there can be. Absoluteness and completeness are meaningless in actuality; these terms can apply only to potency and possibility. Actuality is always incomplete, contingent, and finite.

The Hegelians, though, will persist. Why do potentiality and possibility need to be transcendent? Why cannot all possibility be contained in an eternal subject whose dialectical unfolding will "iron out" mutually incompatible possibilities? Why cannot possibility be simply an inner mode of pure actuality? Why cannot possibility arise out of the contraries inherent in each moment of actuality? Why cannot universals or eternal objects—those terms of which all entities partake—become concrete and actual as well? In sum, why is not the locus of possibility actuality itself?

For process metaphysics it would be inconceivable to restrict the locus of possibility to that which has been actualized or is being actualized in the present moment. It is true that what will happen in the next moment is determined in large part by the previous and present state of things actualized; but each new moment, according to process thought, is also open to the infinite range of possibilities contained in the PN of God, which transcend the limited possibilities contained in previous actual states. In the process view, to be limited only to that which has been actualized is to be impoverished; in fact, there would be no novelty or freedom in life at all. The Whiteheadian God orders possibilities for occasions of experience, but this by no means completely determines the course of their subjective experience. It would seem that the case with the Hegelian system is quite the opposite. As the Hegelian scholar John N. Findlay states: "Actualities are, however, real necessities in the sense that, the conditions and circumstances being what they are, no other outcome is possible. Real possibility is therefore . . . inseparable from real necessity." [29]

If we are to avoid the inadequacies of the philosophies of pure experience—either the sheer determinism of Hegel or the sheer indeterminism of Heraclitus—we are compelled to posit a range of infinite possibility that is always more than the actuality of our present or our past. This transcendent aspect of reality would contain an infinite number of possible objects of experience, which, if actualized at once, would prove mutually incompatible. No amount of Hegelian dialectic or synthesis could reconcile such anarchy and chaos. For process thought the concrete and the actual are superior, but the primordial ordering of possibilities by the abstract nature of God is absolutely necessary for continued existence, order, and satisfaction. Whitehead's eternal objects have no significance or reality whatsoever unless they are seen in relation to particular occasions of experience; yet they are mandatory for experience to continue. Again we have argued ourselves into a dipolar view of reality; again we must conclude that if this dialectic of dipolarity is synthesized, as it is in Altizer's or Hegel's world of pure experience, we then close ourselves to an adequate, logical, and intelligible view of reality.

IV

Certainly one of the most controversial topics in contemporary theology is the relationship between faith and history. Has the past event of Christ redeemed all time? Can one derive authentic existence from a past time and a past happening? Does historical research and criticism have any real relevance for Christian faith? The responses to these questions could be polarized as a thoroughgoing denial from the radical theologians and an enthusiastic affirmation from the new school of Pannenberg and, as we shall see, the process theologians as well. The radicals, following the Barthian disdain for an exclusive use of the historical-critical method, think that it is the overwhelming acceptance of this method as a valid means of investigating reality that is indicative of the death of God in our time. Nietzsche was the first to give this argument radical expression. Jacob Taubes elaborates: "It was Nietzsche who discovered (what Hegel and his pupils may have known but did not admit) the driving force behind the passion of historical research: the death of the Christian God. Historical research, Nietzsche observed, works only as a post mortem, dissecting the body for the sake of anatomical study and writing an obituary." [30]

For Bultmann the Christ event is something that must happen ever anew; the past forms of faith cannot give us spiritual sustenance or lead us to an eschatological mode of existence. Authentic existence is one that is fully oriented toward the future; it always stands before man as a future event and cannot be grasped in terms of philosophical or historical analysis, but only existentially. For Bultmann, one must cut himself off from all past forms of religious security before a truly Christian mode of existence can be realized. "Philosophical analysis can show that my present is always determined by my past. If that is true, my freedom is always a relative rather than a radical freedom. For to be free in a radical sense, I must be freed from my past. This radical freedom can only be a gift, for every endeavor to become free is an endeavor of the old man who is determined by his past." [31]

Bultmann, with his program for a present- and future-oriented theology, sets the stage for much of radical theology's views on the relevance of time and history for Christian faith. One of the most pervasive themes in Altizer's writings is what he discovered in his study of Blake and Nietzsche: A prophetic hatred of memory.[32] With Nietzsche the aversion to all past events is shown in his condemnation of the "It was." The *Übermensch*, according to Nietzsche, will someday have it within his power to declare, "Thus I willed it," instead of merely, "It was." For Altizer the preoccupation with memory and recollection is a sign of allegiance to the transcendent God of the past, the God whose death must be willed ever anew.

This thoroughgoing rejection of past events also includes the complete repudiation of all past forms of the sacred. These, says Altizer, are only objects of idolatry and formalized religion. Allegiance to such forms leads one away from the only true form of the sacred, that found in the immediate moment and in the midst of the profane. Moreover, each new moment in the dialectic of experience carries a new epiphany of the sacred that completely negates its predecessor. In essence then, past events are seen as instances of transcendence—that which is alien and removed from the fullness of the immediate moment. From the preceding sections we have become well aware of Altizer's aversion to all forms of transcendence. It is Altizer's hope that the radical Christian, once freed from the past, will be finally "liberated from every reality that appears beyond the human hand and face." [33]

Accordingly, God must come to fullness and die in each succeeding moment. His death is repeated eternally, for we can never return and expect to receive spiritual life from past forms of the sacred. The sacred reality is not gained by a "recollection" of past sacred events, but by a repetition of a real sacred event in the present moment. In Altizer's view, past, present, and future all collapse into simultaneity. Altizer refers to Nietzsche's concept of the Eternal Now, where "Being begins in every Now." As with Kierkegaard, faith and contemporaneousness are identified. God begins and perishes in every "Now." The full implication of this view is that there is no special time or place where the epiphany of the sacred occurs; it occurs everywhere and in every moment: the sacred center is everywhere and sacred time is anytime. For Altizer the fullness of faith is reached by a total immersion in the sheer actuality and the pure immediacy of the here and now.

Process theology must part radically at this juncture. This problem about the status of past time constitutes one of the most decisive points of disagreement between process theology and death-of-God theology. For Altizer the past, with its tendency to enslave us in priestly forms of religion, is simply an enemy. Time and history appear to be reduced to nothing, if Altizer remains true to his insistence on the Nietzschean Eternal Now. If present, past, and future are simultaneous, then past time is lost and unredeemable.

T. S. Eliot's discussion of time is relevant at this point. In the *Four Quartets* he writes:

> If all time is eternally present
> All time is unredeemable.
>
> ("Burnt Norton," I.)

But man in fact does not live in an eternal present; his existence is bound by time and history. Even the saints and mystics, though able "to apprehend The point of intersection of the timeless With time" ("The Dry Salvages," V) must return periodically to a time-bound world—a world determined by time past and time future.

> Men's curiosity searches past and future
> And clings to that dimension.
>
> ("The Dry Salvages," V.)

> We cannot think of a time that is oceanless
> Or of an ocean not littered with wastage
> Or of a future that is not liable
> Like the past, to have no destination.
>
> ("The Dry Salvages," II.)

Man redeems the time by living in it, clinging to the dimensions of past and future time. "Only through time time is conquered." ("Burnt Norton," II.)[34]

In *History and Hermeneutics,* Carl E. Braaten criticizes Bultmann for not recognizing the "ontological priority of historical reality," and for refusing to accept the fact that it is "the nature of faith to look to past fulfillment as well as future possibility." [35] Braaten represents the other side of the controversy regarding the relationship of faith and history. Faith need not necessarily be identified with contemporaneousness. The fullness of the reality present in such past events as the Incarnation and the Crucifixion is available for Christian men living in our present time. Ogletree's formulation of such a notion is apt and penetrating: "The Incarnation of the Word in Jesus Christ is an eschatological occurrence. It actualizes in advance the goal of the forward thrust of history. *This means that the movement of history cannot exhaust the significance of that which has already occurred. . . . Rather than negating all previous forms of the Word, new manifestations of the living Christ in human history always have an essential and positive connection with the Word which was in Jesus.*" [36] These thoughts are central also to the new school of Pannenberg, in which Christ is seen not as ending time and history but actualizing a new order of history in which men participate and find their redemption. Christ redeems the time, and "only through time time is conquered."

Past events, then, are but the prefiguration of future ones. The first of Eliot's *Four Quartets* opens with these lines:

> Time present and time past
> Are both perhaps present in time future,
> And time future contained in time past.

Similarly, process philosophy sees present, past, and future as distinct but inextricably linked. Simply put, the process view virtually turns on the concept of the retention of all past forms of experience. For a Whiteheadian such as Cobb, the past has an objective ontological status.[37] Not one occasion of past experience is lost; hence, all past time is recoverable and redeemable. Past time is redeemed because it is intimately linked with the formation of present and future moments. The experience of an actual occasion is a selective synthesis of the totality of the past. Each and every occasion of past experience passes into an immortal form that can then be used for the ordering of future occasions. In short, past time is used again; it enriches future moments of experience. Cobb phrases it in this way: "All real relations are the reenactment in the new experiences of elements of old experiences. . . . The past always profoundly affects the becoming present . . ."[38] The only way to the future is through the past. Arguing against the concept of an Eternal Now, Edward Farley contends: "If time is real, future cannot be reduced to the state of present, for the very meaning of present depends on the open possibility of actualizing future states."[39]

Both Altizer and the process view have a concept of eternal dying. For Altizer, however, that which dies, dies completely; it cannot be ontologically constitutive of the living present or future. Whitehead's actual occasions do come into being and perish, but they remain continuous with and constitutive of time present and time future. In other words, an actual occasion experiences a peculiar sort of dying: it passes into God's memory as an immortal object for future experience. While in the process view experience dies for posterity, in Altizer's view the experience of the "Old Aeon" must die completely.

By virtue of this intimate relationship between all modes of time in the process view, we are assured of a fairly well ordered continuum of experience. Each and every occasion of past experience is retained in memory—the memory of God—so that it becomes an integral part of the ordering of future experience. As a result, the cosmos is becoming ever more complex and richer due to the accumulation of past events and past values. Altizer would hold that the richness of experience is due solely to the intensity of feeling and conviction with which we thrust ourselves into the "Now." The Whiteheadians would no doubt affirm this also, for concepts about the intensity of an actual occasion's feelings are an integral part of process thought. A Whiteheadian would hasten to add, however, that the fullness of the moment we face with conviction and feeling is also due in large part to the richness of the past to which that moment is related.

V

Perhaps the most pervasive assumption in the Occidental philosophical tradition has been that there exist unique individuals capable of acting responsibly and morally in an ordered, temporal continuum. It will become clear later in this section that process thought is one of the twentieth century's most sophisticated expressions of this assumption. Altizer, on the other hand, contends that it is precisely this assumption, more than any other, that impedes man's search for a truly sacred reality. Altizer, much like Karl Barth, his predecessor in dialectic theology, believes that autonomous man absolutely precludes the man of faith. In *Oriental Mysticism and Biblical Eschatology* Altizer states, "Insofar as man has become an autonomous being, he has become an alien from God." [40] In *The Descent Into Hell* he admonishes us that the apocalyptic call of faith will pass us by as long as we affirm the inherent reality of a private center of consciousness.[41] A will strong enough to affirm the death of an autonomous, transcendent God is identical to a will strong enough to renounce all claims to an autonomous selfhood.

According to Altizer, the typically Western notion that there exists a God who is self-causing and self-sustaining is the product of a fallen consciousness. The ontology that laid the basis for this doctrine of God also gave form to a concept of the individual, which is seen as self-causing and self-sustaining. The concept of God and individuals as autonomous and self-contained is a unique product of the Western consciousness. In fact, as Leroy T. Howe has observed, the modern (fallen) sensibility is prone to affirm everything that has empirical substantiality as being self-grounded.[42] Such an affirmation, according to either Altizer or Barth, cannot be held by the man of radical Christian faith. Altizer states, "Religion must necessarily direct itself against a selfhood, a history, or a cosmos existing immediately and autonomously as its own creation or ground."[43]

Theologians such as Barth and Altizer do not make these harsh judgments without good reason. As a product of a fallen consciousness, Western philosophy has held tenaciously to the ontological primacy of selfhood and individuality. In modern times, however, this had led to an ontology of alienation. Our modern situation seems to indicate quite clearly that the more modern man stresses the integrity and uniqueness of selfhood, the more he facilitates the operation of those psychic forces which tend to undermine mental and emotional stability. The more he stresses his autonomy, the more he lives the horror of the death of God—a life of total alienation. The modern situation is indeed ironic: While Western man is being driven more and more to existential despair by self-consciousness and increased self-awareness, he nonetheless abhors the thought of the loss of his individuality and consciousness. That which is the source of fallen man's deepest despair seems to be his most prized possession.

This is indeed the modern dilemma, and Altizer, I believe, is quite justified in his attempts to salvage a sacred reality by returning to what in essence are Hegelian concepts of individuality and of what it means to be ultimately real. Altizer makes it quite clear in *The Descent Into Hell* that his view does not lead to a dehumanization of man. On the contrary, he would claim that it is the traditional view of an autonomous man and a self-contained God that has led to a dehumanization of man and the desacralization of flesh and world. Altizer would hold that his view leads to an eschatological existence in which Blake's full "humanity divine" is realized.

In a sense, Altizer is just as doggedly consistent as was Barth. Both have experienced the disdain and rejection of the contemporary sensibility because they hold to assumptions that seem quite incompatible with a modern scientific mode of viewing reality. What both Barth and Altizer demand is the preservation of the absolute sovereignty of the sacred reality. Such dogged theological consistency has proved unpopular and unacceptable to the modern mind, because by preserving the absolute sovereignty of the sacred, they in turn were compelled to deny the ultimate reality of the world and individuals. For Altizer, reality is God as all in all; anything less than that is not fully real—it is a fallen view of world and of God. God *is* (becoming) all reality; God *is* (becoming) "world." Leroy T. Howe attempts to understand Altizer's view with this statement: "From a Christian standpoint it is less blasphemous to identify world and God, than to proclaim the world's absolute autonomy." [44]

The process view does hold to the autonomy of the world and the individual. Accordingly, God is not absolutely sovereign at all; he is, in many respects, limited and restricted. At this point the two views reach a definite impasse. Once more, the difference runs as deep as the opposing philosophical views of the "world" that the two theologies hold. Altizer's view, thoroughly idealistic, must insist that the world is but a creation of mind or Spirit. The world is then secondary and derivative; it has no ultimate reality. For the process view ultimate reality lies precisely in the world of the particular—the myriads of actual occasions that have ontological status in and for themselves. If the world of particularity has it own autonomy, the absolute sovereignty of God cannot be a meaningful concept.

Again an impasse is reached between the two views on another point. Altizer's dialectic of the sacred has a definite and final end. A key word for Altizer is "total." The kenotic view of Incarnation means an eventual "total" emptying of the transcendent divine nature into a world of "total" immanence. In this sense the death of God is a "total" and irrevocable event. Similarly, God becoming all in all in a totally immanent Christ is a total process. In the New Apocalypse there will be nothing that is not the new sacred reality; there will be total and universal redemption.

Both the process view and Altizer's view are teleological and finalistic. However, *telos* in the process view is seen at the level of the actual occasion and its own particular subjective experience and end. For Altizer, the *telos* is seen at the level of all-encompassing Spirit, which is moving from a primordial form to its final form of "total flesh" in the New Apocalypse. All process has a final end: the sacred reality as all in all in a wholly concrete form. For the Whiteheadian, process is eternal; *teloi* are particular and not universal. In process thought, no event can be labeled final, total, or irrevocable.

The ethical implications of the foregoing discussion lead us to yet another impasse between the two views. A distinction can be drawn between a concept of a partially selfless love that has a definite relationship with past events and a strong concept of the individual (the process view), and a totally selfless love based on a renunciation of the reality of selfhood and the elimination of all that is not related to a thrust into the immediate moment with total conviction (Altizer's view). In essence, Altizer's view calls for the end of all traditional forms of ethics. In *The Descent Into Hell* he states: "A fully eschatological faith must repudiate traditional moral language. Above all, it must negate and transcend the language and form of the moral imperative." [45] Altizer believes that individual ethical decision can no longer have any significance; everything must be seen in terms of a total, universal commitment.

The pervasive ethical emphasis of radicals such as Herbert Braun and William Hamilton is to be contrasted to Altizer's unequivocal call for a suspension of the ethical. These radicals would seek to dissolve theology into an anthropocentric ethic. They speak so exclusively about personal encounter, the I-Thou relationship, that God and the sacred are reduced to some dimension of human existence, a notion quite antithetical to Altizer's intentions. Speaking solely in terms of the human dimension is also inadequate for the process theologians. According to them, such radicals as Braun and Hamilton are too exclusively humanistic. The process view, with its panpsychism and its cosmological emphasis, insists not only on an ethical openness to man but also on a sympathetic participation with the whole cosmos. In process thought we see a balance drawn between the individuation required for responsible ethical action and the sense of relatedness to the "All" that participation in the cosmic whole requires.

For Altizer the experience of cosmic love requires the negation of all individuality, all forms of selfhood, even, as we have seen, the selfhood of God. All this is required if one is to participate in the cosmic dance of life and energy in the immediate moment. This dance is the redeeming event, and it seems that for Altizer it is the only thing that ultimately matters. Other selves and societal responsibilities, in the last analysis, appear peripheral and unimportant. In the dance of the New Apocalypse there are no "other selves"; in fact, there is no "otherness" whatsoever. In *The Descent Into Hell,* Altizer states: "Accordingly, visions of a new apocalyptic compassion must inevitably appear in the form of madness or chaos to all those who can still find life or hope in an individual center of consciousness." [46] Earlier in the book he maintains that his view does not call for a "simple anarchism" or a "simple denial of law and authority," but it means the "absolute reversal" of all law and authority.[47] I would suggest, however, that it will be difficult for the conventional mind not to interpret this as a radical anarchism.

In our time the call for self-annihilation and absorption in the moment is indeed a tempting one. But, if we are to model our new Adam after Zarathustra—he who no longer negates nor sets limits—we have not only the possibility of a radical ethic of sacrificial love but also the possibility of a life of moral holiday. A Dionysian sacrificial love is not a responsible love. Leroy T. Howe believes that Altizer's view contains a "renunciation of every quest for genuine and lasting *polis,*" and "that all things *are* becoming one, through God and not man, absolving individuals of every obligation to develop personhood in community." [48] Process thought offers a basis for a personalistic ethics that would be an alternative to Altizer's call for an ethical life of self-annihilation. Process theologians are persuaded that a post-modern selfhood can be maintained in spite of modern alienation and despair. The challenge, then, of process theology would be not so much in its radical conception of God, as Altizer anticipated, but rather in the fact that it strongly upholds the ultimate reality and integrity of the individual.

NOTES

1. Thomas J. J. Altizer, "The Sacred and the Profane," in Thomas J. J. Altizer and William Hamilton, eds., *Radical Theology and the Death of God* (The Bobbs-Merrill Company, Inc., 1966), p. 147.

2. In his most recent book, *The Descent Into Hell* (J. B. Lippincott Company, 1970), Altizer admits that even his own theology has not been sufficiently dialectical. He mentions those who criticize his previous work as being Gnostic and dualistic and confesses that they have some ground for their criticism. *The Descent Into Hell,* however, appears to be a concentrated effort to construct a theology which is fully dialectical.

3. Mack B. Stokes, "The Non-theistic Temper of the Modern Mind," *Religion in Life,* Vol. XXXIV (Spring, 1965), p. 257.

4. Paul van Buren, "The Dissolution of the Absolute," *Religion in Life,* Vol. XXXIV (Summer, 1965), pp. 334–342.

5. Bernard E. Meland, "Alternative to Absolutes," *Religion in Life,* Vol. XXXIV (Summer, 1965), p. 346.

6. Maynard Kaufman, "Post-Christian Aspects of the Radical Theology," in Thomas J. J. Altizer, ed., *Toward a New Christianity* (Harcourt, Brace and World, Inc., 1967), pp. 353–357.

7. Thomas J. J. Altizer, "Introduction," in his *Toward a New Christianity,* p. 13.

8. Thomas J. J. Altizer, "Creative Negation in Theology," *The Christian Century,* Vol. LXXXI (July 7, 1965).

9. Martin Heidegger, *Vorträge und Aufsätze,* 2d ed. (G. Neske, Pfulligen, 1954), p. 183. Quoted in Charles E. Scott, "Heidegger,

the Absence of God, and Faith," *The Journal of Religion,* Vol. XLVI (July, 1966), p. 366.

10. Altizer, "Creative Negation in Theology," p. 866.

11. John B. Cobb, Jr., "From Crisis Theology to the Post-Modern World," in Altizer, ed., *Toward a New Christianity,* p. 249.

12. *Ibid.,* p. 245.

13. Altizer, *The Descent Into Hell,* p. 189.

14. Kaufman, "Post-Christian Aspects," p. 357.

15. The terms "primordial nature" and "consequent nature" are primarily Whiteheadian terms. Hartshorne usually makes a similar distinction in the nature of God with such terms as "absolute-relative" or "necessary-contingent." I am indebted to Charles Hartshorne's article, "Whitehead's Idea of God," in Paul A. Schilpp, ed., *The Philosophy of Alfred North Whitehead* (Tudor Publishing Company, 1941), for some of the material in this section. Using a Hartshornian piece on Whitehead may be confusing the issue somewhat. I am quite aware of the differences between Whitehead and Hartshorne concerning a process doctrine of God. This section deals primarily with Hartshorne's view, but some reference is also made to distinctively Whiteheadian emphases.

16. Charles Hartshorne, *The Divine Relativity* (Yale University Press, 1948), p. 86.

17. *Ibid.,* p. 120.

18. *Ibid.*

19. Hartshorne, "Whitehead's Idea of God," p. 532.

20. Thomas W. Ogletree, "A Christological Assessment of Dipolar Theism," *The Journal of Religion,* Vol. XLVII (April, 1967), p. 96.

21. John B. Cobb, Jr., *A Christian Natural Theology* (The Westminster Press, 1965), p. 243.

22. Edward Farley, *The Transcendence of God* (The Westminster Press, 1963), p. 154. Italics mine.

23. Lewis S. Ford has called to my attention that the theory of dipolarity is not really dialectical, for, although the two poles reciprocally require one another, they are not necessarily in tension with one another, let alone being contradictory. This tension and contradiction of opposites is, of course, quite central to Altizer's theology. For the purposes of comparison and dialogue, however, we will let this minor objection ride.

24. Altizer, *The New Apocalypse: The Radical Christian Vision of William Blake* (Michigan State University Press, 1967), p. 75.

25. *Ibid.,* pp. 67–68.

26. Theodore Runyon, *supra,* pp. 54 f.

27. Hartshorne, *The Divine Relativity,* p. 94.

28. Hartshorne, "Whitehead's Idea of God," p. 531.

29. John N. Findlay, *The Philosophy of Hegel* (Collier Books, 1962), p. 215.

30. Jacob Taubes, "On the Nature of the Theological Method," in Altizer, ed., *Toward a New Christianity,* p. 223.

31. Rudolf Bultmann, Review of Schubert M. Ogden, *Christ Without Myth,* (Harper & Row, Publishers, Inc., 1961), in *The Journal of Religion,* Vol. XLII (July, 1962), p. 226.

32. Thomas J. J. Altizer, *The Gospel of Christian Atheism* (The Westminster Press, 1966), p. 50.

33. Altizer, *The New Apocalypse,* p. 143.

34. T. S. Eliot, *Four Quartets* (Harcourt, Brace and World, Inc., 1943).

35. Carl E. Braaten, *History and Hermeneutics,* Volume II of *New Directions in Theology Today,* William Hordern, gen. ed. (The Westminster Press, 1966), p. 66.

36. Thomas W. Ogletree, *The Death of God Controversy* (SCM Press, Ltd., 1966), p. 80. Italics mine.

37. John B. Cobb, Jr., "Ontology, History, and Christian Faith," *Religion in Life,* Vol. XXXIV (Spring, 1965), pp. 270–287.

38. Cobb, "From Crisis Theology," p. 248.

39. Farley, *The Transcendence of God,* p. 134. Compare with Blake: "I cast futurity away, and turn my back upon that void Which I have made; for lo! futurity is in this moment." Turning from the immediate moment is error. It is wrong for man's curiosity to search "past and future and cling to that dimension." The radical Christian must find "futurity" in the present moment. Cf. Altizer, *The New Apocalypse,* p. 195–196.

40. Thomas J. J. Altizer, *Oriental Mysticism and Biblical Eschatology* (The Westminster Press, 1961), p. 198.

41. Altizer, *The Descent Into Hell,* pp. 196–203, 209–210.

42. Leroy T. Howe, "Altizer on Selfhood: A Critique," *The Christian Advocate,* Vol. XI (Aug. 10, 1967), p. 8.

43. Altizer, *The Gospel of Christian Atheism,* p. 34.

44. Howe, "Altizer on Selfhood," p. 8.
45. Altizer, *The Descent Into Hell*, p. 145.
46. *Ibid.*, p. 210.
47. *Ibid.*, p. 147.
48. Howe, "Altizer on Selfhood," p. 8.

Thomas J. J. Altizer
Response

I

DANIEL C. NOEL POSES A PROBLEM THAT IS SELDOM STATED BY THE-
ologians but that has overwhelming implications for our contemporary theological or religious situation: What is the decisive
difference between the religious ways of pre-death-of-God and
post-death-of-God religion? By understanding pre-death-of-God
and post-death-of-God as stages of religious evolution, Noel sees
a full continuity between what he terms the way of momentary
rebirth and the way of "on-goingness." The latter is understood
as a Christian phenomenon, for a passing through the experience
of the death of God leads to the apotheosis of subjective experience, which itself is a fulfillment of the continuing Incarnation
culminating in the Christification of many. If this analysis is to
stand, it depends upon the actuality of a new form or mode of the
religious consciousness, one that transcends even while existing
in full continuity with the previous stage of religious evolution.
While I am fully persuaded that the death of God is a Christian
phenomenon, and that it promises the Christification of all, I
find that Noel's portrait of "on-goingness" at no point transcends
or goes beyond a pre-death-of-God stage of religious evolution.

Why, it may be wondered, does Noel place such an enormous burden in his argument upon the identification of Jung's process of individuation as a truly new and yet Christian process of continual and interior self-redemption? Whether or not Jung may truly be identified as a Gnostic (and he has so identified himself on numerous occasions), there is nothing in what he describes as individuation that is not far more fully present in classical mystical ways of both the East and West. It is noteworthy that Noel ignores the world of mysticism, preferring to identify pre-death-of-God religion with Eliade's archaic religion, and this leads him to the fantastic historical thesis that interior- and self-redemption arises only with the death of God. No doubt the individuation process will truly appear to be new if one confines all pre-death-of-God religion to the historical world of primitive or archaic man. Jung knew better, for already in 1920, with the publication of *Psychological Types,* Jung demonstrated his own immersion in the mysticisms of China, India, and Europe. Indeed, he never abandoned the theory of the "Self" that was formulated in this work, and the unifying or reconciling symbol of the "Self" ever thereafter remained the foundation and the goal of the individuation process, a process that Jung himself considered to be universally present in the collective unconscious.

In a section entitled "The Relativity of the Idea of God in Meister Eckhart" in the *Psychological Types,* Jung shows how a mystical way can concretely collapse the dogmatic distinction between "God" and the "soul." For Jung believed then, as he continued to believe until his death, that the goal of all the great religions is the subjective withdrawal of libido into the unconscious so that a libidinal power may therein be stored which in the form of "God" or the "soul" becomes the most active force in psychic life. By means of religious or mystical discipline or practice, this libido may be withdrawn from the unconscious, thus bringing about a regenerative attitude and a new life springing out of the reactivation of unconscious psychic energies. The birth of this libidinal power signifies a becoming aware of unconscious contents.

This is an act of conscious discrimination from the unconscious *dynamis,* a severance of the ego as subject, from God
(i.e., the unconscious *dynamis*) as object. In this way God
"becometh." When, through the "breaking-through," i.e.,
through a "cutting off" of the ego from the world, and through
an identification of the ego with the motivating *dynamis* of
the unconscious, this severance is once more resolved, God dis-
appears as object and becomes the subject which is no longer
distinguished from the ego, i.e., the ego as a relatively late
product of differentiation, becomes once more united with the
mystic, dynamic, universal participation (*participation mystique*
of the primitives).[1]

Jung finds this meaning of "God" to be present in Christian, Indian, and Chinese mysticism, and he insists that it is identical
with that "Self" which is the goal of all psychic growth. How,
then, can Jung's individuation process be identified as a post-
death-of-God and specifically Christian way of "on-goingness"?

Initially I was intrigued with Noel's suggestion that the re-
placement of dialectical thinking with metaphorical thinking
would cure the regressive tendencies of my thought. But Noel's
real complaint seems to be that my dialectical method is tainted
because it fails to return to the natural dialectic of Heraclitus and
insists on assigning metaphysical primacy to post-Parmenidean
concepts of contradiction. This is certainly true, for I do not believe that it is possible to reverse history and return to a pre-mod-
ern or primal thinking, whether of a Jungian or a Heideggerian
kind. Unlike Jung and Heidegger, however, Owen Barfield does
embrace the historical evolution of consciousness, and he does so
by way of a radical understanding of the Incarnation. Or is it
truly radical? Of this I am now unsure, particularly in view of
Barfield's most recent writings, to say nothing of the fact that his
most fundamental loyalty has always been to Rudolf Steiner
(whom Noel pointedly ignores). Already in 1927, moreover,
Barfield hailed the backward glance of poetry, for it is by creating
true metaphors that poetry *restores* (Barfield's italics) the pri-

mordial unity of subject and object. At its birth, language is a living unity, but this unity is lost with the development of consciousness.

> Accordingly, at a later stage in the evolution of consciousness, we find it operative in individual poets, enabling them to intuit relationships which their fellows have forgotten—relationships which they must *now* express as metaphor. Reality, once self-evident, and therefore not conceptually experienced, but which can *now* only be reached by an effort of the individual mind—this is what is contained in a true poetic metaphor; and every metaphor is "true" only insofar as it contains such a reality, or hints at it. The world, like Dionysus, is torn to pieces by pure intellect; but the poet is Zeus; he has swallowed the heart of the world; and he can reproduce it as a living body.[2]

In its infancy, language is all poetry. But with the development of conceptual thinking the primordial unity between subject and object is lost from perception. Now the connections between discrete phenomena can be apprehended only as metaphor—for once they were *perceived* as immediate realities—and it is the function of the poet to see these connections as immediate realities, and to make others see them, *"again"* (my italics).

At bottom there is nothing in this theory of poetry as metaphor that goes beyond the romanticism of the nineteenth century, just as there are no ideas of Jung that cannot be traced to a comparable source. If there is one motif that is common to all forms of romanticism—and here I am speaking of romantic theory and not of the actual poetry of the so-called romantic poets—it is a nostalgia for the lost innocence of a primordial beginning and a yearning for an original and undifferentiated form of consciousness. This romanticism was still present in the Nietzsche who wrote *The Birth of Tragedy,* but it was conquered in his prophetic realization of the death of God, and his consequent baptism of time and death in his vision of Eternal Recurrence. Yes, this vision of Eternal Recurrence is an acceptance of death as living in the Now, and it is just for this reason that it is opposed to all pri-

mordial forms of a *coincidentia oppositorum*. It is precisely those
who most deeply refuse our world and the forward movement of
history and consciousness who are now driven to a primordial
way, a way that masks the profane reality of time and death by
apprehending it as being at one with a primordial unity. Nietzsche
points the way to a total refusal of every such primordial call,
and his own thinking and experience is a model for the reversal
of regression. For this reason alone the contemporary Christian
should accept Nietzsche as a prophet and seer. Where else may
one find such a consistent and comprehensive inversion and reversal of a pre-death-of-God stage of religious evolution?

II

There can be no gainsaying the power of process theology in the
contemporary American Protestant theological world, and not the
least source of this power is its ability, or the ability of its proponents, to enter and comprehend the most diverse forces upon the
contemporary theological scene. Despite the fact that I was initiated into systematic theology by Daniel Day Williams, that I am
an alumnus of the established academic center of process theology
—the Divinity School of the University of Chicago—or, most important of all, that I have been in intimate touch with the thinking and criticism of John B. Cobb, Jr., for the past thirteen years,
I continue to find process theology both conceptually and humanly
unreal. First, I find it to be unreal because it is so closely bound
up with the cultural world of liberal Protestantism. As Charles
Harvey Arnold attempts to demonstrate in *Near the Edge of
Battle,* a history of the Chicago Divinity School, there is a full and
unbroken continuity between the liberalism of the early twentieth-
century Chicago theologians and the liberalism of Meland,
Loomer, and Williams. To this day, Cobb is the only process theologian who is even open to the challenge of radical relativism
and nihilism. Thus I must begin my response to this critique
from the point of view of process theology by citing a portion of

Cobb's criticism of Boston Personalism in his *Living Options in Protestant Theology:*

> Personalism has great confidence in the reliability of a kind of common-sense speculation about the cosmos as a whole, whereas sophisticated moderns generally find such confidence naïve and out of date. Even when sympathetic to such inquiry they find the results too suspect and humanly unreal to serve as a basis for ultimate decisions of life and death. Hence, it is not philosophers only, but spiritually sensitive moderns generally, who feel an ultimate frustration and emptiness before Personalism's staggering claims about reason's ability to know God.[3]

Now I recognize that process theology is far more sophisticated than Boston Personalism, and more sophisticated precisely because it is genuinely philosophical, but I fail to detect any substantial or real theological distance between Boston Personalism and Chicago Process Theology, just as I cannot fail to observe that both are so clearly related to the social world of modern American liberal Protestantism.

Whitehead himself, unlike Hartshorne and Ogden, repudiates the deductive method and the demonstrative claims of classical rationalism and, rather, attempts to arrive at a metaphysical system that will bring a consistent meaning and coherence to the critical ideas, mostly scientific, of his own time and world. We might then expect that process theologians who are in continuity with Whitehead would attempt to establish a theological system that brings a consistent meaning and coherence to the theological ideas or the religious practices and beliefs of the contemporary Christian world. After two generations of process theology this is finally, perhaps, being attempted; but surely it is a fact of some significance that process theology could exist for nearly forty years even while ignoring virtually all of the central or unique affirmations of the Christian faith. At no other point is there such an enormous distance between the English Whiteheadian theologians—e.g., William Temple and Lionel Thornton—and the Chicago School. Of course, Temple and Thornton were more classically Christian than philosophically Whiteheadian. But this leads to the inevitable question: Can Whiteheadianism be a conceptual vehicle for the Christian faith? Indeed, the common theological charge against process theology is that it is quite simply non-Christian. Here, we find no awareness of the Fall (except as a means of affirming total personal responsibility), no doctrine of sin as opposed to evil, no past or future eschaton, no atonement (except as a moral example), and no Incarnation (except as a "renewal" of the sense of the present immediacy of God). Does process theology not in large measure confront us with a contemporary expression of a traditional natural religion or natural theology? At what point do the theological affirmations of process theology decisively differ from the common-sense beliefs of traditional Western culture and society? Above all, is it because process theology has chosen to affirm the eternal reality of God that it is unable to speak specifically of Fall or eschatology or Christ?

Gier makes a major point of insisting that the retention of the past is a basic philosophic tenet of process theology. Now what can the retention of the past mean in a theological context? Surely it cannot refer to physical time, which for Whitehead is perpetual perishing. Does this mean that the "living immediacy" of temporal occasions is preserved in the consequent nature of God? If the consequent nature of God is "the judgment of a tenderness which loses nothing that can be saved,"[4] does this mean that every positive value is everlasting in God? And does every such positive value provide a specific aim for some new occasion to realize in the future? Is not this very conception in full continuity with the classical liberal understanding of progress and progressive evolution? Is this not, furthermore, a religious way of providing an ultimate sanction for whatever has occurred or happens to be? Does not such a total affirmation of the past foreclose the possibility of a truly new or revolutionary future? Such a judgment must inevitably occur from the perspective of a radical Hegelian understanding of history, as can be seen from Engels' interpretation of those primal words of Hegel, "All that is real is rational; and all that is rational is real":

And so, in the course of development, all that was previously real becomes unreal, loses its necessity, its right of existence, its rationality. And in the place of moribund reality comes a new, viable reality—peacefully if the old has enough intelligence to go to its death without a struggle; forcibly if it resists this necessity. Thus the Hegelian proposition turns into its opposite through Hegelian dialectics itself: All that is real in the sphere of human history becomes irrational in the process of time, is therefore irrational by its very destination, is tainted beforehand with irrationality; and everything which is rational in the minds of men is destined to become real, no matter how much it contradicts existing apparent reality. In accordance with all the rules of the Hegelian method of thought, the proposition of the rationality of everything which is real resolves itself into the other proposition: All that exists deserves to perish.[5]

What can it mean to speak of the richness of the past in the context of our revolutionary situation? Is process theology yet another priestly and counterrevolutionary assault upon that actual future which now lies before us? How can we retain all past forms of experience and move forward to a truly new future?

At no point do I feel a greater distance from process theology than in its affirmation of the absolute value and reality of the unique and individual person. Here, process theology is in full continuity with Boston Personalism, as it is with liberal Protestantism in general. In brief, my response to this fundamental affirmation of liberal Protestantism would be that the idea of the ultimate value and reality of the individual is historically limited to the classical period of modern Western culture, and that it can have neither a living meaning nor a truly human form in a post-modern or post-liberal period of history. When theologians affirm that every quest for a genuine and lasting *polis* is identical with the development of "personhood" in community they should be aware that—at least from a Marxist or revolutionary political point of view—they are serving as ideological spokesmen for a modern Western or bourgeois conception of politics and society.

Hopefully, radical theology is truly apolitical and nonethical, if responsible ethical and political action are identified with the established forms of modern Western politics and ethics. Now I cannot pretend that I have reached a positive ethical or political way, but so far as I am aware a positive *and* radical ethics or politics has not yet been reached by any school or movement of theology. The only positive ethics or politics that we possess are clearly grounded in historical worlds of the past, and for this reason alone responsible theologians have opted for the retention of the past. But there can be no avoiding the truth that in our historical situation an affirmation of the past is at the very least in grave danger of negating and opposing an actual and real future.

No, as opposed to Gier, I continue to believe that the great challenge of process theology is in its doctrine of God, rather than in its conception of the personhood of the individual. For apart from what process theology affirms as the absolute presence of God there would be no ground for the ultimate reality and responsibility of the individual. If each new moment, according to process thought, is open to the infinite range of possibilities contained in the primordial nature of God, then is possibility as such finally grounded in God's purely conceptual and unchanging envisagement of eternal objects? Whitehead conceived the primordial nature of God as this timeless envisagement of possibilities, and God's ordering of the eternal objects is such as to specify the initial aim for each new occasion. While God is the sole ground of the initial aim of each occasion, every actual occasion is a novel addition to the universe. "Creativity" is inescapably an aspect of every such entity, but as Cobb interprets Whitehead, "God must be conceived as being the reason that entities occur at all as well as determining the limits within which they can achieve their own forms." [6] In view of this fundamental metaphysical conception of the relation between God and the world, Cobb's understanding of the otherness of God as absolute nearness can be seen as a way of affirming the sovereign and primordial power of God.

If process theology is truly a rebirth in a contemporary form of an ancient natural religion or natural theology, then we should expect that process theology is unable to envision a truly new creation or new humanity. A dipolar conception of God seems to promise a genuine theological understanding and affirmation of creativity, and even of a forward-moving creativity, but, rather, the truth would seem to be that the God of process theology forecloses even the possibility of a new humanity. Once the primordial nature of God and its timeless ordering of eternal objects is envisioned as the ground of novelty, then not only can there be no fundamental or ontological change of reality, but potentiality as such must be limited to a primordial envisagement of possibility. God is manifest solely as the Creator, for even the consequent nature of God is God's physical pole, his prehension of the actual occasions constituting the temporal world. It is not accidental that process theology cannot speak of Christ or eschaton, for the eschatological goal of humanity is limited to a renewal of the sense of the present immediacy of the Creator. No contemporary form of theology has given us such a full and genuine conceptual understanding of God as has process theology, but the price that process theology has been forced to pay for its doctrine of God is its negation of both the meaning and the reality of Christ.

It is instructive at this point to contrast Whitehead's metaphysical understanding of the primordial nature of God with Hegel's dialectical understanding of Spirit. If the primordial nature of God is absolute because it always retains its self-identity, a fully dialectical form of Spirit is absolute because it is identical with itself even when it fully exists and is finally real as its own inherent otherness. The question of the fundamental meaning of "identity" is paramount here. In the *Science of Logic,* Hegel conceives identity as being nonidentical with itself. The essential moment of identity is that in which it is determined as being its own negativity even while being different from "difference." Its difference is not from an "other," but from itself: it is not itself, but its *own* "other." Thus the fullest moment of identity is that in which it passes beyond itself into self-dissolution. It is not accidental that it is in this very section of the *Science of Logic* (Vol.

I, Bk. II, Sec. I) that Hegel identifies the law of contradiction as the alternative expression of the law of identity, insisting that both are synthetic rather than analytic, and that when each is thought through to its own inherent conclusion they both cease to be formal and abstract and, rather, transcend and negate themselves by making "contradiction" manifest as the root of all movement and life. Accordingly, the pure or formal reason of *Verstand* is not opposed because of an opposition to reason as such. On the contrary, pure reason is here understood to pass beyond or to dissolve itself, and it is just this self-negation of pure reason which makes manifest the active and dialectical reason of *Vernunft*.

No one who has even the slightest knowledge of Hegel's dialectical method of thinking, or who is aware of its immense impact upon the contemporary world, could think that his conception of identity and contradiction is simply absurd or arbitrary. Nor need the Christian Hegelian necessarily feel threatened in the presence of the logical power of the Christian Whiteheadian. What is at issue theologically is the question of whether Hegelian or Whiteheadian thinking is the best philosophical vehicle for the contemporary expression of the cognitive meaning of the Christian faith. And not the least claim that can be made for the Hegelian method or mode of thinking is that it is truly and fully a cognitive expression of the eschatological and Christological ground of the Christian faith. Thus the Christian Hegelian can say that God is most truly and fully himself when he transcends and passes beyond his *own* identity and becomes "other" than himself in the eschatological event of Christ. God is identical with Christ, yes; but this is a dialectical identity, for it is only insofar as God dissolves himself as God that he is manifest and real as Christ. Apart from such a movement of "self-negation," there can be no new creation in Christ, and no advent of a new world or new humanity. Does a Whiteheadian dipolar conception of God make possible either an eschatological understanding of Christ or a Christological understanding of eschaton? Surely this is one point at which Whiteheadian and Hegelian theological thinking could engage in fruitful dialogue, and perhaps the course of this dialogue will reveal that each is closer to the other than either is to any other system of thought. After all, both are genuine forms of "process" theology, just as both are full and genuine expressions of modern thinking. Is there any other contemporary theological movement about which these judgments could be made?

NOTES

1. Carl G. Jung, *Psychological Types,* tr. by H. G. Baynes (London: Brace, Trench and Trulner, 1923), p. 316.

2. Owen Barfield, *Poetic Diction: A Study in Meaning* (McGraw-Hill Book Company, Inc., 1964), p. 88.

3. John B. Cobb, Jr., *Living Options in Protestant Theology* (The Westminster Press, 1962), pp. 82 f.

4. Alfred North Whitehead, *Process and Reality* (The Macmillan Company, 1929), p. 525.

5. Karl Marx and Friedrich Engels, *On Religion* (Schocken Books, 1964), p. 217.

6. John B. Cobb, Jr., *A Christian Natural Theology* (The Westminster Press, 1965), p. 211.

Part V

ALTIZER AND
THE HISTORY OF RELIGIONS

Winston L. King
Zen and the Death of God

Since Zen Buddhism does not believe in God in any recogniz-
ably Christian sense, and since, for radical (Christian) theology,
the Christian God is "dead," a comparison of the two suggests itself. Nor is their comparison a merely captious joining of two
"atheisms." On the Japanese Buddhist side there is considerable
interest, because the death-of-God language seems to approximate
the historical Buddhist Dharmakāya language.[1] And at least
with Thomas Altizer—whom we shall take to represent death-of-
God "theology"—there is a considerable return interest in Buddhism. Further, and perhaps ironically, Altizer specifically rejects
Buddhism as inadequate because, in its quality as an Oriental
mysticism, it seeks regressively to return to a transcendent primordial Unity for salvation.[2]

The question to be raised here is whether Zen (Buddhism) in
its rejection of (Buddhist) "Oriental mysticism," and Altizer in
his rejection of Christian *and* Buddhist transcendentalism, do not
finally come to approximately the same position—though by somewhat different routes. To this end we shall sketch the rejection-

From *Japanese Religions*, December, 1967, with some editorial
changes.

affirmation modes of each party to the comparison and in the third section draw our conclusions.

I

For Altizer the contemporary and very much alive Devil is Dualistic Transcendence. As a Hegelian he believes that the only *creative* form of dualism is of the dialectical sort in which every entity is always moving into union with its opposite. This kind of "contradiction" is "the root of all movement and life." [3] But the traditional dualistic transcendencies of religion and philosophy are separated by an infinitely wide and deep chasm of irrelevance and unreality from the living immediacy of the ongoing world-process. Here "transcendence" is always and everywhere synonymous with the abstract, the empty, the meaningless, the past, the distant, and the dead in everlasting opposition to and separation from the concrete, the significant, the present, the near at hand, and the living. [4]

Hence Altizer's war to the death against "God." For "God" as portrayed in Christian theology and embodied in the institutions and rituals of Christendom is the essence of evil transcendence and the root cause of all that is wrong in Christianity today. It is impossible for Altizer to be too emphatic here. "God" as mystery must be rejected since mystery means "silence and apartness from history and life." [5] With Nietzsche he holds that "God" is "the deification of nothingness," in polar opposition to the world, "the contradiction of life," one who "crushes the life of man," "the deepest embodiment of . . . No-saying, [i.e.,] absolute life and self-negation." [6] Such a God is the author, or the excuse for "the alien power of the moral imperative" which is "addressed to man from a beyond" and imprisons him "by an obedience to an external will or authority." [7]

The Christian theological tradition has created in "God" a uniquely monstrous transcendence "whose very sacrality is absolutely opposed to the life and immediacy of man's existence in the world" . . . a feat unequaled even by Muslim or Jew![8] Hence one must "kill" the sacred-transcendent God.[9] He must be specifically and deliberately pronounced dead by the Christian community, and even the putrefying corpse of his memory must be deeply buried lest its infection bring Christianity to *its* total death. Of course the death of the traditional Christian God calls for the death of traditional Christianity as well:

> The modern prophet . . . has been given a vision which abolishes all that humanity has thus far known as light. Both the ancient and modern prophet must speak against every previous epiphany of light, calling for an absolute reversal of a fallen history as the way to life, with the hope that the destruction or dissolution of an inherited and given history will bring about the victory of a total epiphany of light.[10] If Christ is truly present and real to us in a wholly incarnate epiphany, then the one principle that can direct our search for his presence is the negative principle that he can no longer be clearly or decisively manifest in any of his previous forms or images. All established Christian authority has now been shattered and broken.[11]

Thus only in knowing and declaring that God is dead can the Christian live as Christian. But it is precisely at the point of the death of God and the abolition of traditional Christianity that true (radical) Christianity is to be differentiated both from "religion" (false transcendence per se) and its supreme embodiment in Oriental mysticism:

> Christianity, and Christianity alone, proclaims the death of the sacred; and only in Christianity do we find a concrete experience of the factuality and the finality of death. . . . No other higher religion in the world calls its participants to a full experience of the pain and darkness of the human act of dying as the way to transfiguration and rebirth. Unique, too, is the way in which the Christian is called to share or to coexperience Christ's death, where a sharing of the passion of Christ becomes participation in the process of salvation.[12]

But before we can fully understand Altizer's call for the death sentence upon all sacred entities in general, and God in particular, we must add Altizer's emphasis upon *kenōsis,* the Self-emptying of God into historical being. Now with this we are obviously moving into the area of affirmation. Altizer's basic affirmation is precisely here, the kenotic emptying of all transcendence into the immanence and particularity of *incarnation.* For him the basic and uniquely Christian truth is the Incarnation.

What then does incarnation mean for Altizer? In general it means the dialectical (*not* dualistic) movement of God's *total* being into his "opposite," the world of flesh-in-history, or historical being in flesh. It is assumed that this movement must be total and absolute; were any part or particle of God left behind, in terms of sovereignty or transcendent being, there could be no incarnation worth speaking of. Now was God's movement into historical being in Christ unique and once for all, or is there a perpetual ongoing movement of God into historical being? The answer is both. Thus:

> It [the Incarnation] is . . . a real movement of God himself, a movement which is final and irrevocable, but which continues to occur wherever there is history and life.[13] . . . If we conceive the Crucifixion as the original enactment and embodiment of the self-reversal of all transcendent life and power, then we can understand the atonement as a universal process present wherever there is life and energy, wherever alienation and repression are abolished by the self-negation of their ultimate source.[14]

Ultimate source means "transcendent God," of course.

Now the dualistic sin of the Christian church, its original heresy, is that of resurrecting Jesus into the heavens with God in glory and the designation of the church as Christ's mystical body on earth.[15] In *actuality* this doctrinal pronouncement represents a *reversal* of God's kenotic movement into humanity in Christ's flesh and in his death, for contrary to the spirit of kenotic incarnation, the church has become ever more sacredly apart from the profane, and the resurrected Savior ever more transcendent

of the world. Not only so, but the church-style incarnation confines it to *one* man at *one* time in history. But though this is a
primary manifestation, and initially occurred in Christ,[16] the incarnation cannot be understood and participated in save as a total
and perpetual process which moves on toward a supreme consummation:

> At no point in this process does the incarnate Word or Spirit
> assume a final and definitive form, just as God himself can
> never be wholly or simply identified with any given revelatory
> event or epiphany, if only because the divine process undergoes
> a continual metamorphosis, ever moving more deeply and fully
> toward an eschatological consummation.[17]

This eschatological consummation will be the death of the transcendent God, his self-negation by a total incarnation of actualization "throughout the total range of human experience,"[18]
his "kenotic passion" fulfilled in a "new and liberated humanity"[19]—a humanity liberated from even the memory of God to
become its own Divine Self.[20]

In conclusion to this sketch of Altizer's affirmations we must
say a word about his affirmation of the eschatological quality of
Christianity which, he holds, most definitively and radically separates Christianity from "religion" in general, and Eastern mystical religion—the essence of "religion" as such—in particular. In
this context Christianity is characterized as *forward-looking*—
toward the eschatological consummation of God's full movement
from transcendence into immanence. It is thus to be contrasted
to the religious and Eastern-mystical *looking backward* from
concrete, present historical reality to a primordial blessed Oneness
of mystic peace as the final consummation.

Now Christianity has produced its own false form of apocalyptic
in which the apocalyptic goal (eschaton) is thought of in a
chronological sense as some far-off divine event toward which
all creation and all history move. But this is a reversal of the true
kenotic-apocalyptic process, for in the guise of moving forward
it would instead be moving backward toward a repetition of the

primordial unity and harmony. And in so doing it forsakes its uniquely Christian quality and becomes an Oriental-mystical type of "religion." It is here precisely that radical (true) Christianity must be separated from Buddhism:

> At this point Buddhism presents an instructive contrast to Christianity, for here [in Buddhism] one discovers unbelievably complex systems of meditation centering upon the image of *death,* but here death is a way to a *dissolution* of the human condition, and therefore to the abolition of pain and suffering.[21]

That is, by the salvational dissolution of the human condition, Buddhism reverses incarnation and rejects the immanental consummation of true Christianity.

II

In Zen, as in death-of-God, we encounter a radical critique of the parent tradition. However, it should be observed at the outset that Zen does not seem to be as finalistic and radical in its rejection. For Zen Buddhists are still quite willing to be called Buddhists in the full sense, and in many ways are quite indistinguishable from other Buddhists. Perhaps part of the difference of tone lies simply in Eastern and Western temperament and cultural conditioning. Western dialectic is sharp, hard, definite. Eastern dialectic is softer and more indirect. And, after all, in the Buddhist-Eastern view, words and arguments never contain the definitive essence of matters religious.

Nevertheless there have been both rejection and criticism of the mainstream Buddhist tradition by Zen. One way of characterizing the Zen reversal is in the famous words falsely attributed to Bodhi-Dharma, but truly descriptive of Zen principles:

> A special transmission outside the scriptures;
> No dependence upon words and letters;

Direct pointing to the soul of man;
Seeing into one's nature and the attainment of Buddhahood.[22]

This is a kind of antitraditional Buddhism, so to speak. The real, radical teaching of Buddhism, according to Zen, is the "secret transmission" of the original enlightenment (Satori) experience directly from master to disciple in person-to-person confrontation, not by the scriptural or doctrinal route. Accordingly, as even a casual reader can observe, Zen tradition is full of aspersions cast on theoretical learning. Again and again one reads of a master who answers a disciple's philosophical question with a complete and insulting *non sequitur* of nonsensical quality. The learned-in-the-scriptures disciple is held up to derision. And on occasion the sacred manuscripts have been used *practically,* i.e., for kindling a fire. So too, disregard, even insult, has been sometimes directed toward the Buddha. What is he? A dung stick, three chin of flax. The Buddha image? Fine for a fire to keep warm by. You must "kill the Buddha" before you can gain enlightenment, in the words of some of the Zen masters.

Yet some of this should not be taken too literally. One young Zen monk, concerned that Westerners should think that "Kill the Buddha" statements meant habitual insult of the Buddha in Zen circles, invited us to witness a Founder's Day service at a Zen temple. Not only was there a majestically magnificent temple, but numbers of gorgeously robed priests, and a ritualistic order of service that put Greek Orthodox and Roman Catholic liturgists to shame in the elaborateness with which the Buddha was honored by reverential and multiplied bowings and meticulously crafted ritual forms. It is also true that a Zen meditator in training hears numerous sermons on Buddhist truth, and frequently chanted scriptures; he participates in a rigidly prescribed manner of life that has no allowable variation save in that awful moment of truth when he confronts the *rōshi* on his own and must speak forth what he himself knows of enlightening truth. In short we might say that Buddha and scripture denials are primarily methodologically and psychologically oriented; they are designed to shake one loose from easy dependence upon the mere *forms* of piety and open to him the deeper truth of his own being.

But the question of rejection or denial must be pressed on a deeper and more existential level than this. What does Zen reject? *Dualism,* in all its forms, and on every level. It finds the cerebral-visceral, thought-action, reflection-participation, abstract-concrete, intellectual-existential, good-bad dichotomies of most contemporary men to be unrelievedly tragic. It is the mark of their unsaved status, or in Buddhist terms, their inability to realize their own essential, i.e., Buddha, nature at every moment and in every action. This dichotomized or unsaved man, unable to perform any action with the totality of his being, is not as well-off even as the animal. Dr. Daisetsu Suzuki used to point to one of his cats and remark: "When that cat jumps, it doesn't have to think: I am about to jump. It just jumps," in a perfect unity of thinking, feeling, being, and acting.

There are many other types of destructive dichotomy to be found in human life. For example, there is the distinction which men make between themselves as souls, selves, or thinking beings, over against the inanimate world of rocks, trees, and mountains. Dr. Suzuki was fond of saying that when a man sat in a garden contemplating a rock it was not a one-way operation, but that "something" returned from the rock to the man. Or, to reverse it: A man must somehow feel-think-intuit himself into that mode of being which is the rock's. And in discussing this very situation, Professor Keiji Nishitani was quite unwilling (on a Zen basis) to allow one to speak of the mind of man as "including" the object of thought, i.e., the rock, in a way *superior* to that rock itself. The rock and its human observer were different, to be sure, but not in any hierarchical sense, nor in any fully separative manner.

Again, and fundamental to all Zen thinking, is the evil of the subject-object dichotomy. Because our basic modes of consciousness are always experienced in the context of subject vs. object, we can never see things as they truly are, nor see into our own true nature. For the subject-object relation is an assertion of ego, one's ordering the world about his subjective, personal consciousness, and as such it offers a handhold to all of the invidious evaluations that separate men from things, from each other, and from their own deepest life itself.

Naturally, Zen also has much to say about the evil dualism of the transcendent and the immanent. If transcendence is to be thought of as apartness from, standing in opposition to, then it is to be condemned here just as roundly, if not as violently, as in the death-of-God view. Zen will have nothing to do with a "holiness" which is holy by virtue of being apart from the rest of life; it must be "sacred" by being *intrinsic* to life, or it is not sacred at all. The final state in the famous ten Oxherding pictures, which are a parable of the Zen quest for enlightenment, is that of the fully enlightened man who

> is found in company with wine-bibbers and butchers;
> he and they are all converted into Buddhas.
> Bare-chested and bare-footed, he comes out into the market place;
> Daubed with mud and ashes, how broadly he smiles!
> There is no need for the miraculous power of the gods,
> For he touches, and lo! the dead trees come into full bloom.[23]

For Zen, not even the individual "self" is ever to be thought of as transcendent of the physical-mental events that constitute its present content. They *are* the self, in its totality and essence. As mind, or "no-mind" equally well, they are an integral part of the universal flux of events.

So too, more ontologically speaking, Zen rejects the noumenal as over against, within, or beyond the phenomenal; there is no other reality "behind" appearances. There *is* perhaps a depth dimension in which all realities are to be seen, but it is not separate from them in any way. Thus, says Suzuki, when Western-Christian-oriented Tennyson looked at the tiny flower in the crannied wall, first of all he plucked it. Then he began to think thoughts about "God and man" or about being "all in all," which he hoped would enable him to understand the mystery of all creation. But when Bashō the Zen poet saw a flower he left it there and unromantically writes thus:

> When closely inspected,
> One notices a nazuma in bloom
> Under the hedge.[24]

No more, no less. No need to bring in a God-thought at all. The flower is simply there to be totally sensed. Its perceived existence is its sacredness. In totally and perceptively sensing it, in ceasing to try to dominate, categorize, or change it in any way, one experiences in the very act of sensing it the totality of reality.

Here we are on the ground of affirmation. And indeed negation in Zen is difficult to separate from affirmation, for Zen insists that they are the same. To negate dualism is to affirm oneness; to negate separation is to affirm unity; to deny the unreal is to affirm reality—without defining them. To negate anything is to affirm something else. In a true vision of reality, the distinctions of one and many, large and small, better and worse will be bypassed—or transcended, if you will, by a *non*transcendent kind of awareness. The greatest is the smallest and the smallest is the greatest. One finds the three million worlds in the tip of a single hair. Individuality cannot be separated from totality, nor vice versa. Each implies the other; or better, each is present *in* the other. And with regard to *God,* if he is to be thought at all, he is not transcendent or other, but present in, consisting in, the holiness of all that is. For isness is holiness; holiness is isness, just that and no more. To live a holy life is just to live life in all its natural fullness. For the moment we may then summarize the Zen radical immanence in this well-known passage:

> Again, you and I sip a cup of tea. The act is apparently alike, but who can tell what a wide gap there is subjectively between you and me? In your drinking there may be no Zen, while mine is full of it. . . . In my case the subject has struck a new

path and is not at all conscious of the duality of his act; in him life is not split into an object and subject, or into acting and acted. The drinking at the moment to him means the whole fact, the whole world.[25]

III

Zen immanental terms are not precisely death-of-God incarnational terms, but they seem to be within shouting distance of the latter. Therefore I wish to raise again the question in this final section as to whether Altizer, despite his rejection of Buddhism as definitely different from and lesser than Christianity, has not in the final analysis come full circle and embraced a Buddhist type of radical immanentalism. In support of this suggestion I will make four comparisons, drawing in part on statements already made, and in part upon further statements, particularly from the Zen side.

1. Though beginning from somewhat different bases, both death-of-God and Zen reject all transcendence modes that separate ultimate reality from contemporary living event. Zen begins with the ordinary individual who is separated from his own true Buddha nature by the false dichotomies of a "Buddha" far back in history, or now in Nirvana; or, more existentially, man as separated from the world around him by a subject-object dualism. For such a man rivers are rivers, mountains are mountains, and trees are trees, things of differing natures, apart both from each other and from the man who observes them. But after Zen meditation there comes a time when one is not certain of this ordinary sort of realism. A mountain as such is not a sharply separate entity. In itself and by itself it is not fully real. Not only does it imply all other things—trees and rivers as well— indeed it may be said to have tree-and-river nature within it, to be *inseparable* from tree and river in reality. And the meditator becomes troubled and confused. What *is* true reality?

But if he persists, the third and final step of enlightenment ensues. And how does he *now* see things? He sees trees as trees, rivers as rivers, and mountains as mountains. Mere word play? No. We have returned to the first condition, but spiralwise on a higher level. We now behold all things in their genuine imma-nental reality. They are in their very particularity, universal as well; to be universal is to be particular. There is nothing "be-yond" this immediate reality, no substrate of Being, no mystically apprehended noumenon, no God who "clothes" himself mys-teriously in phenomenal beauty and power. We—things and per-sons—just are; but in being, we are both many and the One.

Do not death-of-God Christianity and Zen here unite? For Altizer there is no longer a God out there, back there, up there, anywhere. All the God that is, is incarnate in the concrete reali-ties of the here and now. We make him alive by killing him in his transcendence. We encounter him simply by immersion in living. True, Altizer from his Christian context speaks of in-volvement in "history," whereas the word "history" hardly ever crosses a Zen lip. And again, perhaps because of Christian back-grounds, Altizer has a certain preference for God's incarnation in "human face and hand," rather than rocks, mountains, trees, and rivers. *Perhaps* these distinctions are crucial; but to me they seem peripheral.

2. Historical particularity is obviously, at least in Altizer's case, a close corollary of immanentalism and incarnationalism. But two brief quotations will give it further point:

> What is new in the Christian name of Jesus is the epiphany of the totality of the sacred in the contingency of a particular moment of time: in this name the sacred appears and is real only to the extent that it becomes actual and realized in history.[26]

In the modern historical consciousness, only two hundred years old, there has been

> an eclipse of the transcendent realm, an eclipse resulting in the birth of a unique sense of historical particularity. . . . For the

first time historical events appeared as radically particular, as confined in their meaning and value to the actual but singular process in which they occur, and thus as being wholly detached from a universal order or law.[27]

Note that again we have the prevalent "historical" motif; the Altizer particularity is *historical* particularity or event. And again this grows out of the general Christian context from which Altizer speaks.

With Zen, particularity is of a somewhat different sort by virtue of the Buddhist context of its assertion. And that Buddhist context has led many Christians to deny that the integrity and value of the particular can be had in Buddhism, especially that of the *personal* particular. Thus the late Paul Tillich in his *Christianity and the Encounter of the World Religions,* written shortly after his visit to Japan some years ago, says: "Only if each person has a substance of his own is community possible, for community presupposes separation. You, Buddhist friends, have identity but not community." [28] It seems that quite logically Altizer should share in this general opinion, and see in the Buddhist pattern a denial of the humanistic, historical, and particularistic, for the sake of the Primordial Whole.

But contemporary Zen Buddhist scholars vigorously reject Tillich's interpretation. In the above-mentioned person-and-rock discussion in which he rejected the superiority of the person's nonstone capacity for "inclusion" of the stone in his field of thought and action, Professor Nishitani maintained that Zen Nothingness (*śūnyatā*), because of its *indeterminate* character, could include *both* the person and the rock in a "loving" relation, in which (1) each party could relate to the other in the true meaning of "love," without let or hindrance; and (2) at the same time respect the true identity of the other being without coercing it into any preformed, or prejudged, relational framework.

So also there was a specific rejoinder to Tillich's statement by Professor Masao Abe, which I doubt that Tillich ever read.

Is not the dialectical nature of the Christian community and separation really not dialectical, thus not reaching the core of ultimate reality? Buddhist communion takes place as the communion of the "Realizer of Nirvana" with everything and everyone in the topos of the absolute *Mu* (i.e., nothingness) in which everything and everyone are *respectively absolute,* being just as they are, and thus *absolutely relative.*

True Śūnyatā, being the negation of sheer emptiness as well as sheer fulness, is an active and creative Emptiness which, just because of being itself empty lets everything and everyone be and work respectively in their particularity. . . . The several rocks with different shapes and characters which are placed here and there on the white sand are nothing but the self-expression of the true Śūnyatā which lets everything stand and work. Each rock is not simply something with a particular form but, *equally* and *respectively,* the self-expression, through the taking form, of the true Śūnyatā, that is, the True Self which is beyond every form.[29]

Again we see differences between death-of-God and Zen. But again, they unite in strenuously affirming the holiness of particularity: Altizer, the human historical particular; Zen, every particular as such.

3. As noted earlier, it is at the point of eschatology that Altizer makes his stand most particularly for the radical uniqueness of Christianity. Its uniqueness consists in its forward-looking eschatology as opposed to the backward-looking mysticism of "religion." He chides Christian theologians in general for not seriously taking history as a dynamic forward movement into God's future. But whether this is a valid distinction must be judged on the basis of the essential quality of eschatologies. For, contrary to much Western opinion, Zen also contains a species of eschatology, in which worlds are passing away and the Great Death of cataclysmic change must take place before the New Order can enter in.

Of course in the Christian sense Buddhism has no genuine

eschatology. There is no prospect of an Absolute End to this present world order in the flaming fires of judgment, or the birth of a new order forged in its flame. To be sure, there are world endings, some of them quite catastrophic. But there have been and will be *many* of them.

But Zen makes little, if anything, of such eschatological materials of even the limited sort that are available to it in its own Buddhist heritage. Yet it has its own immanental apocalyptic, of a most intense and radical sort. For what is the nature of life itself? A moment-by-moment succession of states of existence, each one of which dies before another can be born. Indeed human "existence," so called, is nothing but a tenuous film of shadow-being stretched over the great abyss of nonbeing. There is no solid ground underneath our feet, no solid place to stand on, only the foundation of the Abyss of the Void.

> The eschatological myth of older ages that the cosmos must someday necessarily be burned up in a cosmic fire also entered into Buddhism. Buddhists, however, in their interpretation of this myth have always accepted it on the dimension of religious existence and transformed the idea of the end of the world into an existential problem. Viewed from this standpoint, this world as it is, with the sun, the moon and the numerous stars, with mountains, rivers, trees, and flowers, is as such, the world ablaze in the all-consuming cosmic conflagration. The end of the world is an actuality here and now, is a fact and a fate directly underneath our very feet.[30]

And how shall one escape this existential fiery abyss? By the Great Death: the great death of his own ordinary selfhood in all its dimensions; by a complete reversal of his hitherto-followed, conventional, ordinary subject-object modes of thinking, feeling, and acting. The same author writes further:

> The very procedure of stepping out into the field of the scientific world view (from our religious teleological, human-oriented world views) is here translated into a decision to

accept the universe with its feature of bottomless death as the place for the abandoning of oneself and the throwing away of one's own life. . . . When he presented the eschatological situation of the world in terms of an unspeakably awesome cold, the Zen master offered to the questioner—and through him to all things in the world—a place for their Great Death. The myth of eschatology was thus de-mythologized and turned into the religiosity of the Great Death of the questioner as well as of the world itself.[31]

What then is the quality of Altizer's eschatology? It sometimes preserves the Christian *form* in words of forward-moving progress into the future. In an essay entitled "William Blake and the Role of Myth" he speaks of "final Eschaton," "dawning Kingdom," of a dynamic and forward-moving process that will lead on to the "realization of a final paradise which must wholly transcend the paradise of the beginning." [32] It is "a forward-moving process revolving about the absolute negation of the old cosmos of a totally fallen history." [33] Thus the radical apocalyptic is at least dynamically going somewhere, in opposition to the Buddhist reversal process.

But where is somewhere? This is the crucial point. There are phrases like "The Great Divine Humanity" of Blake, in which God has become man and destroyed his own transcendent Godhood in the process; there is God's progressively greater *kenōsis* into "energy and life," [34] "energy and joy of body," "ever more fully into the depths of the profane";[35] there is the Spirit, a la Hegel, "come to its own fulfillment in the immediate and sensuous present," [36] as final reality "in the actual and contingent processes of history";[37] and Jesus as "the body of humanity," [38] or as the Christian name for the totality of experience of a "new humanity liberated from all transcendent norms and meanings," [39] and a "movement of Incarnation [that] has now become manifest in every human hand and face." [40]

Can the conclusion be resisted that it is not into history as going somewhere chronologically or teleologically, but in "history" as individualized human existence in whatever form, that Altizer's God incarnates himself? And how, save in peripheral terminology, does this distinguish itself from Zen existential apocalypticism? Indeed Altizer *also* speaks of the "extension of an eschatological future into the present." [41] Not even Altizer's assertion that this does not mean a mere submission to the brute realities of historical process clearly differentiates it from Zen.

4. Finally there is the almost inevitable result that neither Zen nor Altizer has any clear ethical direction to present. Writes Altizer:

> The Christian who bets that God is dead risks both moral chaos and his own damnation. . . . [He] must do so with a full realization that he may very well be embracing a life-destroying nihilism; or, worse yet, he may simply be submitting to the darker currents of our history, passively allowing himself to be the victim of an all too human horror. . . . [There is the] very real possibility that the willing of the death of God is the way to madness, dehumanization, and even to the most totalitarian form of society yet realized in history. [42]

This of course is spoken out of Altizer's conviction that all the Christian past—historical, theological, ecclesiastical, ethical—must be obliterated if incarnation is to be perfectly fulfilled. And consonantly with this, one looks in vain on the pages of Altizer for any moral-social direction the radical Christian should take, beyond that of plunging with all one has in him into contemporary "historical" action. The only discernible direction, ethically and historically, is into life, without asking or knowing where "life" and "history" are going or even what they are.

Not surprisingly we read a kindred passage in Professor Abe's review of Tillich's book referred to above, which sets forth a Christian-Buddhist contrast here in fine style:

> It may well be said that the [acceptance of man] *in-spite-of* [his sin] character of the Christian faith, by means of prophetic criticism and the "will to transform" based upon divine justice,

functions as a militant element in the realm of human society and history, whereas the *just-because-of* [human sin and selfishness acceptance] nature of Buddhist realization, . . . functions as a stabilizing element running beneath all social and historical levels. The *in-spite-of* character of the Christian faith is apt, I am afraid, to increase as well as decrease tension among people, to cause a new dissension as well as a great unity, thus falling into a false endlessness. On the other hand, there is always the risk, in the *just-because-of* nature of Buddhist realization which accepts everything indiscriminately, even social and historical evil, that one's attitude toward the world will be, because of a false sameness, indifferent.[43]

In the end, is a radical Christian total involvement in, and affirmation of, everything that happens to man, any different from an indiscriminate acceptance of everything, of even social and historical evil? Perhaps only in its greater degree of enthusiasm.

NOTES

1. Professor Shōjun Bandō, of Ōtani University in Kyōto, finds the death-of-God theology significant because it divests the Christian god of his specific and personalistic attributes, his historical purposiveness, and his transcendence. Thus the final result seems to approximate Buddhist *Dharmakāya,* that Absolute Reality or Ground of Being which is basic to all and in all existent beings.

2. To use one book as a basis of comparison is admittedly limited, but in Thomas J. J. Altizer, *The Gospel of Christian Atheism* (The Westminster Press, 1966), all of the basic Altizer themes are to be found. It may be noted in passing that Altizer is in some sense the victim and product of the most extreme degree of that very dualism which he abjures so strongly in the name of Hegel. Its presence is on every page that he writes. We encounter the radical, abyss-wide oppositions of life and death, beginning and end, innocence and

Fall, the light of Spirit and the darkness of flesh, the certainties of primordial Being and the uncertainties of history, the abstract and the concrete, God and the world. Hence also that dramatic apocalypticism which likewise appears on every page.

3. Altizer, *The Gospel of Christian Atheism,* p. 80.

4. *Ibid.,* pp. 22, 39, 42, 45, 54, 67, 73, etc.

5. *Ibid.,* p. 85.

6. *Ibid.,* p. 94.

7. *Ibid.,* p. 127.

8. *Ibid.,* p. 93.

9. *Ibid.,* p. 51.

10. *Ibid.,* p. 152.

11. *Ibid.,* p. 137.

12. *Ibid.,* p. 51.

13. *Ibid.,* p. 43.

14. *Ibid.,* p. 113.

15. *Ibid.,* p. 102.

16. *Ibid.,* p. 108.

17. *Ibid.,* p. 104.

18. *Ibid.,* p. 108.

19. *Ibid.,* p. 111.

20. *Ibid.,* p. 113.

21. *Ibid.,* p. 51. Italics added.

22. D. T. Suzuki, *Zen Buddhism,* ed. by William Barrett (Doubleday & Company, Inc., Anchor Edition, 1956), p. 61.

23. D. T. Suzuki, *Essays on Zen Buddhism,* First Series (London: Luzac & Co., 1927), p. 366.

24. D. T. Suzuki, *Essentials of Zen Buddhism,* ed. by William Barrett (London: Rider & Co., 1963), pp. 360–361.

25. Suzuki, *Essays,* p. 265.

26. Altizer, *The Gospel of Christian Atheism,* p. 57.

27. *Ibid.,* p. 74.

28. Paul Tillich, *Christianity and the Encounter of the World Religions* (Columbia University Press, 1963), p. 75.

29. Masao Abe, "Review Article," *The Eastern Buddhist, New Series,* Vol. I, (Sept., 1965), pp. 118–119.

30. Keiji Nishitani, "Science and Zen," *The Eastern Buddhist, New Series,* Vol. I (Sept., 1965), p. 88.

31. *Ibid.,* p. 91.

32. Thomas J. J. Altizer, "William Blake and the Role of Myth," in Thomas J. J. Altizer and William Hamilton, eds., *Radical Theology and the Death of God* (The Bobbs-Merrill Company, Inc., 1966), p. 186.

33. *Ibid.*, p. 189.

34. Altizer, *The Gospel of Christian Atheism*, p. 75.

35. *Ibid.*, p. 110.

36. *Ibid.*, p. 118.

37. *Ibid.*, p. 46.

38. *Ibid.*, p. 70.

39. *Ibid.*, p. 73.

40. *Ibid.*, p. 136.

41. *Ibid.*, p. 84.

42. *Ibid.*, p. 146.

43. Abe, "Review Article," p. 121.

Thomas J. J. Altizer
Response

UPON FIRST READING THIS ESSAY I WAS SIMPLY OVERWHELMED, FOR Winston L. King has carried my position to a conclusion that I myself was unable to reach, and he has done so on the basis of an understanding of Buddhism that is fuller and more solid than mine. So far as I am aware, Winston L. King and myself are the only Christian theologians who have entered into a dialogue with Buddhism with the purpose of attempting by this means to enrich and even reconstruct the present shape and structure of Christianity. Thus it was with both delight and fearful apprehension that I followed the argument of this essay, for it challenges my own theological choice at the deepest level. Nor does it challenge it simply in a negative sense, for it opens horizons that had previously been closed to me and offers ideas and images with which to voyage into those horizons.

Before taking up this challenge, however, I wish to object to two of King's points. Both of these points have to do with what King terms "Dualistic Transcendence"; and, at this point, I wish to state only that I do not regard such transcendence as false in a literal or ordinary sense, nor do I believe that a genuine dualistic transcendence is to be found outside of the Christian tradition. From my point of view, God himself negated and reversed his own transcendence in the Incarnation, and the Christian is called to will the death of God as a way of opening himself to the gift or "Body" of God in Christ. Buddhism has never known any form of a truly transcendent realm or deity, hence I concur with the common judgment that from the Christian point of view Buddhism is atheistic. Moroever, it is precisely its "atheism" that makes possible the richness and power of Buddhism, and most particularly so in its Madhyamika and Zen expressions. But I do not regard Buddhism as being either false or inferior to Christianity. On the contrary, I regard Buddhism as a "true" apprehension of the primordial Totality, and as being *religiously* superior to Christianity. While I believe that Christianity is called to a negation and reversal of both the way to and all images of a primordial Totality, I nevertheless believe that such negation should be dialectical in the Hegelian sense, and therefore it must ultimately entail an affirmation of the primordial Totality.

If nothing else, King's Christian apprehension of the dialectical way of Zen offers a demonstration of a form of Buddhist dialectical life and power that is apparently not present in Christianity. And how embarrassing it is when my efforts at dialectical thinking are contrasted with Zen! As King notes, my own thinking appears to be almost totally dualistic in this perspective, and I can only plead that I fear that this is inevitable. Yet Zen's total transcendence of dualism can point the way to a Christian transcendence of dualism, a transcendence that can lie only in our future, for it does not exist in anything that we can know as our Christian past. I must confess that it had never even occurred to me that Zen could be understood as a way of negating Buddhist transcendentalism so that its negation fully parallels the radical Christian negation of transcendence. Perhaps this is true, although such a momentous point cannot easily be understood or assimilated. Here, I can only take up the question of the relation between Zen and Christian affirmation. King astutely and succinctly captures the quality of Zen affirmation in one sentence:

"To negate dualism is to affirm oneness; to negate separation is to affirm unity; to deny the unreal is to affirm reality—without defining them." The all too significant qualification of this last point itself defines a gulf between Buddhism and Christianity. For despite the profundity and profuseness of the purely theoretical or philosophical expressions of Buddhism, these expressions, at least in their Zen and Madhyamika forms, follow a totally negative way. Thereby they not only refuse all positive statement or definition, but they identify such definition as a turning away from the all-embracing life and truth of "Emptiness." Accordingly, Zen affirmation is not susceptible to what we know as definition, and therefore it can appear to us only as pure negation.

Insofar as we remain bound to the meaning and reality of "history," we will also be closed to the positive ground of Zen affirmation. It is not simply that Buddhism knows nothing of what we have known as history, but also that Buddhism is closed to everything that we have known as world and self-affirmation. King's portrait of Zen particularity makes manifest how Zen can affirm the immediately real even while dissolving all apprehension or awareness of a differentiated real—thus the disappearance of the distinctive or differentiated categories of nature, deity, and selfhood goes hand in hand with the appearance of the immediately real. Nothing that we have known as "will" is present in this affirmation, nor can affirmation here be understood as a human, a moral, or a religious act. The Taoist category of *wu wei* ("doing nothing") illuminates the meaning of Zen affirmation, for it is an affirmation in which nothing is done or said. Or, at least, there is nothing present in Zen affirmation that approximates to a Western or Christian language and action. From our point of view, nothing really happens in Zen. Zen knows nothing of a "Fall," nor does it know anything of what we have known as redemption and salvation. Consequently, Zen is closed both to forward-moving process and to backward-moving regression. Nothing is present here of what we have known as goal or direction, and perhaps only the advent of modern Western nihilism opened the West to the meaning and power of Buddhism.

I was particularly taken with the manner in which King, following Nishitani, related the Buddhist image of the "Great Death" to Zen acceptance and affirmation. Now if it is only by the abandoning of oneself and the throwing away of one's own life that Zen affirmation is possible, then obviously this parallels the Christian way of finding life through death. But a crucial difference between the two immediately presents itself. Just as the Christian celebrates an ultimate death or Crucifixion that is both actual and historical, so likewise a Christian dying with Christ is a dying to a particular and actual human condition. Not only is the Christian called to die to a fallen form of selfhood, but he is also called to die to that form of selfhood which is most immediately real to him. That is to say, the Christian must die to or in an individual and personal form of selfhood, a form of selfhood that is historically real and that is actually and indubitably real to a fully individual or differentiated mode of consciousness. Not only does Buddhism know little or nothing of such a form of selfhood, but Buddhist "death" or enlightenment entails an obliteration or dissolution of any awareness of selfhood as such. Accordingly, Zen knows nothing of an actual abandoning of oneself, for there is no self to abandon.

It may well be possible to speak of Zen existential apocalypticism as King does, but we should be aware that this is a form of "apocalypticism" in which nothing actually happens, in which there is neither world- nor self-transformation. Even as Zen repudiates all actual ways to enlightenment, so in the last resort nothing is gained by enlightenment of *satori,* and thus the life of the sage is no different from the life of ordinary men. Of course, in one sense these Zen formulations are paradoxes that are intended to instill nonattachment and nonaction (*wu wei*). But in another sense they are celebrations of "Emptiness" that are intended to point the way to total calm or peace. I do not see how it is possible, at least from a Christian or Western point of view, to avoid identifying Zen as a backward way to an original or primordial Unity. True, such an identification is not possible from the perspective of Zen itself, if only because Zen transcends any distinction between backward and forward or future and past. But we must inevitably look at Zen from our own perspective or point of view, even if our glances at Zen still and uproot our own vision. Indeed, it is only our discovery of Oriental religious or mystical ways that has initiated us into the full meaning of what must appear to us as "backward" ways to a primordial Unity or Totality. But thereby we have been given a new way into the "forward" way of eschatological faith.

Now if we entertain the possibility that a new and total way of eschatological faith has dawned in the modern world, one way into the meaning of that faith may well be by relating it to its Oriental counterpart. For both ways are total ways, therefore they are radical ways, and nothing whatsoever is untouched by their vision or practice. Initially, I was delighted with King's judgment that the "history" which a Christian atheism claims to be the total consequence of the Incarnation is identical with Zen particularity. While such a "history" may indeed be present in the fullest expressions of the modern imagination, theology has only begun to understand that "history," and thus I must respond that King's judgment is premature. Nevertheless, I believe that King has pointed to a legitimate goal of radical theology, although I would insist that an apocalyptic or total "history" must be in continuity with the actuality of the history that we in the West have known. Perhaps at no other point can such a continuity so immediately establish its importance as in the ethical or moral arena. King closes his essay with a discussion of what he terms "ethical indirection," claiming that neither Zen nor my own work has any clear ethical direction to present. No doubt this is true, but I would regard ethical indirection as an inevitable consequence of a total or radical way, if only because a total way uproots and dissolves or reverses all individual or particular ways, including the ethical way or direction. It is not accidental or insignificant that ethical ways disappear or are invisible as such in both the total ways of the Orient and in the most radical expressions of modern Western thinking and vision.

Nietzsche's symbol of "Yes-saying" is a symbolic evocation of a total way, and it has inevitably been fiercely rejected and opposed by its theological critics. Theologically, however, we cannot understand Nietzsche's Yes-saying unless we are aware of its atheistic ground and realize that it entails not only a negation but also a reversal of transcendence. On the one hand, this all too modern symbol of Yes-saying unveils the impotent passivity and the inhuman detachment of Christian faith in God, of Christian dependence upon and submission to God, the demonic consequences of which are so passionately portrayed in Ivan Karamazov. On the other hand, Nietzsche's symbol of Yes-saying calls upon its hearer to become God, or to freely accept the total responsibility of God, a responsibility that Christianity had identified with the total sovereignty of the Creator. Once God is dead, the transcendent realm is emptied, and it is no longer possible to find life or hope in the beyond. But Nietzsche's symbol of Yes-saying points the way to transforming transcendence into immanence, so that the emptying of heaven becomes identified as the transformation of heaven into "earth." As a consequence of this apocalyptic transformation or reversal, a new man or new creation dawns who embodies in himself the total life and power of the Creator. From the perspective of the old man or the old creation, this new power is terrifying, for it demands not only a total immersion in the here and now, but also a total responsibility for the world. Nothing whatsoever stands outside of this responsibility, for total Yes-saying demands not only an acceptance but also an affirmation of the All.

Is the Yes-saying of Nietzsche's affirmation identical with the total affirmation of Zen? R. H. Blyth, among others, does not hesitate to draw this conclusion. I would rather suggest that just as Zen knows nothing of what we have known as transcendence, so likewise it has no awareness of what we are coming to know as total immanence. When we remember the overwhelming emphasis that Nietzsche gives to the "Will to Power," we are forced to recognize the chasm separating the total way of a modern Yes-saying from the total way or no-way of Zen. Nietzsche calls for an actual acceptance and affirmation, for a total willing of our real present as our own creation. This is at the opposite extreme from a total passivity or indifference to history, for it demands that the Yes-sayer assume total responsibility for both his own identity and his own world. Or, rather, world and individual identity here come together and are indistinguishable —thereby truly paralleling Zen—but their very identity is of such a kind that the individual not only wills but also enacts his total responsibility for the world. Nietzsche's Yes-saying is a call to total freedom, but it is also a demand for total responsibility, and in demanding that responsibility it negates every form of responsibility or ethical direction that rests upon the authority or the power of the beyond.

Mircea Eliade
Notes for a Dialogue

SOME MONTHS AGO I GLADLY ACCEPTED THE INVITATION TO DISCUSS
Thomas Altizer's book, *Mircea Eliade and the Dialectic of the
Sacred*.[1] Unfortunately, I did not have the time to write the
"critical dialogue" that I originally had in mind. But while re-
reading Professor Altizer's book, I made a series of rather loosely
connected critical notes and comments. These are certainly inadequate, and I had hoped to develop and articulate them more
fully.

I am happy to be included in a volume devoted to Professor
Altizer's works, if only to express publicly my friendship for the
man and my admiration for the author. The issue of agreeing
or disagreeing with his theological innovations is, at least in my
case, irrelevant. I am interested in Altizer's writings for their
own sake; I consider them original and important spiritual ad-
ventures.

My notes are largely confined to certain of Altizer's interpretations with which I find points of disagreement and misunderstanding. I did not feel it necessary to be concerned with what
I may call the positive aspects of his analysis.

1. A preliminary remark is that the book is personally im-

Previously unpublished.

portant for Altizer, because it uncovers the direction of his own thinking. This does not imply that it is not a "serious" or "scholarly" work; it is, but, as happens with so many other scholarly products, it is also a deeply personal undertaking. Altizer does much more than present, discuss, and criticize my contribution to the understanding of *homo religiosus*. He writes original and always stimulating chapters on Nietzsche, Dostoevsky, Proust, Freud, and Teilhard de Chardin. His comments on Nietzsche, especially, are of great consequence, for they reveal Altizer's deepest level of preoccupation and commitment. Indeed, a few years after the publication of this book, he became the most popular champion of the "death of God" theology.

2. I have the impression that the reader must finish the volume feeling rather disappointed with Altizer's declaration that my work utilizes the dialectic of the sacred in a "revolutionary" way. This is not surprising; for after Nietzsche's splendid proclamation of *"in jedem Nu beginnt das Sein,"* Proust's discovery that "the only paradise is always the paradise we have lost," or Freud's heroic transformation of metaphysics into metapsychology, how can one be attracted to the ideas of an author whose books bear such titles as *Shamanism, Yoga,* or *The Forge and the Crucible?* Or, to put it even more bluntly: how can the works of a historian and phenomenologist of religion display problems, discoveries, and splendors comparable with those found in *The Idiot, Thus Spake Zarathustra, The Interpretation of Dreams,* or *The Phenomenon of Man?*

3. Of course, one recognizes Altizer's design: convinced that my interpretation of the dialectic of the sacred is timely for Christian theology, he wanted to show that other thinkers and artists have anticipated this type of dialectic or have proposed similar paradoxical recoveries of the sacred. I can only be thankful that he chose to discuss my work in the context of so many giants. But all of them are *creative* authors, and Altizer, who relied exclusively on my "scholarly" studies published in English and French, has ignored the complementary part of my *oeuvre* written in Romanian (eight novels, two volumes of short stories,

five volumes of philosophical essays and literary criticism). Of course, these works are not yet available in English and only a few are translated into French and German; but I do not understand why Altizer did not consult *Forêt interdite* (a rather large novel of almost seven hundred pages), which could have helped him grasp more acutely my personal ideas on time, history, destiny, etc.

The fact is that "situations" and "messages" comparable, for example, with those deciphered in Kierkegaard, Camus, or Sartre, could be found in my literary and philosophical writings rather than in, say, *Shamanism, Yoga,* or even in *The Sacred and the Profane*. Thus, when Altizer states that "Dostoevsky's novels demonstrate that a Christian sensibility can be open to the profane—indeed, can be immersed in the profane—while yet remaining indubitably Christian" (p. 113), he describes what I have tried to show in most of my fiction. Likewise, he could not have written that I "remain closed to the *religious* power of the profane" (p. 196), if he had read *Sarpele* (Bucharest: Editura Ciorne, 1937; in German translation published as *Andronic und die Schlange,* Munich: Nymphenbürger Verlag, 1939) or other of my novellas and short stories.

4. Altizer could reply that I did not manifest the same "openness to the profane" in my historical and hermeneutical works. Here, it seems to me, is a rather serious misunderstanding. In all my "scholarly" studies I attempted to illustrate a rigorous and relevant hermeneutics of the sacred. I did not intend to elaborate a *personal* philosophical anthropology. My principal objective was to forge a hermeneutical method capable of revealing to modern, desacralized man the meaning and spiritual values of archaic, Oriental, and traditional religious creations. I am truly grateful to Altizer for understanding so well, and expressing so sympathetically, my endeavor to disclose the coherence and richness of "primitive" and Asiatic religions. However, one can again detect a certain kind of *malentendu*. Reading his enthusiastic analysis of *Yoga, Shamanism, The Forge and the Crucible,* etc., one can receive the impression that these books constitute a

cryptic philosophical anthropology. Altizer appears to be convinced that I present the "situation" of the shaman, the yogi, the
alchemist, and particularly the "archaic mode of being in the
world" as models for modern man. Naturally enough, he opposes this nostalgia as a regression to the archaic. "Like the
Oriental mystic," he writes, "Eliade conceives of the way to the
ultimate sacred as a *return* to the 'nontime' of the primordial
beginning." And after quoting a passage from *Patterns in Comparative Religion*[2] he adds: "As always, Eliade, in such statements, reveals his non-Christian ground; he is unable to say
Yes to the future, to envision a truly New Creation, to look
forward to the Kingdom of God" (p. 195).

Altizer has unraveled intentions in my works of which I am
not aware.[3] My scholarly enterprise was always more modest and
more related to the labor of a religious hermeneut. I was striving
simply to disclose the meaning and relevance of non-Western
and non-Christian religions. I still think that such a "creative
hermeneutics" is an important contribution to contemporary
culture. This is not because it proposes "models" for a modern
man, Christian or agnostic, for I never suggested that we must
go back to the archaic or Oriental modes of existence in order
to recapture the sacred.[4] The possible relevance of my hermeneutics lies elsewhere—it contributes toward filling the gap, so
to say, between the modern, Western or Westernized, world
and the "eccentric," dark, and enigmatic "primitive" and Oriental worlds. To *understand* the archaic or Asiatic modes of
being, that is, to realize the religious foundation of their existence, is for me already a considerable accomplishment, not only
because it helps a Westerner to communicate meaningfully with
the representatives of Asia and the Third World, but, more so,
because through such a hermeneutics Western spiritual creativity
can be immensely stimulated.

5. It is true that the effort to understand non-Western and
non-Christian values cannot succeed without a certain "sympathy" on the part of the hermeneut. This is the case especially
when one tries to elucidate the meaning of archaic, and some-

times rather aberrant, religious creations. But such a "sympathy" does not imply either an adhesion to, or a nostalgia for, archaic creations. I have emphasized "primitive" religions only because I felt that previous exegesis, illustrated by so many famous anthropologists, sociologists, and psychologists, did not do them full justice.

Altizer repeatedly refers to the "prophetic" quality of my work. Were I tempted to accept such an exalted appraisal, I would specify that it is a "prophetism" directly related to our historical moment, namely, the coming together of previously separated worlds, the "planetization" of culture. Indeed, I am convinced that *this* is the most recent and the most pertinent discovery of the West: the religious, cultural, and political *existence* of Oriental and "primitive" worlds. For a theologian, real "modernity" is not only the confrontation with the technological, desacralized societies of the West, but the dialogue with the religions that originated and unfolded outside of the Judeo-Christian traditions.

This is surely *not* a rejection of history, but an anticipation of the creative acts of the future. It is true that I have used the expression the "terror of history," but I was referring particularly to peoples that did not have the possibility or opportunity to "make" history, and to epochs when history was made exclusively by a handful of masters and terrorists, whatever they chose to call themselves. It is against the different types of post-Hegelian "historicisms" that I rebelled rather than against history as such.[5]

6. Altizer's most serious criticism concerns my understanding of the dialectic of the sacred as a hierophany. He interprets this as meaning that the *sacred* abolishes the *profane object* in which it manifests itself. But I have repeatedly pointed out that, for example, a *sacred* stone does not cease to be a *stone;* in other words, it preserves its place and function in the cosmic environment. In fact, hierophanies could not abolish the profane world, *for it is the very manifestation of the sacred that establishes the world,* i.e., transforms a formless, unintelligible, and terrifying chaos into a cosmos.[6] To quote what I wrote elsewhere:

It was the experience of the sacred which gave birth to the idea that something *really exists,* that there are absolute values capable of guiding man and giving a meaning to human existence. It is, then, through the experience of the sacred that the ideas of *reality, truth,* and *significance* first dawned, to be later elaborated and systematized by metaphysical speculations. The apodictic value of myth is periodically reconfirmed by rituals. Recollection and reenactment of the primordial event help "primitive" men to distinguish and hold to the Real. By virtue of the continual repetition of a paradigmatic act, something shows itself to be fixed and enduring in the universal flux.[7]

In short, the hierophany is an ontophany—the experience of the sacred gives reality, shape, and meaning to the world.

Altizer seems very impressed by the archaic and Oriental obsession with the "beginnings." In the nostalgia for a mythical *illud tempus,* he sees essentially the inability of the "primitive" to affirm the present and the "primitive's" fear of the future. But this is only partially true, for the models revealed *in illo tempore* serve to renew the world and to reinforce human life. Although apparently only imitating models supposed to have been revealed in the primordial, mythical time, *homo religiosus* also conquered the material world. One must always keep this *fact* in mind when assessing the meaning and function of myth.

NOTES

1. Thomas J. J. Altizer, *Mircea Eliade and the Dialectic of the Sacred* (The Westminster Press, 1963). References to pages in this book are included in parentheses in the text rather than in the notes.

2. Mircea Eliade, *Traité d'histoire des religions* (Paris: Payot, 1949); *Patterns in Comparative Religion,* tr. by Rosemary Sheed (Sheed & Ward, Inc., 1958), p. 408.

3. Sometimes Altizer misunderstands me, as for instance when he writes that "Eliade has confessed that, in the purer expressions

of the sacred, the sacred is both inside and outside of 'time'; here, the sacred and the profane are no longer in simple opposition" (p. 195). He refers to my *Méphistophélès et l'Androgyne* (Paris: Librairie Gallimard, 1962), p. 87; but in that passage I was only analyzing an experience related by Warner Allen in his book, *The Timeless Moment;* I was not conveying my own understanding of the sacred "inside" or "outside" of time.

4. I do not understand why Altizer considers that a correct exegesis of the yogic types of "knowledge" should imply the allegiance to Oriental modes of cognition and the rejection of Western philosophy also. Thus, after quoting two passages from my *Yoga: Immortality and Freedom,* tr. by Willard R. Trask (Bollingen Series LVI, Pantheon Books, Inc., 1958), pp. 51 f., he writes: "At this point it will be sufficient to note that Eliade is seeking a form of knowledge in which cognition, as the Western thinker understands it, will have disappeared. Rebelling against the 'secular' thought which has now overwhelmed the West, he seeks an authentic mode of understanding the sacred that will allow the sacred to be itself" (pp. 33–34). As a matter of fact, in my book on yoga I tried to elucidate only a specific, and extremely suggestive, Indian mode of thinking. I did not put forward my own philosophical presuppositions.

5. Altizer insists on the ahistorical character of my works. However, in *Yoga,* in my *Birth and Rebirth* (tr. by Willard R. Trask [Harper & Brothers, 1958]), and in other minor monographs I tried to describe the transformation of religious patterns by the very fact of their involvement with historical time. Moreover, the synchronic approach is as valid as the diachronic one. I concentrate primarily on structures because I am convinced that such a method is the most adequate for uncovering the meaning of religious phenomena.

6. Altizer asks himself: "Can Eliade remain content with the idea that the goal of man's choice of the sacred is simply to arrive at a precosmic state? If so, he will be forced to abandon both his dialectical method and his Christian ground" (p. 104). Here again, I do not recognize my thinking. For the last thirty years, and in hundreds of pages, I have stressed the paradigmatic value of the cosmogonic myth, showing that the cosmogony constitutes the exemplary model for all kinds of "creations." The reintegration of the

precosmic state is only *a moment* in the cosmogonic process, and it is superfluous to indicate the religious function of such ephemeral recoveries of the primordial Chaos. There are, certainly, examples depicting the desire to *remain definitely* in a precosmic state, but these are exceptions belonging mostly to "sophisticated" stages of some high religions (for example, post-Buddhist India).

7. Mircea Eliade, Preface to Thomas N. Munson, *Reflective Theology* (Yale University Press, 1968), pp. viii-ix.

APPENDIX

Walter D. Love

MERCY FOR MISS AWDY, IN A VILE ACTING OF THE SACRED

A Dissolution of the Many into One Act (Which is Indubitably an Epiphany of Eternal Being, Immanent in that Act, which is History, but which inevitably shatters History, and is thus Dialectically Transcendent, and so on.— To be continued in the program notes for other deep and radically contemporary plays, such as *Biblical Scatology and Old Rented Mistresses,* etc.)

Scene:

Arena University. Professor Oldteaser's *office, a dim room of the Freud Building. Upon the walls are prints of Chinese tapestries, visions of Hell, Dionysian orgies, and a number of pink and fleshy nudes. Among the books, all of which either wear their contemporary paper jackets or are recent paperbacks, on the shelves that climb the walls, are displayed plastic reproductions of such things as a Tibetan prayer wheel, African masks, a cross or two, a grinning gargoyle, several Indian-temple loving couples, and (standing in a corner) a crosier. There are also stones of various sizes, shapes, and colors, several Coca-Cola bottles, and many other objects sacred and symbolic. All are entirely new and wholly relevant.*

The play takes place in deeply modern times.

The Professor is at his desk, squatting on his swivel chair in a Yoga posture (āsana), concentrating on a single point, the "O" key on his typewriter. There is a knock at the door, which the Professor acknowledges, having put his feet down on the floor. The door opens, and MODERN WOMAN *is manifest. She bursts into tears.*

MODERN WOMAN: Oh, Professor Oldteaser, I am profoundly disturbed about your class, Bible 101. You have destroyed my faith.

OLDTEASER: Good! Good! Sit down and tell me about it, Miss Awdy.

MODERN WOMAN: [*Sobbing*] I've begun to see that you are right. God died.

OLDTEASER: Yes. God is dead. That is what Nietzsche has taught us. He is the greatest prophet of the modern world. God is dead (*Gott ist tot*)—the German, you know. Theological language. It is very important to find the words relevant to our times. So many English words aren't.

MODERN WOMAN: I see. I do admire the way you use *all* the languages, Western and Eastern. But [*still sobbing*], I think I'm losing my mind.

OLDTEASER: Good! Good! How do you know?

MODERN WOMAN: [*Now calmer*] Well, I keep having these funny little experiences of . . . I don't know what to call them . . . I don't know how to describe them . . . I just feel unreal.

OLDTEASER: Good! Good! Don't you know what all the greatest contemporary writers, without exception, have taught us?

MODERN WOMAN: Something you told us in class?

OLDTEASER: Yes. They have taught us that when you feel the most unreal, why then obviously you are most in contact with the profoundest reality.

MODERN WOMAN: Oh? But that isn't what it feels like to me. I feel like nothing is real and feel *un*real myself. What's that you say over and over in class—"wholly other"? That's it. That's what happens to me; I go along all right, and then all of a sudden I feel wholly other all over.

OLDTEASER: Good! Good! That is precisely what is to be expected in our times. Especially at the moment when it becomes wholly manifest to Modern Man—or Woman—that it is existentially true that God is dead (*Gott ist tot*). You are just where Modern Man—or Woman—*must* be, Miss Awdy; in order to begin. You must deny God in order to affirm him.

MODERN WOMAN: Oh? Why must I do that?

OLDTEASER: Well, it is not enough to deny him by wondering vaguely whether he exists or not. Lots of students do that, and start taking classes in philosophy. You can study the proofs for the existence of God—ontological, cosmological, scatological, and so on—but they are not wholly relevant. You must deny God radically.

MODERN WOMAN: Radically?

OLDTEASER: Yes, radically. It is very important to do everything radically. If it is worth doing, it is worth doing radically. Go all the way.

MODERN WOMAN: I quite often do.

OLDTEASER: Well, yes. But now you must deny God by saying he is dead. Say it existentially.

MODERN WOMAN: I'll try. God is dead.

OLDTEASER: And the rest of it.

MODERN WOMAN: *Gott . . . ist . . . tot.* Okay?

OLDTEASER: Okay. Now that you have denied God utterly, you can move directly to the wholly opposite. You can affirm him.

MODERN WOMAN: How?

OLDTEASER: Well, actually, just saying "God is dead (*Gott ist tot*)" is so *radical,* that it is the very same as saying he is wholly alive, even if we *are* in deeply modern times. That's dialectic. Negation is affirmation. Coincidence of opposites (*coincidentia oppositorum*). Isn't it exciting?

MODERN WOMAN: I suppose so.

OLDTEASER: Of course it is. And you have made the right beginning in negation. You start with the radical denial, negate that, and that negation of course posits the negation of the negation, which is the radical affirmation. Or did I put in too many negations? Never mind. The point is that you, Miss Awdy, are on the *tao* (way) to wisdom. Notice how I pronounce that "t" as if it were a "d"—that's because it's Chinese, you know. The Chinese don't spell like we do, because they're so archaic.

MODERN WOMAN: Oh. Do you mean that I'm going to *like* saying God is dead because I'll still be thinking he isn't?

OLDTEASER: Oh, yes. That's *wisdom.* Saying the opposite of what you think. You see, when you take this college course it is *not* so that you can be instructed about the mere content of the Bible. That would only be *knowledge.* The goal of our quest in Bible 101 is wisdom. You can't get there with mere knowledge, which is radically profane, and deeply modern. It's what the sciences have. The humanities are supposed to teach you to *think.*

MODERN WOMAN: Oh, is *that* what they're for? I have often wondered. They're so boring.

OLDTEASER: That is because the people who teach most of them only know how to think profanely, and are so utterly irrelevant.

MODERN WOMAN: Right. And some of them *are* crude.

OLDTEASER: My courses are designed to make you think deeply and profoundly. That is to say, of course, I teach you to think dialectically.

MODERN WOMAN: Doing something to opposites, you mean.

OLDTEASER: You've got the crucial notion.

MODERN WOMAN: To make them stop being opposite?

OLDTEASER: Something like that.

MODERN WOMAN: Could I use it in my other courses?

OLDTEASER: Of course. *Everybody* should use it. I wish I could get our so-called political scientists to teach statesmen how to think dialectically.

MODERN WOMAN: Why?

OLDTEASER: Because then they could solve the world's problems. For instance, American statesmen should make everybody else in the world mad at the United States. They should simply utterly alienate all the other countries in the world. Alienate them radically and completely and wholly. Then we would stand radically opposite to them in perfect enmity. And of course the moment the absolute extreme was reached it would immediately become transformed into its dialectical opposite—friendship. Everybody in the world would love us, and there would be perfect peace.

MODERN WOMAN: That would be nice.

OLDTEASER: But of course, as Nietzsche, the greatest prophet of the modern world, has taught us, profound chaos is our destiny in the world. So it doesn't actually matter what statesmen do.

MODERN WOMAN: Yes, it's chaos that I've been feeling.

OLDTEASER: That's because you're so wholly contemporary, Miss Awdy. That's the best way to be, because it keeps you relevant. But you need help.

MODERN WOMAN: I certainly do.

OLDTEASER: Well, now you have taken a number of courses at Arena University, and all have given you knowledge.

MODERN WOMAN: Well . . .

OLDTEASER: Of course they have. But now is precisely the time to start using dialectic. Negate your knowledge. The result obviously will be wisdom, because wisdom is of course the radical opposite of knowledge. You see?

MODERN WOMAN: No.

OLDTEASER: Well, that is to say, it is time for you to wholly obliterate from your mind all the knowledge you have put in it. That will be your negation. Rebel! Rebel against knowledge, Miss Awdy! Rebel against Arena University!

MODERN WOMAN: I'd like to do that. I really would. But I don't think I can do anything radical just now. Because, like I told you, I think I'm losing my mind.

OLDTEASER: Oh, yes. I remember. Good! Good! Deeply exciting. Could you describe in a little more detail these feelings of unreality you've been having?

MODERN WOMAN: Well, just this morning I was sitting down, just sitting down, and all of a sudden it happened.

OLDTEASER: What happened?

MODERN WOMAN: Just the minute I sat down, at the second that I touched . . .

OLDTEASER: Touched what?

MODERN WOMAN: When I touched . . . well, *bottom* . . . I had a vivid impression of having touched bottom just like that before.

OLDTEASER: Oh, of course. Modern Man—or Woman—is often thinking of the past. It's a sign of the end of our Civilization. Just like the man who reviews his life between the time he's jumped off the top of a building and before he's reached the ground. Thinking historically is the greatest fault of contemporary sensibility. The terror of history.

MODERN WOMAN: It was terrible, all right. It was like I was touching bottom at this moment and touching bottom in the past moment, both at the same time. I felt like I was back *there*. And *here*, at the same time. Oh dear, I'm not explaining it very well.

OLDTEASER: [*Profound pause*] Miss Awdy, you don't have to explain it. I understand perfectly. You have had a Proustian experience. I am amazed! [*Pause*] Did you like it?

MODERN WOMAN: I don't know.

OLDTEASER: Of *course* you did. Your joy and ecstasy confirm existentially that it was nothing other than a Proustian experience.

MODERN WOMAN: Pardon me, Dr. Oldteaser. What *is* a Proustian experience?

OLDTEASER: You don't *know* what a Proustian experience is? I am deeply shocked, Miss Awdy. You haven't read Proust?

MODERN WOMAN: I don't think so.

OLDTEASER: *Everybody* has read Proust. He was the last flower of the Ironic Age, but wholly contemporary. And utterly profane. He wrote the most immoral novel that has ever been written.

MODERN WOMAN: Really? I *would* like to read that.

OLDTEASER: Well you can't read it. You have to *live* it. You will live through the passing away of absolutely everything *and* be pervaded by sorrow. Doesn't that sound exciting?

MODERN WOMAN: I'm not sure.

OLDTEASER: Well you can listen to it then. Because it is a wholly contemporary vision of the Western Self, fully orchestrated by a Buddhist.

MODERN WOMAN: I can't think how a novel would sound in an orchestra. I can't think how a vision of a self would sound either.

OLDTEASER: Don't try. You can just read it after all. And in it you will find Proustian experiences which exactly parallel what you have described in your own experience this morning.

MODERN WOMAN: I will?

OLDTEASER: Yes, it was essentially a vision, a vision of the Eternal in Time. It was a Moment with a capital letter. An illumination (*illumination*). Or—and here is one of the seventeen greatest words in the language of dialectical theology: an epiphany.

MODERN WOMAN: A what?

OLDTEASER: Epiphany. Or hierophany. They are different, of course, but exactly parallel. I usually say "epiphany." That's because Modern Man has found so many epiphanies in Flaubert, Rilke, Mallarmé, Rimbaud, Joyce, and all those other

last flowers of the Ironic Age. And there are even more in
the genuinely contemporary writers, Kierkegaard, Kafka,
Blake, Nietzsche, and all the artists of the Modern Age.
E . . . Pi . . . Funny. Can you remember it?

MODERN WOMAN: I think so. Epiphany.

OLDTEASER: That's precisely right. Now Proust's novel, since it
is radically profane, is . . . wholly sacred! He *embraces time*
with those Proustian experiences. Stubbing his toe on stones,
breaking plates with his spoon, drooling into his napkin, and
choking on all those nasty little cakes. He embraces time
radically by embracing these times so utterly and by making
other times manifest inside them! So he dialectically reveals
the Eternal as incarnate in fragments of time, and . . .

MODERN WOMAN: What did you say the name of it was?

OLDTEASER: I was careful *not* to say. In English it is called *The
Remembrance of Things Past,* which is wholly misleading,
because it completely fails to suggest the *quest* Proust made.
That is, his quest for the mystic ecstasy of his little accidental
moments of Proustian experience. The true name is in the
French. It is called *A la recherche du temps perdu* (research
for lost time). You must remember that when you're reading
or living it. Remember it's really scientific research, and you
won't forget how contemporary it is, and profane.

MODERN WOMAN: But I can't read anything now. [*Starts to
sob again*] I'm losing my mind.

OLDTEASER: Now, Miss Awdy, stop crying. It's so bourgeois. You
must learn to think dialectically, so you won't feel anything.
Of course you're losing your mind. That's because you're so
contemporary. But it is precisely at this point that you must
negate. Negate madness. Annihilate it. And what then stands
forth? What could it be other than that you are *gaining* your
mind? Your funny experience of unreality was a Proustian
epiphany, remember? And there is nothing more *real* than
that.

MODERN WOMAN: I suppose the reason it seems so *un*real is

that it wasn't just that *one* moment before—of touching bottom—that I seemed to return to this morning. It was more
bottom-touchings. It was like all the bottom-touchings I'd
ever felt *and* every bottom-touching anyone else had ever felt.
Since the beginning of the world.

OLDTEASER: Since the beginning of the world? *That* sounds like
the exact parallel of the experience of archaic man, as revealed
by Eliade. I am amazed, Miss Awdy! You experienced the
Eternal Return in bottom-touchings! The archaic experience
is to go *back* to the Primal Bottom-Touching. Out of time.
It is utterly sacred. And you've had it! You know Eliade of
course.

MODERN WOMAN: I forget.

OLDTEASER: I deeply hope you do. He is the greatest living contemporary interpreter of the whole world of primitive and
archaic religion. Also of alchemy in both East and West, as
well as in the North and South. And of all the various forms
of Yoga, and all fifty-two positions. He is the exact parallel of
Sir Francis Bacon. Bacon profanely took all knowledge for
his province. Eliade takes all *wisdom* for his.

MODERN WOMAN: [*In tears again*] But what does he have to
do with touching my bottom?

OLDTEASER: Since he is a true historian of religions, he is able
to write with authority and understanding and relevance
about the whole vast realm of the sacred. So he can help us
to recognize the archaic experience of the sacred, no matter
what arena it is manifested in. And I think that it manifested
itself in *your* arena this morning, Miss Awdy. Yes, you have
indubitably been opened to the archaic sacred.

MODERN WOMAN: Which shows that I *am* losing my mind?

OLDTEASER: Not at all. It reveals your utter sanity. I thought
you had experienced nothing but the profanity of the Proustian experience. But now I see that you were engaged in a
deep dialectic. Your experience was also a genuine coincidence
of the opposites (*coincidentia oppositorum*). It was merely

profane in bringing together your contemporary bottom-touching with a past bottom-touching. You were still bound to history, with all its terror. But with your sensation of the repetition (*anamnesis*) of *all* bottom-touchings, you have manifested a Cosmogonic Act. That is a Return to the Eternal. You have abolished and shattered history, Miss Awdy! Isn't that wonderful?

MODERN WOMAN: I should say so. Only I wish I'd done it sooner. Before I took History 101 and 102. Still it will help some of my friends. How did I finally get rid of it?

OLDTEASER: Like this: During your epiphany you simply were not living in time at all, because you were far too archaic. You were living in Eternity, which is to say, *in illo tempore* (in those days). And I can tell you, Miss Awdy, Eternity is the only time worth living in. Especially now, in deeply modern times, when history is such a terror. It's just been *asking* to be abolished and shattered. And the best way to do that is to become radically archaic with Eliade. Rebel, Miss Awdy! Be a primitive man. Or Woman. Negate!

MODERN WOMAN: I quite often am, quite primitive. And utterly archaic. Especially on dates.

OLDTEASER: Please do not tell me about your personal life, Miss Awdy.

MODERN WOMAN: But, Dr. Oldteaser, I *want* to tell you all about myself. That's what I came to your office for. You help me so much. To think, and all. It's so exciting to negate and rebel. I want to know you. Please, Dr. Oldteaser . . . Tim? . . . Call me Elly.

OLDTEASER: No, Miss Awdy. I can't do that. You may be a shaman, but you are still a student in Bible 101.

MODERN WOMAN: [*Sighs*] I see.

OLDTEASER: But you *are* the first shaman I've had in Bible 101. It *is* exciting. By making contact with the profane like Proust, and with the sacred at the same time, like Eliade, you are existentially immersed in the most profound dialectical relationship to yourself. Having become radically *archaic* you have of course inevitably manifested yourself as radically *modern*. That's dialectic.

MODERN WOMAN: I see. All my friends are very modern. But I don't think any of them are as archaic as I am on dates.

OLDTEASER: But, Miss Awdy, impressive as your revelation of the sacred is, and profane as your bottom-teaching is, and as deeply dialectical as you are, I am afraid you have not gone far enough.

MODERN WOMAN: I haven't? My friends think I've gone much too far.

OLDTEASER: No. Your creation of the profane bottom-touching is radical and your creation of the sacred bottom-touching is radical, but they're just not radical enough. Radical, yes, but not *truly* radical.

MODERN WOMAN: I'm sorry. What can I do?

OLDTEASER: I don't know. I'm afraid we have reached the limits of your sensibility. Unless . . .

MODERN WOMAN: Unless what?

OLDTEASER: Unless you could remember something especially concrete and thus utterly profane, grounded in your modern consciousness this morning. It would have to be at the Moment of bottom-touching. As you were sitting down, did you think of any particular concrete, historical, and thus more radically profane thing that your bottom had touched?

MODERN WOMAN: Well, now that you mention it, I do believe I did think of something. I thought of sitting down on . . .

OLDTEASER: On what, Miss Awdy?

MODERN WOMAN: On my father's knee.

OLDTEASER: [*Profound pause*] Really? That *is* profane. Your father's knee! Your *father*. I'm having an insight! I've got it! Do you know what this sitting on your father's knee *means*?

MODERN WOMAN: What does it mean, Dr. Oldteaser?

OLDTEASER: It means that your vision was not only Proustian and Eliadian, it was *Freudian*. And that *is* more radically profane.

MODERN WOMAN: I know it's not a very nice word.

OLDTEASER: Of *course* it's nice. Because it's so profane. All profanity is sacred. Remember that.

MODERN WOMAN: I'll try.

OLDTEASER: You have revealed your deep Oedipus Complex this morning.

MODERN WOMAN: [*Bursts into tears again*] I knew it. I *was* crazy. I've lost my mind.

OLDTEASER: Shut up, Miss Awdy. You have *not* lost your mind. You are simply on the *tao* (way) to wisdom. By a dialectical route. *Everybody* has an Oedipus Complex.

MODERN WOMAN: They do?

OLDTEASER: Of course. Haven't you read Freud?

MODERN WOMAN: I don't think so.

OLDTEASER: You haven't read Freud? I'm deeply shocked, Miss Awdy. *Everybody's* read Freud. And the good news is that everything he wrote is indubitably true and real. Insofar as it has met with such a profound response from the contemporary sensibility. Can't you see that your sensibility has responded profoundly to him? He is even more deeply profane than Proust.

MODERN WOMAN: Did he write immoral novels too?

OLDTEASER: Unfortunately, no. He was much too busy with his hysterical patients and with his Analysis. You know what that is, don't you?

MODERN WOMAN: Oh, yes. It's very expensive. Some of my friends . . .

OLDTEASER: Well, it didn't cost him anything. Because he was able to do it to himself. Which exactly parallels the polyeroticism of his greatest interpreter, Norman Brown. It was the first analysis. The Primal Analysis.

MODERN WOMAN: How nice.

OLDTEASER: And while engaged in the quest, he discovered that Oedipus, a Greek king (*rex*), lay right in the center of his vision. That was the discovery of the Oedipus Complex.

MODERN WOMAN: How lucky. Did he patent it?

OLDTEASER: No. He couldn't genuinely do that, because he was so unoriginal. I'm sorry to have to tell you that Freud was only the authentic descendant of Nietzsche, the greatest prophet of the modern world. He prophesied the whole modern world, including Freud.

MODERN WOMAN: That's too bad.

OLDTEASER: No. It's really good. Good for Nietzsche's reputation, which needs a boost. Freud never read Nietzsche, of course. Nietzsche was so rich that Freud could make no more sense of him than anybody else and gave it up completely. That's why we say he was an authentic descendant. We're speaking dialectically of course. It's because Freud got *none* of his ideas from Nietzsche.

MODERN WOMAN: I'm not sure I understand that.

OLDTEASER: You will when you're older and more contemporary. What excites me now is that in your very vision of the profane and sacred bottom-touching, in your epiphany of the Eternal in a fragment of time this morning, you touched bottom to your father's knee and felt wholly other all over.

MODERN WOMAN: That's right.

OLDTEASER: [*Pause*] Now think carefully, Miss Awdy. I want you to think very carefully.

MODERN WOMAN: Not dialectically then?

OLDTEASER: No. Just try to remember. [*Pause, deepens voice*] Are you sure it was your father's *knee* you sat down on this morning?

MODERN WOMAN: This morning?

OLDTEASER: Yes, this morning. And in Eternity (*in illo tempore*) too, of course. Don't evade the crucial issue, Miss Awdy. Was it your father's *knee?*

MODERN WOMAN: [*In a low voice*] No.

OLDTEASER: What was it then?

MODERN WOMAN: [*Almost inaudibly*] You know.

OLDTEASER: Of course I do. And that *is* profane. What could be more radically and genuinely profane than that? Though not particularly contemporary.

MODERN WOMAN: Nothing, I guess.

OLDTEASER: [*Loudly*] *What* did you say?

MODERN WOMAN: [*Raises her voice*] I said, "Nothing."

OLDTEASER: Good! Good! Miss Awdy, that is the profoundest statement you have made in our times. Nothingness is precisely what is more profane than the mere object of your Oedipus Complex.

MODERN WOMAN: I would have thought *it* was better than nothing.

OLDTEASER: No, Nothing is better than it. You have of course read *La nausée,* the first and most important novel of Jean-Paul Sartre?

MODERN WOMAN: I don't think so.

OLDTEASER: You haven't read *La nausée* (*Nausea*)? Then surely you have read *L'être et le néant* (*Being and Nothingness*)?

MODERN WOMAN: I don't think so.

OLDTEASER: You haven't read *Being and Nothingness?* But it is Sartre's *magnum opus* (big work). It reveals to Modern Man —or Woman—that Nothing is the key to Sartre's system. It is the "hole of being," right in the middle of everything in his book. Have you ever thought of that?

MODERN WOMAN: Well, now that you mention it, this morning, while I was sitting and feeling wholly other all over, I did begin to imagine that a big hole gaped below me.

OLDTEASER: Are you sure?

MODERN WOMAN: Oh, yes. The biggest hole you ever saw. It made me sort of dizzy.

OLDTEASER: Of course. Nausea at the sheer isness of the world. In that hole. Because the world, properly negated, *is* nothing other than a hole—absolute Nothingness. You were really negating more radically than I realized, to see that, Miss Awdy. To see the world as a hole. But what was happening to your father at this Moment? What was happening to his knee and all?

MODERN WOMAN: I was sort of pushing him out. Into the hole.

OLDTEASER: Good! You were annihilating him, profane as he is. And making him into Nothing, which is even more deeply profane.

MODERN WOMAN: Oh, he's not so bad.

OLDTEASER: I am speaking theologically. Don't bring in any moral judgments.

MODERN WOMAN: All right. Well, anyway. I was pushing him out, and while I was doing it, my mind was going completely blank, just as empty as that hole. But just as it went blank my father somehow rose up, somehow changed—changed so that he wasn't just a man anymore, but a woman too. He was both at the same time, floating up from under me to fill the whole world around. Oh! [*bursts into tears*] That's worse than an Oedipus Complex. I must have been completely insane by that time.

OLDTEASER: Not at all, Miss Awdy. You weren't even in time, remember? You had destroyed history. You had manifested the Eternal in your bottom-touching Moment. All that radical sacred. And you had in those days (*in illo tempore*) also embraced your radically profane father. Still more radically profane, you could push him out of your . . . uh . . . vision and embrace a hole, a hole full of Nothing. And you did it with joyful nausea. I congratulate you on your profanity.

MODERN WOMAN: Thank you.

OLDTEASER: But *now* you have revealed that you were also witness, in the midst of doing all these other exciting things, to a big Archetype. The Male-Female Archetype. That's what came floating up from under you. Do you know what it means?

MODERN WOMAN: What?

OLDTEASER: The big Archetype.

MODERN WOMAN: What does it mean?

OLDTEASER: Well, Miss Awdy, when the Male and Female are wholly interpenetrated and androgynous (male and female) [*male et femelle*], they are manifesting a cosmological principle. And cosmological principles are Archetypes. Can you see that?

MODERN WOMAN: I'm not sure I can.

OLDTEASER: Well, I hope you aren't thinking of a *Jungian* archetype.

MODERN WOMAN: I don't think I am.

OLDTEASER: Good. Jung, I'm sorry to say, has next to no claim to contemporaneity, though he lived a very long time. He just gradually became increasingly irrelevant with age. Every step he took after he left Freud took him farther and farther away from the world of Modern Man—and Woman. Ultimately, myth prevailed in his system, and his thought lost all semblance of rational meaning. Isn't that too bad?

MODERN WOMAN: I suppose so.

OLDTEASER: *Your* Archetype is Eliadian. And he says that the interpenetrated Male and Female are nothing other than the primary symbol of the primordial Totality. That is to say, they are Everything. Totality. See what your Nothingness has turned out to be?

MODERN WOMAN: What?

OLDTEASER: Everything. Because right in the center of Nothing, in that hole, you manifested precisely the right Archetype. I again congratulate you on your morning's work, Miss Awdy. How did you do it?

MODERN WOMAN: I don't know. When I think back on the way it happened, it seems to me I just pushed and pushed and out went my father's . . . uh . . . knee and all. Out went my father. In came the Archetype—or whatever you call it—and then out again. In and out, until even the hole was gone. Nothing below me and nothing above. In fact, my mind was a complete blank.

OLDTEASER: Good! Good! A complete blank. That is truly a radical vision of the sacred and Eternal, by far the best way you have described your morning's Moment. And you just *pushed?*

MODERN WOMAN: Yes. I couldn't help it. I had to. I suppose it was mad. But I just pushed them out and my mind went utterly blank while I did it.

OLDTEASER: "Pushed them out"! What are you saying, Miss Awdy? [*Pause*] Listen carefully to me, Miss Awdy. Open yourself to me wholly. I have just had a profound insight into your Vision. Where *were* you this morning when you had it?

MODERN WOMAN: I never said.

OLDTEASER: I know. Now I want you to.

MODERN WOMAN: Do I have to?

OLDTEASER: Indubitably. I must know. I must know because it is of the greatest importance that you embrace still more radically the historical moment in which the epiphany was manifested. Let's do that now.

MODERN WOMAN: Why?

OLDTEASER: Do I have to explain to you again the principles of Dialectic? You have now revealed to me that in your Moment you reached the goal of the most radical, radical sacred. Your mind was completely blank.

MODERN WOMAN: That's right. It did.

OLDTEASER: Now to reach the higher goal of *coincidentia oppositorum* (coincidence of opposites) you must have let stand forth the most radical, radical profane. Tell me now, where was your epiphany manifested? In what room?

MODERN WOMAN: Oh, Dr. Oldteaser, do I have to say?

OLDTEASER: Yes, you do.

MODERN WOMAN: In the bathroom.

OLDTEASER: I knew it. This is deeply exciting. And you were sitting down?

MODERN WOMAN: [*Whispers*] Yes.

OLDTEASER: And you touched bottom.

MODERN WOMAN: Yes.

OLDTEASER: You actually touched bottom to the toilet seat, didn't you, Miss Awdy? You just *thought* of touching your father's knee and all.

MODERN WOMAN: [*Sobs*] Yes, I did. I didn't want to tell you that part of it. What my bottom touched.

OLDTEASER: Well, I'm glad I found it out. Don't be embarrassed. Genuinely modern people are frank, you know. We embrace the profane. And I think you did that too, this morning.

MODERN WOMAN: I suppose so.

OLDTEASER: Good. So now listen carefully to me again. This is of the greatest importance. It is precisely at this point that I must ask you, precisely what action were you engaged in— existentially—while you sat there, having your epiphany?

MODERN WOMAN: What do you mean?

OLDTEASER: I mean what were you *pushing out*—existentially— into the hole beneath you? Tell me.

MODERN WOMAN: Oh dear, Professor Oldteaser; I can't say it.

OLDTEASER: Come on now. Don't be bourgeois. Rebel. Say it.

MODERN WOMAN: Well. [*Whispers*] *Faeces*.

OLDTEASER: Oh, my God. *Nobody* says *faeces* anymore except psychoanalysts. Don't you know that the grossness and absurdity of psychoanalytic language is beyond satire? The language of dialectical theology, I'm proud to say, is not. Say "shit."

MODERN WOMAN: Shit.

OLDTEASER: Good! Now that we have settled that, this is precisely the point at which I must tell you that your epiphany, at such a moment, is of the profoundest significance. Your mind was completely blank, so you were in direct contact with the radical, radical sacred. At the same moment you were engaged in pushing out shit, which is the profanest thing you could have been doing. The radical, radical sacred and the radical, radical profane, Miss Awdy. They coincided in you this morning! The coincidence of opposites (*coincidentia oppositorum*), you see. That is precisely the goal of the dialectical movement. Aren't you pleased?

MODERN WOMAN: I guess so.

OLDTEASER: *And* at the same time, you have been witness to the deeply anal character of Western Man—or Woman—as in Brown. Norman Brown, who will someday stand forth and be manifested as Freud's greatest interpreter. He has penetrated into the anal character of Western Man in the most exciting part of his book, *Life Against Death*.

MODERN WOMAN: Life against what?

OLDTEASER: Life against death. He has his dialectic too, like all truly contemporary artists. Instead of the sacred and the profane, he has life and death. You could probably make them coincide, too, now that you have learned how.

MODERN WOMAN: But not now please. Actually I don't think I'm through with the sacred and the profane. There was a little more, one thing more, in my Moment this morning. Do you want me to tell you?

OLDTEASER: Yes, very much. Please do.

MODERN WOMAN: Well, while I was having my epiphany and all, sitting there . . . on the toilet . . . pushing out . . . shit, and my mind a total blank, a funny little phrase suddenly came into my vision, and I don't know what it means. I'm afraid it is quite mad.

OLDTEASER: What was it?

MODERN WOMAN: It may sound funny. I don't know what it means. It was this: "The just lives by faith."

OLDTEASER: What? Miss Awdy, are you serious?

MODERN WOMAN: I think so.

OLDTEASER: Are you sure? Is that indubitably the phrase you heard?

MODERN WOMAN: Oh, yes. I'm sure. It was plain, running through in a tinkly little voice, like water on tin.

OLDTEASER: Miss Awdy, I am amazed! Your epiphany, then, is an exact parallel to that of Martin Luther. Those were precisely the words he was meditating on when he had his experience in the tower.

MODERN WOMAN: What was that?

OLDTEASER: He had a message from the Holy Spirit while he was on the privy in the tower of a monastery in Wittenberg in the sixteenth century. And that was the beginning of the Reformation. The anal character was particularly deep in Luther and all the Protestants who came after him. He was doing precisely what you were doing when he had his experience in the tower. And the same phrase came to you as had come to him in the midst of a profound epiphany! What a Moment!

MODERN WOMAN: Mine or his?

OLDTEASER: Both. But especially yours. How did you feel about it at the time this morning?

MODERN WOMAN: Of course my mind was a complete blank, except for the little phrase. It was sort of nice to have the little phrase there while I was feeling so wholly other all over, and . . . uh . . . doing what I was doing. I felt strongly that I would like to have it *keep* happening. I would like it to keep happening over and over, for ever.

OLDTEASER: You felt *that*, Miss Awdy? That's wonderful! You willed that Moment to come back to you eternally. What could that be other than Nietzsche's Eternal Recurrence, his greatest doctrine? I often put it in capital letters. That's when I'm thinking of it joyfully, and metaphysically. When it seems to me as if the future would be awfully tiresome with all these moments coming back again and again, then I put it in small letters, and think of it existentially, to show my anguish (*Angst*). Or is it the other way—capitals for existential thinking, and . . . —anyhow the distinction is crucial.

MODERN WOMAN: I'll bet it is.

OLDTEASER: You'd win. Of course Nietzsche said I *should* be horrified at the thought of eternal recurrence. He thought of it while he was swallowing a snake, and he was utterly horrified, thinking of coming back to Germany again and again and again, having to write over and over all those books that have to be in archaic English, even though he was not archaic himself, since he was so contemporary and wholly relevant. And then think of having all those rumors about his sister repeated eternally, when there has been such an effort to quash them. But now you, Miss Awdy. You are going to have this morning forever. You have willed it, joyfully. Isn't that a nightmare? It takes the deepest courage to embrace it, but I believe that you, Miss Awdy, are open to it. Have you ever swallowed a snake?

MODERN WOMAN: I don't think so.

OLDTEASER: I'm sure you can do it.

MODERN WOMAN: I'm glad you believe in me.

OLDTEASER: I do, more and more. You have come so far in the quest, the quest for wisdom. You were engaged from the first in trying to return to *illo tempore* (those days), in your archaic experience of eternal bottom-touching. But in that effort you are actually trying to go *backward,* to primitive nontime. That was only an Eternal Return, which was created by Eliade. I put that in capital letters. I forget what it means when I put it in small letters, so I guess the distinction is not crucial.

MODERN WOMAN: Apparently not. But what is the distinction between Eliade's doctrine and Nietzsche's?

OLDTEASER: They are an exact dialectical parallel. Nietzsche's doctrine is Eternal *Recurrence,* instead of Return. He wills the eternal repetition of the profane moment in time, and so looks forward to the *future,* instead of the past. It is his triumphant hymn of joy in praise of a vast and meaningless cosmos.

MODERN WOMAN: Meaningless?

OLDTEASER: Of course. In the stance you took this morning, you yourself are witness to the truth of the vision of the world as shit.

MODERN WOMAN: Oh, Dr. Oldteaser.

OLDTEASER: You are. And it is the profoundest truth you have ever manifested. But you have embraced wholly that truth. For you have willed the eternal Recurrence of shit. You needed to do that, or you would have been left only with the Eternal Return of the sacred bottom-touching. Now you have embraced them both: the most radical, radical profane—shit—and the most radical, radical sacred—the utter blank of

your mind when your bottom is touched. All together, immersed and dissolved in your morning's Moment! But what a
Moment!

MODERN WOMAN: Yes. I am beginning to see that it was something. At first I just thought that I was losing my mind. And
I'm not sure, quite, that I haven't lost it. Though you do help
me so much. I think I see that you mean that I finally got
in my Moment to the coincidence of opposites you talk about
in Latin so much, or whatever language it is. So they ought
to stop being opposite now. Does that mean I'm through with
my dialectic?

OLDTEASER: No, Miss Awdy. The end is of course precisely the
beginning. There is one thing about your Moment you have
forgotten.

MODERN WOMAN: What is that?

OLDTEASER: That it is a *Lutherian* Moment. As well as Proustian,
Eliadian, Freudian, Sartrian, and Brown.

MODERN WOMAN: So?

OLDTEASER: So you have willed the Eternal Recurrence of the
Reformation!

MODERN WOMAN: The Reformation? What's that?

OLDTEASER: That's what Martin Luther started in the privy.
And so all the real Christians left Rome. I've often feared I
might have to go back, but I won't worry any more, since we
are to have the Reformation again in our time. This is precisely what is the dearest hope of Eliade: the rebirth of a new
Man—or Woman. I have been so busy with the employment
of this or that modern artist as a route to a new form of theology, that I just haven't had time to make any contacts like
yours. Now we can work together. You make the contacts,
when you have time, and I'll open myself to the truly paradoxical language that the new theology will need to employ in
the contemporary Christian dialectic. It never occurred to me
that the new contemporary and radical theology would be
precisely the Recurrence of the Reformation, until you revealed it to me, Miss Awdy. Now we must get busy. Let's see

now. Luther spread the glad tidings of the advent of the new man and new theology, by nailing 95 theses to the church door. Or was it 94? That is precisely what we will do. Now, where's some paper? Here. We need a long one. That legal pad. Now. 95 theses. Maybe only 94. Here we go: "Number one. All traditional theological thinking has become wholly meaningless, now that civilization has ended in our deep and modern times." I wonder if that is strong enough. "Number two. The first requirement of a contemporary theological method is a full understanding of the death of God. *Gott ist tot.*" Of course *everybody* knows that by now. "Number three. Modern Man—or Woman (that is a reference to you, Miss Awdy)—is engaged in the quest of a Christian dialectic between the sacred and the profane in the context of our present situation." I will use you, Miss Awdy, to show them *how* profane our present situation is. Though of course some people are more profane than others. And some are more contemporary, too. I do feel sorry for those who aren't sufficiently contemporary and modern and radical, Miss Awdy. They must feel utterly sad, in their antiquity pockets, being so irrelevant. Now you and I, Miss Awdy . . .

[PROFESSOR OLDTEASER *pauses and looks up.* MODERN WOMAN *has risen from her chair, walked into the exact center of the room, hoisted her skirts, and manifested herself right into the most characteristically modern of genuinely contemporary dance positions—the defecating. Her eyes stare, and her expression seems a perfect blank. She is concentrating on a single point. She shudders slightly.* PROFESSOR OLDTEASER *jumps to his feet and cries out*]:

Wait! No! Not *here,* Miss Awdy. Don't have an epiphany here. Not in my office! Not on my floor! Stop!

[MODERN WOMAN *does not move*]

Listen to me, Miss Awdy. I think this sort of thing is not an epiphany after all. You are not having visions. You *are* losing your mind. You really are. I know I said it was not madness, but a vision, and I was negating. Well, now I negate the negation. You *are* losing your mind. Miss Awdy, listen to me. You are as mad as a hatter. Get out! *Va-t'en! Schnell!* Get out of my office!

[MODERN WOMAN *is still motionless. She is grounded in dead center, and looks neither forward nor backward. The stage slowly dims until it is wholly black, as black as the terrible night created by the death of God. At once, inevitably, as in a* coincidentia oppositorum, *there is a blinding flash. Light appears in precisely those corners which are most filled with darkness. It gradually focuses down upon the exact center of the stage, where* MODERN WOMAN *is still manifest, skirts around her waist, and there is revealed to us in these our modern times nothing but*

> *The Profoundest,*
> *Deepest,*
> *And Most Radical*
> *End.*]

Bibliography of the Works of
Thomas J. J. Altizer

Books

Oriental Mysticism and Biblical Eschatology. The Westminster Press, 1961.

Truth, Myth, and Symbol, ed. by Altizer, William A. Beardslee, and J. Harvey Young. Prentice-Hall, Inc., 1962.

Mircea Eliade and the Dialectic of the Sacred. The Westminster Press, 1963.

Radical Theology and the Death of God, ed. by Altizer and William Hamilton. The Bobbs-Merrill Company, Inc., 1966.

The Gospel of Christian Atheism. The Westminster Press, 1966.

Toward a New Christianity, ed. Harcourt, Brace and World, Inc., 1967.

The New Apocalypse: The Radical Christian Vision of William Blake. Michigan State University Press, 1967.

The Descent Into Hell. J. B. Lippincott Company, 1970.

Articles

"Incarnation," in *A Handbook of Christian Theology,* ed. by Marvin Halverson and Arthur A. Cohen. Meridian Books, 1958, pp. 186–188.

"Religion and Reality," *Journal of Religion,* XXXVIII (October, 1958), pp. 251–262.

"The Romantic Achievement of Sigmund Freud," *The Emory University Quarterly,* XIV (October, 1958), pp. 171–183.

"Science and Gnosis in Jung's Psychology," *The Centennial Review,* III (Summer, 1959), pp. 304–320.

"The Religious Foundations of Biblical Eschatology," *The Journal of Religion,* XXXIX (October, 1959), pp. 263–272.

"Demythologizing and Jesus," *Religion in Life,* XXIX (Fall, 1960), pp. 564–574.

"Nietzsche's Influence Upon Contemporary Theology," *The Emory University Quarterly,* XVI (Fall, 1960), pp. 152–163.

"The Challenge of Modern Gnosticism," *Journal of Bible and Religion,* XXX (January, 1962), pp. 18–25.

"Mircea Eliade and the Recovery of the Sacred," *The Christian Scholar,* XLV (Spring, 1962), pp. 267–289.

"The Religious Meaning of Myth and Symbol," in *Truth, Myth, and Symbol,* pp. 87–108.

"Nirvana and Kingdom of God," *Journal of Religion,* XLIII (April, 1963), pp. 105–117. Reprinted in *New Theology No. 1,* ed. by Martin E. Marty and Dean G. Peerman. The Macmillan Company, 1964, pp. 150–168.

"Amerika und die Zukunft der Theologie," *Antalos,* September, 1963, pp. 424–436. Appears in English in *Radical Theology and the Death of God,* pp. 9–21.

"A Comment on 'Teaching World Religions,'" *Journal of Bible and Religion,* XXXII (January, 1964), pp. 23–24.

"Theology and the Death of God," *The Centennial Review,* VIII (Spring, 1964), pp. 129–146. Reprinted in *Radical Theology and the Death of God,* pp. 95–111.

"Creative Negation in Theology," *The Christian Century,* LXXXII (July 7, 1965), pp. 864–867.

"William Blake and the Role of Myth in the Radical Christian Vision," *The Centennial Review,* IX (Fall, 1965), pp. 461–482. Reprinted in *Radical Theology and the Death of God,* pp. 171–191.

"Word and History," *Theology Today,* XXII (October, 1965), pp. 380–392. Reprinted in *Radical Theology and the Death of God,* pp. 121–139.

"The Death of God: Is This Our Situation?" *The Christian Advocate,* IX (October 7, 1965), pp. 9–10.

"Discussion: The Tri-unity of God," *Union Seminary Quarterly Review,* XXI (January, 1966), pp. 207–210.

"The Sacred and the Profane: A Dialectical Understanding of Christianity," in *Radical Theology and the Death of God,* pp. 140–155.

"The Significance of the New Theology," in *The Death of God Debate*, ed. by Jackson Lee Ice and John J. Carey, pp. 242–255. The Westminster Press, 1967.

"Theology's Response to the Challenge of Secularism," *The Centennial Review*, XI (Fall, 1967), pp. 474–481.

"Radical Theology and Political Revolution," *Criterion*, VII (Spring, 1968), pp. 5–10.

Reviews

Of C. G. Jung, *The Practise of Psychotherapy, Journal of Religion*, XXXV (January, 1955), pp. 53–54.

Of Winston L. King, *Introduction to Religion, Journal of Religion*, XXXVI (July, 1956), p. 196.

Of Mircea Eliade, *Birth and Rebirth: The Religious Meanings of Initiation in Human Culture, Journal of Religion*, XL (April, 1960), pp. 131–132.

Of Roger Caillois, *Man and The Sacred, Journal of Religion*, XL (April, 1960), p. 132.

"A Theonomy in Our Time?" Review of Paul Tillich, *Christianity and the Encounter of the World Religions, The Christian Scholar*, XLVI (Winter, 1963), pp. 356–362.

Of Owen Barfield, *Worlds Apart: A Dialogue of the 1960's, Journal of Bible and Religion*, XXXII (October, 1964), pp. 384–385.

"Still Burning Bright." Review of Jean H. Hagstrum, *William Blake: Poet and Painter, An Introduction to the Illuminated Verse, The Christian Scholar*, XLVIII (Summer, 1965), pp. 165–167.

Of Regis Jolivet, *Sartre: The Theology of the Absurd*, and Charles N. Bent, *The Death of God Movement, The Journal of the American Academy of Religion*, XXXVI (June, 1968), pp. 162–163.